BANKING AND FINANCIAL INSTITUTIONS LAW

IN A NUTSHELL

SIXTH EDITION

By

WILLIAM A. LOVETT
Joseph Merrick Jones
Professor of Law and Economics
Tulane University School of Law
New Orleans, Louisiana

THOMSON
—————★————— ™
WEST

Mat #40254536

PREFACE

This book is intended for lawyers, law students, economists, bankers, and business people seeking to understand recent developments in banking and financial institutions law and policy.

Major changes have occurred. Broader rivalry developed among banks, thrift institutions, securities firms, mutual funds, insurance companies, pension funds, various retirement and investment accounts. Considerable deregulation has been achieved; yet the next steps remain controversial. Unfortunately, a costly wave of U.S. bank and thrift failures came in the late 1980's—early 1990's. This brought tougher laws in 1989 and 1991, and large-scale bailout and restructuring efforts, especially for S&L's and savings banks. But, as economic conditions stabilized and bank margins improved, capital was replenished for most U.S. institutions since the early 1990's. More recently, a wide consolidation and merger movement began to affect depository and other financial institutions in the U.S.

Meanwhile, a longer term trend toward globalization linked financial markets from many countries more closely. Debt overload strains affected many countries in the 1980's, with extensive rescheduling arrangements. As confidence revived, capital flowed more freely, in the 1990's, and many emerging markets received large investments. Speculative booms followed in many countries. Disruptive crises and devaluations occurred in some nations, although an overall expansion in global finance seems fairly well established. Increasingly, finance has become internationalized, with serious challenges for supervision and transparency.

This book explains the economic, historical, and legal background for banking and financial intermediaries. Each of these industries tried to strengthen their position against others—with uneven results. Law and policy-makers tried to compromise conflicting interests, with a view toward improved competition and overall performance. But consolidation and global integration pose important further questions.

Extensive literatures and law exist in each area summarized by this book. But hardly any legal writing that properly integrates these developments for banking and financial intermediaries as a whole. This book meets that need, and has been heavily revised for recent developments.

WILLIAM A. LOVETT
Joseph Merrick Jones
Professor of Law
and Economics

Tulane Law School
New Orleans, Louisiana
June, 2005

OUTLINE

LIST OF TABLES
AND CHARTS

―――――――

TABLE OF CASES

References are to Pages

BANKING AND FINANCIAL INSTITUTIONS LAW

IN A NUTSHELL

SIXTH EDITION

*

CHAPTER I

EVOLUTION OF BANKING AND FINANCIAL INSTITUTIONS LAW

A. INTRODUCTION

Modern industrial societies need money, banking, and financial institutions to trade and prosper. Money serves as our medium of exchange and standard of value. Money and financial deposits are convenient, liquid stores of value for individuals, families, businesses, and other organizations. Banks and financial institutions collect money and deposits from all elements of society, and invest these funds in loans, securities and various other productive assets. Every healthy economic system requires that money, banks, and financing intermediaries provide this service efficiently and reliably. Production, saving, investment, and efficient industrial development are facilitated thereby. Such work is vital for the transactions flow of each nation and the world economy.

Each country legislates its own currency, with unique regulations for the network of banking, credit, and financial transactions within its jurisdiction. These arrangements, hopefully, should ensure that money, banking and finance operate smoothly.

1

In many ways, such arrangements are often similar. But considerable differences exist among national laws with respect to: (1) the scope for private enterprise; (2) permissible entry into banking and finance, and the latitude for chartering and branching; (3) competition among financial institutions, their number, size and variety; (4) the role of monetary controls and interest regulations; (5) public finance, revenues, taxes, and deficits; and (6) the macro-economic policies designed to coordinate fiscal, monetary, trade and capital flows, foreign exchange and other regulatory activities.

This book emphasizes the law and policies affecting banking and financial institutions in the United States of America. But we must never forget that money, finance and commerce are increasingly international in character. Financial markets, transactions, and credit-borrowing flows are world-wide. And the entire network is experiencing an onslaught of technical change. Electronic communications, funds transfer, coding, access, cards, telephone, and computerized linkages are transforming finance and accounting. These changes, along with conflicting pressures from industry groups, moderate and conservative, together with liberals and socialist reformers, in various countries, have made the law of banking and financial institutions an exciting, if somewhat unsettled field of activity. Our purpose is to summarize the American legal arrangements in detail, and put them in the context of powerful international forces and technological trends.

B. EARLIER MONEY AND BANKING

In traditional societies, money consisted almost entirely of "specie" (usually gold or silver). The supply of specie money was limited to the supply of metal available for coinage, which increased slowly each year by the amounts newly mined. A great virtue of this arrangement was relative stability in the specie money supply. So long as governments avoided debasement of the coinage, specie retained its value and served reliably as the medium of exchange.

Credit was granted by wealthier asset holders (landowners, merchants, temples, or artisans), who could afford to lend to borrowers. Stable money values provided a convenient measuring rod for debt transactions, but loans were often extended in kind—food, seed, animals, tools, materials, and so forth. Payment obligations were expressed commonly in money, although shares of crops, production, or other profits were often specified. Thus, credits flowed from the affluent to some of the more needy, or at least, to those considered capable of using credits responsibly and repaying their loans.

Early banking was provided by leading merchants, money changers, goldsmiths, or nobles, who took specie deposits from other merchants and individuals for safekeeping and convenience. These "stronger" houses provided care for specie deposits, frequently paid interest, and the "banker" could lend out the accumulated deposits (at higher interest) to borrowers. Generally the banker would provide receipts or "notes" in place of actual specie, so that risk of loss in handling specie could be minimized. Soon thereafter bankers discovered the advantage of "fractional reserves," a profitable innovation. If bankers merely loaned out a portion of their deposits received, they would serve merely as financial intermediaries or trustees. But bankers go beyond this level of lending, and grant more loans (in return for promissory notes and mortgages) than the original amount of deposits.

How is this possible? So long as banks keep enough cash as a reserve fund, the confidence of original depositors can be retained, and their needs for occasional withdrawal will be satisfied. Bear in mind the banks are still solvent, *at least to the extent that "good" loans and security exist* for the additional issue of receipts, notes, checks, etc. Provided most borrowers are able to repay their loans and meet interest obligations, this expansion of bank note "money" (or even checking account "money") will be highly profitable for bankers. (The small proportion of defaulting loans can be covered by a slight increase in the interest risk premium charged to borrowers.) Meanwhile, the city, province or country served by the bankers benefits from enlarged access to credit, increased liquidity and investment potential, and expanded prosperity. In this way, through fractional reserve banking, the specie (gold and silver) money supply can be multiplied several-fold, or even more in the course of modern industrial development.

1. NATIONAL BANKS AND CURRENCY

Private banking enlarged the financial potential of city states, republics, kingdoms, and empires through much of history. Financial activity might flourish with military success or expanding trade and prosperity. But risks were inherent in private family (or partnership) banking. Depositors received no more assurance than private fortunes and reputation could guarantee, and banker's notes in circulation might fluctuate in value and suffer significant discounting. To achieve stronger, more reliable banking activity, many countries in the Mercantilist era created national banks, such as the Bank of Amsterdam, Banque Royal, Bank of England, Bank of Sweden, Banque de France, Bank of Prussia (later the Reichsbank), along with the first and second Bank of the United States. These institutions were early "central banks," and some of them survive today.

Early national banks were typically quasi-public corporations, with much broader access to deposits, and substantial government support. Shareholders were wealthy citizens, and might include the government, too. The national bank's notes usually became legal tender, or "currency," along with the country's coinage.* This added another dimension to the money supply, along with potential for excessive currency issue. Countries learned, however,

* Currency could be created directly by government "fiat" as well, with great potential for debasement or inflation if specie redemption or convertibility were not assured.

that a currency would be more stable in value if its convertibility into specie were guaranteed. Thus, apart from unfortunate inflationary experiences like Chinese paper currency, John Law's Banque Royal in France, (1716–1720), the French revolution's assignats, the American "continentals" in its revolutionary war, or the Southern Confederate currency, such "paper" money should not be enlarged unreasonably beyond the specie or liquid capital reserves available to back the currency.

2. SPREAD OF CORPORATE BANKING

In most countries, additional corporate banks were chartered to supplement national banks and private family (or partnership) banks. Gradually, corporate banks outgrew private banks, and took over the leading role in bank finance. This allowed more banking activity and competition, which flourished when checking accounts and bank drafts became almost as reliable as currency. Wealthier individuals would provide the initial corporate bank capital, and additional shares might be sold to the general public. Some risk of insolvency existed, though, for corporate banks that lacked the support and guarantee of deposits that governments could provide. Although a large, successful bank corporation might offer more strength and reliability than most private family banks, the danger of mismanagement, a weak loan and investment portfolio, or bad luck in depressions or financial panic meant that runs and failures might occur. These risks increased with easy entry for small, under-capitalized banks, that often popped up in rural areas, or when bank leadership fell into questionable or incompetent hands.

A serious problem, therefore, in the evolution of modern banking law was to regulate, and reduce the risk of financial panics, disrupted business, and enlarged unemployment. As industrial specialization and inter-dependence increased, this need for banking and financial regulation led to stronger reforms, greater supervision and restriction, and, in some countries, even partial or complete "nationalization" of banking.

A great variety of policies have been employed to strengthen bank integrity, along with protectionist measures designed more narrowly to favor parochial interests. Central banks frequently received a monopoly of the note issue privilege; less favored institutions might have their notes taxed, limited, or prohibited altogether. Checking account deposits gradually evolved as a close substitute, however, for banknote issue, and by-passed these restrictions. Central banks normally became "lenders of last resort" to the corporate and private banks, and regulated interest rates and economic conditions through the rate (or discount rates) at which such loans were allowed.* Legal restrictions were usually placed on bank charters and new entry, sometimes drastically limiting bank competition. Capital re-

* Central Bank loans to banks might be made directly, or by discounting the promissory notes and commercial paper received by the banks in their normal extension of credits to businesses and the public.

quirements became common (especially for initial capitalization), along with percentage reserve (or liquidity) requirements. Limits were sometimes placed on the interest payable on deposits to limit competition and/or cushion established banks. In periods of serious financial crisis, emergency government loans, suspension of customer payments, or increased capitalization requirements could be employed. These techniques evolved in many countries during the last several centuries. Most, at one stage or another, are illustrated by banking law and regulation in the United States.

C. BANKING DEVELOPMENT IN THE UNITED STATES

United States banking history is dominated by federalism. National and state chartered banks struggled for ascendancy from the beginning. It took until 1913 (or nearly 125 years) for a relatively weak Federal Reserve System to be enacted. And only the Great Depression and New Deal Reforms led to a stronger system of national supervision, federal deposit insurance, and more systematic federal regulation of banking and financial markets.

1. FIRST AND SECOND BANK OF THE UNITED STATES

The first Bank of the U.S. (1791–1811) was a centerpiece of Hamiltonian finance. Its share capital was $10 million (20 percent held by the federal government), a substantial note issue followed, and it played an important role in public finance and tax collection. But the states chartered more than a hundred banks in the same period, and their aggregate deposits and notes issue became more important. Agrarian and state banks interests prevented rechartering of the national bank in 1811.

But difficulties in raising federal loans for the War of 1812 (1812–1815), unreliable state banknotes, and shaky finance generally led to a second Bank of the U.S. (1816–1836). The new national bank had $35 million share capital (20 percent held by the federal government), its notes were declared legal tender, and convertibility into specie was required for all banknotes (national or state chartered) used for payments to the federal government. Soon this latter authority was employed to crack down on loose lending practices and excessive note issue by state banks, although at the cost of a substantial deflation-recession (1819–22). Nicholas Biddle of Philadelphia then led the Bank of the U.S. (and some state systems) into a period of healthy expansion, with sounder banking. The Suffolk system in New England (1824–1858) and the New York Safety Fund (1829–1837) also helped to strengthen banking in the states. (The Suffolk system in Boston featured prompt redemption of country bank notes, provided sufficient deposits were placed in leading Boston banks to back them up. The New York Safety Fund was a compulsory state insurance against bank failures, financed by small percentage assessments from all their banks.)

But President Jackson and agrarian interests in the South and West opposed the Bank of the U.S., being suspicious of its Northeastern leaders and shareholders, and preferring to rely only on state banks. Jackson vetoed charter extension in 1832, and won re-election over Henry Clay (who supported the national bank). Soon thereafter Jackson began transferring federal deposits to selected state "pet" banks. When national bank supporters failed to elect enough Congressmen to override a second veto, Biddle accepted defeat and liquidated the Bank of the U.S. in 1836. (It was reorganized as a Pennsylvania state bank, but failed in the subsequent depression.) In these Jackson years state banks multiplied nearly three-fold. Between 1830–1837 state banknote issue more than doubled, and their loans and discounts increased from less than $200 million to more than $500 million. Alarmed at this expansion, Jackson finally tightened up on federal land sales, requiring specie (instead of state banknotes) for payment. This triggered a collapse of the speculative land-boom, excessive note issue caused many bank failures, and a general depression ensued (1837–42).

2. FREE BANKING ERA

Between 1836–1863 the states served as sole chartering authority for banking institutions. Even more significantly, standards for new charters relaxed considerably. In many states, including New York, access to bank charters became more automatic or freely available, provided that moderate initial capital requirements were satisfied by the incorporators. States varied in their regulatory policies, but a general lesson seemed to be that firm capital requirements, reasonable supervision, and/or enforcing specie convertibility would yield sound banking. Laxity in these respects allowed frequent bank failures. Among the "stronger" systems were New York's tightened reserve system (after 1843), the Suffolk system in New England (from 1824 until 1858), Indiana's government sponsored state bank (between 1834–1855), and Louisiana's 100 percent "reserve" system, one-third specie and two-thirds 90 day commercial paper (between 1842–1862). In stronger states, clearing operations among banks improved greatly in the 1850's. But many states allowed loose practices, and in those areas state banks had unreliable note issue, suffered frequent runs, and did not enjoy full public confidence.

3.   NATIONAL BANKING ACT AND THE DUAL BANKING SYSTEM

During the Civil War, with eleven Southern and agrarian states out of the Congress, it was possible to enact stronger federal banking legislation. The National Banking Act of 1863 encouraged federal chartering of state banks with modest capitalization requirements, but imposed stronger reserve requirements and limitations on the note issue of federally chartered banks. Within two years Congress increased federal taxes on state bank notes to onerous levels (10 percent), and by late 1866 there were 1,644 "national" banks with $280 million in banknote circulation. State banknotes largely disappeared from circulation. This was less significant than it seemed, though, because checking accounts were an easy substitute for banknotes. (Checks had become more important in the volume of transactions even in the 1850's, and by the late 1880's less than 10 percent of the total volume of business transactions was in currency, i.e., greenbacks and national banknotes.)

State banking reached a low ebb after the Panic of 1873 and the subsequent depression, when many more state banks failed than national banks. In 1878 there were 2,056 national banks with $653 million deposits, and only 475 state banks with $143 million in deposits. But rivalry in chartering, less restrictive requirements, and the growing importance of checkbook money led to a more rapid revival of state banks.* The country seemed to like easier banking.

| | **National Banks** | | **State Banks** | |
	No. of Banks	Deposits	No. of Banks	Deposits
1868	1,640	$ 744 million	247	$ 52 million
1888	3,120	$1,716 million	2,726	$ 850 million

* Congress liberalized access to national bank charters in the Currency Act of 1900, and as a result, 3,046 new national banks were created between 1900–1908, two-thirds with initial capitalization of less than $50,000 each. State chartering standards were eased, too, and the ranks of state banks increased from 8,696 in 1900 to 18,478 in 1912.

Another factor explaining the proliferation of smaller banks was a prohibition on national bank branching in the National Bank Act of 1864.

	National Banks		State Banks	
	No. of Banks	Deposits	No. of Banks	Deposits
1912	7,366	$ 8.1 billion	18,478	$ 8.4 billion ·
1929	7,530	$ 21.6 billion	17,440	$ 27.5 billion
1945	5,015	$ 76 billion	9,111	$ 59 billion
1985	4,909	$1,008 billion	9,376	$ 749 billion
1991	3,918	$1,534 billion	8,321	$1,093 billion
1995	2,942	$1,617 billion	7,236	$1,291 billion
2003	2,048	$2,293 billion	5,768	$1,914 billion

For these reasons, unfortunately, the problems of fragility and periodic panic were never fully solved until the reforms of the 1930's.

Money and banking remained controversial until 1913 and the Federal Reserve Act. Western and agrarian states felt inadequately served, state bank interests complained of favoritism, and the limited national banknote issue was a constraint on access to liquidity in some areas. Populist movements for enlarged greenback issue (fiat currency) and more silver coinage reflected this dissatisfaction, too. And yet, overall economic growth and prosperity allowed the country to get along with an imperfect system, partly because checkbook money proved adequate for most business purposes. The most serious problem was vulnerability to periodic panic and failures, especially among smaller banks and this provoked recurrent concern about banking regulation. Finally, the Panic of 1907, though relatively brief, triggered serious effort toward more reliable banking.

4. FEDERAL RESERVE SYSTEM AND THE GREAT DEPRESSION

The Federal Reserve System of 1913 evolved out of a search for consensus among bankers, politicians, and some academic experts. It was a move toward "central bank" regulation in the European sense, though weaknesses were not evident until the Great Depression. The major features were: (i) an association of District Federal Reserve banks regulated by a Board of Governors, appointed by the President of the U.S. (ii) Every national bank had to be a member and state banks were allowed to become members. (iii) Member banks had to purchase district bank stock equal to 6 percent of their capital and surplus. (iv) Member banks had to maintain reserves against their demand and time deposits (from 12–18 percent and 4 percent, respectively). (v) Member banks could get loans from their district bank by discounting commercial paper. (vi) District banks would issue Federal Reserve notes ("currency") fully secured by commercial paper and gold reserves. (vii) District banks could purchase and sell government obligations under regulations established by the Board of Governors. (viii) District banks would operate a check clearing system for their member banks. (ix) District banks would be managed by nine member boards—three representing banks; three representing business, commerce and agriculture; and three representing the public at large. This legal structure is the foundation for most subsequent monetary and banking policy developments, and influenced later regulation of savings institutions by the Federal Home Loan Bank Board.

These reforms seemed to resolve the outstanding problems in money and banking. Federal Reserve banknotes could grow with expanding commercial paper and economic prosperity, and assure a more adequate, reliable monetary growth. Government borrowing capacity was firmly established to support emergency finance and war-time needs. And yet, ample safeguards were provided in stronger reserves, Federal Reserve lending authority, and discount rate discipline (like the Bank of England had developed). By standards of past American history, the country had brought its banking laws up to date.

Unfortunately, responsible leaders in the Federal Reserve system, Congress, and the President failed to act boldly, and with big enough emergency credits in the 1929–32 crisis. With hindsight's wisdom, economists now believe the Federal Reserve could have greatly restricted the scope and duration of the Great Depression, provided that leadership from the President and support from Congress had been available. Special legislation and emergency funding would have been required soon after the stock market crash in 1929.* But things were allowed to get out of hand, and the growing depression reduced revenues, and deficits weakened the will of politi-

* Also, the severity of the stock market crash could have been limited substantially by earlier restrictions on excess stock margin speculation and margin accounts.

cians to act. There was a rapid and tragic decline in business and employment. Gross national product was cut in half, and unemployment reached a peak of 24 percent of the work force. Large financial losses for businesses and families put loans into default through much of the economy, and brought insolvency to a large portion of the nation's banks. These banking problems were most acute in agricultural areas, where greatly reduced farm prices made loans hard to collect, and low land prices greatly weakened collateral values. Smaller rural banks failed in large numbers.

5. NEW DEAL REFORMS

Roosevelt's administration responded immediately to the banking and financial crisis with a bank holiday, emergency loans for banks, and suspension of the gold standard. (Britain and many other countries had devalued earlier, and there were substantial gold outflows from the U.S.) Within several months, the Federal Reserve received authority to increase the currency issue, more authority to use government obligations as collateral for banknotes, and yet, powers to restrict undue credit expansion. New law prohibited the payment of interest on demand deposits, to help limit "destructive competition" among banks. And most importantly, the Federal Deposit Insurance Corporation was created to insure all accounts up to $2,500 (later $10,000) for virtually all banks. The FDIC was financed by modest insurance premiums imposed on insured banks, and armed with auditing, examination and receivership authority, along with other corrective powers to deal with troubled banks. Meanwhile, new federal securities legislation imposed major responsibilities for disclosure of financial information with respect to publicly owned corporations; and investment banking (or the underwriting of stock and bond issues) was legally separated from commercial banking. The Securities and Exchange Commission was created in 1934 to enforce these disclosure requirements, and to regulate the stock exchanges and brokerage industry. In 1935, further legislation strengthened the Federal Reserve Board (taking its present form, with 14 year terms), and created the Federal Open Market Committee (comprising the seven Board members and five representatives from district reserve banks). A more flexible, wider range for reserve requirements was established, with Board discretion to set reserve ratios according to economic conditions. And the Board received authority to limit interest rates on time deposits, later implemented under Regulation Q.

The Federal Reserve Board became a much stronger central bank as a result, and social insurance (FDIC protection) of smaller bank deposits greatly alleviated the dangers of bank failure, and virtually eliminated runs on banks. The "Fed" encouraged monetary ease, with excess reserves and low interest rates through most of the 1930's. But this stimulus, by itself, only partly restored economic activity. Moderate government deficits were carried also in the New Deal years, but full employment was not achieved until World War II mobilization, when much larger deficits expanded industrial output to record levels.

6.   WORLD WAR II FINANCE

The war brought concern for inflation, and the Federal Reserve began tightening reserve requirements and credit in the fall of 1940. But the Treasury ran increasingly huge deficits in the war years, and forced the "Fed" to support low interest rates on massive government borrowing. Government debt expanded from $48 to $260 billion, and the money supply increased from $48 to $106 billion during the war years. Price and wage controls, along with some rationing, and a big savings bond program were used to contain and drain off excess inflationary pressure. On the whole, these policies were successful, and consumer prices went up only 25 percent between 1941–45. When controls were lifted after the war, however, more inflation occurred, raising the cost of living another 33 percent by 1948. But strong fiscal restraint, budget surpluses between 1946–1948, and a rapid postwar conversion of industry (assisted by low interest rates) stopped inflation in the 1948–49 recession. In these years, banking policy had been subordinated to war finance and borrowing needs.

7. POSTWAR PROSPERITY AND POLICIES

Bankers and the Federal Reserve wanted to restore normal market conditions for money and credit markets reasonably soon in the postwar era. When inflationary pressure cooled and it seemed likely that regular debt service could be handled satisfactorily, it was time to free the "Fed" from responsibility to support government borrowing at pegged rates. During the Korean War (1950–53), the "Fed" began to tighten money and increase interest rates to help limit inflation, even though the Treasury sought resumption of low interest rates to support renewed borrowing. Early in 1951, the FOMC broke with Treasury policy, and sold part of its bond portfolio (for open market operations) at a discount to raise effective interest rates. This led to the famous "Accord of 1951," under which the Federal Reserve gradually achieved its independence as the dominant force in monetary policy. This led to firmer monetary policy, and helped tighten bank free reserves. Interest rates moved up somewhat. This action combined with partial price controls, increased taxes, and modest surpluses to limit inflation during the Korean War.

During subsequent years, monetary management by the Federal Reserve has become an important element in macroeconomic policy. Along with government budgets, tax and fiscal management, and various forms of wage-price guidance and industrial encouragement, monetary policy has played an increasing role in efforts to coordinate overall economic performance. In general, Federal Reserve monetary policy since 1953 can be characterized as an effort to provide restraint against inflationary pressures, and a relaxation or easing of this restraint when significant recession and unemployment developed. This has required estimates, forecasts, and judgments about bank reserves, monetary growth, interest rates, price levels, excess capacity, unemployment, international trade, the balance of payments, and economic expansion that were often controversial. Inevitably, these issues have become entangled with Presidential politics. (Recent targeting procedures for monetary growth, ease, and restraint, and the controversies involved in their use, are discussed at greater length in later chapters. But this requires a review of Eisenhower, Kennedy, Johnson, Nixon, Ford, Carter, Reagan, Bush, Clinton, and Bush administration policies in some detail, because specific Federal Reserve monetary policies need to be understood as part of their evolving macroeconomic context.) Hence, monetary policy for the Federal Reserve is closely linked to national economic policy.

Another significant development in postwar banking law was the increased importance of antitrust policy, and concern for adequate competition in financial markets. Because new entry into banking slowed greatly since the 1930's, while bank mergers, holding companies, consolidations, and branching became more widespread, Congress and the antitrust authorities imposed constraints. The Bank Holding Company Act of 1956 limited chain banking. The Bank Merger Acts of 1960 and 1966 (along with the U.S. v. Philadelphia Bank decision in 1963 by the Supreme Court) limited larger bank mergers in the same cities or metropolitan areas. In 1970 Bank Holding Company Act amendments narrowly restricted diversification by banks into other industries. But then, in 1974, Supreme Court merger policy relaxed with the Marine Bancorporation decision, which allowed leading banks to make major bank acquisitions in other cities within the same state. In 1980 a Presidential Committee urged that branching be liberalized, and that interstate banking should be allowed. Later in the 1980's many states began to allow regional interstate bank holding companies (often on a reciprocal basis), and more frequent bank failures led to some increased consolidation. During the 1990's, more branching and interpenetration of financial markets was allowed. In 1999 the Gramm–Leach Financial Services Modernization Act authorized Financial Holding Companies to operate in banking, insurance, and securities markets. Thus, even more consolidation in banking and some conglomerate financial integration is occurring recently.

Greater competition for banks had come from saving institutions, too. Savings and loan associations traditionally collected passive, medium term deposits with slightly higher interest rates than banks, and invested these funds mostly in long term

real estate mortgages.* This specialized intermediation could be handled with minimum staff and
paperwork, and often involved low margins for savings institutions in competitive markets. Banks concentrated more on collecting demand and short-
term deposits, and invested in shorter-term loans
and highly liquid securities. Deposits in all savings
institutions, i.e., savings and loan associations and
credit unions, were approaching the scale of domestic commercial banking in the late 1960's. In the
1970's some of the larger savings institutions began
to offer NOW accounts (close to demand deposits)
with interest rates, and sought broadened lending
opportunities. This rivalry among financial intermediaries was accentuated in the late 1970's by new
competition from money market funds.

Money market funds were an outgrowth of mutual funds sponsored by the securities and brokerage
industry. Because interest rates on savings deposits
had been kept down artificially in the 1970's under
Regulation Q, in order to protect savings institutions and banks, this led to an increasing gap in the
late 1970's between passbook rates and world market interest rates. Although banks and savings institutions were forced to create large denomination
money market certificates for big depositors, they
resisted any rapid lifting of Regulation Q ceilings
for small depositors. Passbook rates in 1978–1981
were still 4¾–5½ percent—with ¼ percent more allowed for savings institutions, while money market

* The savings institutions industry began modestly in the 19th
century, but grew rapidly with post-World War II prosperity and
housing investments.

certificates, money market funds, and world market interest rates ranged from 10–20 percent. Money market funds offered by major brokerage firms greatly reduced their initial deposits and allowed prompt withdrawal. Naturally, money market fund deposits grew rapidly, with an additional advantage of interstate operations and national advertising.

These increased competitive pressures led to the Depository Institutions Deregulation and Monetary Control Act of 1980. This compromise featured uniform reserve requirements for banks and savings institutions (but not money market funds) to be phased-in over 7 years, the gradual elimination of Regulation Q limits on interest rates over a 6 year period, broader investment and service authority for federal savings and loan associations, and immediate authority to offer NOW accounts for most financial institutions. In addition, the DIDMCA strengthened Federal Reserve authority to regulate and supervise growth of the monetary aggregates.

In the fall of 1982, the Garn–St. Germain Act gave further impetus to the erosion of boundaries between banks and savings institutions. It added more federal savings institution powers, led to liberalized real estate investment authority, allowed mergers between weakened savings institutions and banks, and mandated new money market accounts equivalent to and competitive with money market mutual funds. But later, as many savings institutions got into trouble and failed in the later 1980's, extensive mergers were allowed, and banks began to acquire them in some areas.

During the postwar era another important development was the spread of international banking in London, Switzerland, Germany, Japan, and various other countries, including many off-shore tax-havens. Multinational business found it increasingly profitable to relocate many of their financial activities abroad to avoid domestic regulation and taxation, often involving Eurodollar banking. Banks in Europe were eager to encourage this business, and the biggest U.S. banks followed their customers overseas through proliferated branch networks. An increasing flow of deposits also was collected worldwide from international entrepreneurs, who generated higher profits by skillfully routing production, sales and service transactions to minimize taxes. Much of this activity escaped effective regulation, but a growth of foreign bank branching (in one form or another) into the U.S. led to the International Banking Act of 1978. This legislation imposed restrictions on foreign banks in the U.S. similar to those already affecting American domestic banks.

Further legal developments since the late 1960's brought important federal regulation to protect consumers, and to limit discrimination based upon sex, race, religion, national origin or age in access to credit. Truth-in-Lending disclosure requirements were imposed in 1968 upon consumer loans and retail credit transactions, with rulemaking delegated to the Federal Reserve Board, and enforcement by federal financial regulatory agencies, the Federal Trade Commission, and private lawsuits. Additional consumer safeguards and limits on liability with respect to credit cards followed in 1970, with regulation of consumer credit reporting services in 1974. Congress outlawed discrimination in access to credit with respect to sex or marital status in 1974, and extended this policy in 1976 to other bases for discrimination, including race, receipt of public assistance, religion, national origin or age. And in 1978, the Electronic Funds Transfer Act protected consumers and defined rights, liabilities, and responsibilities with respect to bankcards and electronic funds transfer systems. More recently, improved privacy and internet safeguards are receiving more attention, with tighter regulations likely.

D. ECONOMIC STRAINS AND ELECTRONIC FINANCE

Two major themes dominate recent concerns about the regulation of banking and financial institutions. The first is anti-inflation and macro-economic policy, and the second involves the potential for restructuring financial markets through cost savings, service improvements, new roles resulting from electronic funds transfer, and changing boundaries between financial institutions.

Inflation used to be associated mainly with wartime disruption, scarcities and related strains in finance. But in the late 1960's–1970's, significant peacetime inflation spread to many countries, including the United States. Inflation picked up momentum at significant annual rates of increase.

Concern for inflationary distortions, lower saving and investment, reduced productivity, distributional inequities, and gradual demoralization caused most economists to urge that inflation be minimized, if at all possible. But a sustained reduction in inflation requires strong fiscal and monetary discipline for a considerable period of years. Other policies to improve saving, investment, productivity and healthy competition will be helpful, too.

Important controversies on inflation and recovery policy include: (i) proper growth of monetary deposits and the supply of credit; (ii) the extent to which interest rates should fluctuate; (iii) procedures for measuring and targeting growth of the money supply; (iv) the role of government deficits and borrowing requirements; (v) the need for improved incentives for saving, investment, and other tax reforms; (vi) the ways in which more capital formation, greater productivity, and better wage-price discipline could be encouraged by government policy; and (vii) the impact of world capital markets, exchange rates, interest rate differentials, and the desirable scope for international lending, investment, and trade-capital flows. All these problems impact on the regulation of banks or other financial institutions.

Added complications come through cost reduction, service improvement and new competitive forces associated with electronic funds transfer and other innovations. Traditional boundaries and roles in financial markets eroded substantially. When inflation rates increased, strains of disintermediation affected some financial institutions. Legal restrictions often added to these difficulties, and slowed market adjustments. Thus, pressures for structural change combined with inflation to challenge some of the accumulated law and regulation affecting banks and savings institutions. Then anti-inflation policy, emphasizing higher interest rates (especially between 1979–82, but continuing somewhat into the 1980s—due to budget deficits), brought deflation pressures. Subsequent loan losses developed in many areas (developing country debts, agricultural loans, highly leveraged corporations, and commercial real estate lending by thrifts and banks). Bank and thrift failures increased greatly in the 1980s—early 1990s (with 1,000 failed thrift institutions and 1,500 failed banks). This brought stronger capitalization requirements, renewed supervision discipline, overhaul and recapitalization of the deposit insurance system. (See FIRREA of 1989—Chapter IV, at 284, and the FDIC Improvement Act of 1991—Chapter III, at 128). But these regulatory improvements, together with eased inflation and monetary policies from the Federal Reserve that favored commercial banking, helped to replenish bank capital in many institutions. Thus, most surviving banks were stronger again by the mid 1990's and beyond.

In the 1990's, U.S. and European budget deficits eased, inflation was minimized, and international commerce thrived. International investment, trading, and financial flows mushroomed. Prosperity followed in this decade for much of the world.

Unfortunately, speculative booms and loose lending followed in many nations. Financial panics, capital flight, currency declines, and bank failures were common, especially in Asia and Latin America. Earlier mistakes of U.S. financial looseness, weak regulation and naiveté, were repeated in many emerging market countries. U.S. financial and regulation history provided helpful lessons and helped to guide reforms. But in the U.S. stock market bubble of the late 1990's, and the slump of 2001–2002, "Enron-style" corporate scandals showed that even the U.S. had to relearn the lessons of prior financial reforms.

More recently, however, the U.S. experienced a big foreign capital inflow surge, with increasing (and unsustainable) trade and current account deficits. Although some dollar devaluation seemed unavoidable, other issues are unresolved—unbalanced trading, currency realignment, import restrictions, and relative interest rates. To what extent should globalization be regulated and how? These challenges are controversial, and flow from unevenly open markets in world trade. Consensus has been difficult, with many nations using neo-mercantilist policies. International institutions (like the Internal Monetary Fund (IMF) and Bank for International Settlements (BIS) are important forums for coordination efforts, but collaboration among leading nations is vital, too.

It is natural, though, that all these financial reform developments build upon established practices. Law in this area reveals traditional momentum, with a taste for gradualism, reflecting the fear of costly mistakes. For these reasons, the law of banking and financial institutions reflects considerable continuity, while these markets cope with new competition, technical innovation, and the financial strains resulting from uneven growth, monetary restraint, trade imbalances, and global markets.

CHAPTER II

MONEY AND BANKING

A. MONEY, CENTRAL BANKING, AND THE FEDERAL RESERVE SYSTEM

Congress has the power, under the United States Constitution, to establish the currency, to regulate money and foreign exchange, to borrow funds, collect taxes and regulate commerce, and to carry on expenditure programs within the broad authority of the federal government. Each year Congress appropriates spending authority to federal agencies and carefully defines the tax laws. But the President and the executive branch of government strongly influence these policies through detailed recommendations, and exercise of delegated authority to administer programs and regulations. The President's Office of Management and Budget (formerly the Budget Bureau) is the principal executive oversight agency for spending; the Treasury Department collects the revenues and manages debt financing. Their leaders, OMB Director and Treasury Secretary, are normally among the President's top economic policy makers, along with the Council of Economic Advisors.

Considerable latitude has been granted, within this framework, to the major bank regulatory agency, the Federal Reserve Board of Governors and its Federal Open Market Committee. Although extensive federal and state legislation regulates chartering, growth, and supervision of banks and other financial institutions, the Federal Reserve System has great influence over bank reserves, monetary expansion, and interest rates. Yet it would be inapt to say, as some suggest, that the "Fed" simply *controls* the money supply, as easily as one might turn a faucet of water. Actually, the supply and demand for money, bank deposits, and liquidity is more complicated, subtle, and partly the result of self-operating, market forces (both national and international). Government budgets, deficits, and public sector borrowing also have important effects on money markets and interest rates, especially when large deficits and borrowing requirements are involved. Nonetheless, the Federal Reserve System has become increasingly significant as an independent force in shaping monetary policy, especially in recent years.

This dual structure of (i) centralized finance for government, with a strong Treasury Department (or Ministry of Finance) and an executive economic staff, and (ii) a more decentralized financial services industry for the rest of the economy, coordinated and disciplined by a quasi-independent "Central Bank" is typical of many modern countries. In the United States, with a larger, more complex economy than most, these agencies have become bigger and more complicated.* Coordination of their policies is

* Under U.S. federal regulation the Office of the Comptroller of the Currency (OCC) within the Treasury, the Federal Deposit

not always easy, especially when new circumstances, e.g., wars, depressions, inflationary momentum or stagflation, place awkward strains on accumulated compromises. Even in smaller countries, the same dual structure is the normal pattern, with somewhat simpler, and more informal bureaucracies.

Remember that the United States evolved rapidly over 230 years from a small country of 3 million to a large industrial society of 300 million. Its institutional development of money, finance, and banking institutions is the accumulated legacy of that lively history. Bear in mind that national economic crises, like war, depression or major inflation, have tended to provoke emergency actions from government finance or special regulation. These interventions correct, or at least alter, the previous momentum of government finances and decentralized banking. Yet a country's financial arrangements normally exhibit great continuity, and build up strong traditions that may inhibit "reforms," all reflected in its present working compromises. Nonetheless, serious economic strains have typically brought, sooner or later, significant adjustments, usually led by executive leadership, treasury actions or central bank policy.

Insurance Corporation (FDIC), and the Federal Reserve Board are the key bank regulatory institutions.

Table II–1

Growth of U.S. Commercial Banking, 1792–2003

	National Banks				State Banks			
	No. of Banks	Assets	Deposits	Bank Note Circulation	No. of Banks	Assets	Deposits	Bank Note Circulation
1792	1	(1st Bank of U.S. $10m capital)		—	16	17.1*		11.2
1804	1	(1st Bank of U.S. $10m capital)		—	59	42.6*		22.7
1811	1	(1st Bank of U.S. Expired, 1811)		—	88	42.6*		22.7
1816	1	(2nd Bank of U.S. $35m capital)		—	246	89.8*		68
1820	1	47	6.5*	3.6	307	102.1*	31.2	40.6
1830	1	69	16	13	329	110.1*	40.7	48.2
1836	1	77		23	713	622	165	140
1840		(2nd Bank of U.S. Expired, 1837)		—	901	657	119	106
1861	—	—	—	—	1,601	1,015	357	207
1868	1,640	1,572	744	294	247	163	52	34
1876	2,091	1,826	842	294	671	406	n.a.	1
1888	3,120	2,731	1,716	155	2,726	1,219	n.a.	—
1900	3,731	4,944	3,621	265	8,696	4,115	3,172	—
1912	7,366	10,857	8,061	708	18,478	10,638	8,396	—
1921	8,150	20,475	15,142	704	22,306	23,194	18,289	—
1929	7,530	27,260	21,586	649	17,440	35,181	27,499	—
1933	4,897	20,813	16,742	727	9,310	19,698	15,336	—
1945	5,015	81,491	76,534	—	9,111	64,754	59,262	—
1970	4,638	314,334	255,819	—	9,052	220,598	178,540	—
1981	4,454	958,156	703,674	—	9,848	716,181	560,390	—
1985	4,909	1,392,787	1,008,000(e)	—	9,376	956,828	748,512	—
1991	3,918	1,964,000	1,534,000	—	8,231	1,411,000	1,093,000	—
1995	2,942	2,299,000	1,617,000	—	7,236	1,871,000	1,291,000	—
2003	2,000	3,834,000	2,332,000	—	5,713	2,834,200	1,881,000	—

SOURCES: *Historical Statistics of the U.S., 1789–1945,* Bureau of the Census, U.S. Dept. of Commerce, 1949; *Historical Statistics of the U.S. from Colonial Times to 1970,* Bureau of the Census, U.S. Dept. of Commerce, 1975; *Annual Statistical Report 1981,* Federal Reserve Board (domestic banking only). Federal Reserve Bulletin, Jan., 1987 (domestic banking only); *Annual Reports 1991 and 1995,* Federal Financial Institutions Examination Council, 1992 and 1996. Federal Reserve data, 2000, 2003.

* Bank Capital

NOTE. All financial figures in millions of dollars, i.e., for bank capital, assets, deposits and bank note circulation.

1.   FINANCIAL BEGINNINGS AND THE BANKS OF THE UNITED STATES

The British colonies in North America suffered a shortage of specie. Tools and capital goods imported from the mother country absorbed a heavy deficit in payments from the colonies with substantial net credits from English merchants and bankers. And while the balance of payments with the West Indies was favorable, leading to a steady inflow of Spanish dollars, the better coins were sent back to England. This left a scarce supply of specie in the colonies, featuring a considerable residue of worn and clipped dollars. For this reason, the colonists constantly sought additional forms of money to serve their needs. Leading commodities in each section were employed early as a medium of exchange, including furs, corn, livestock, tobacco, rice, and even Indian wampum (sea shells). These were supplemented later by merchant bank notes and periodic note issues from colonial legislatures. When such paper was used with reasonable restraint, and not as a substitute for taxes to pay current expenses, results were satisfactory. But with excessive circulation, serious depreciation naturally followed. British policy, meanwhile, tried to restrict and inhibit colonial paper, fearing losses to their merchant creditors, and wanting to bring specie home to the mother country. This conflict left an important impression in colonial minds at Independence, and sympathy for paper money circulation.

The Continental Congress issued $242 million in paper money to finance the Revolutionary War, which depreciated rapidly during the conflict. The states issued another $209 million of separate paper, which depreciated at varying rates. Meanwhile, $8 million in foreign specie (mostly French funds) were borrowed, much of which remained abroad to cover drafts on supplies. Of this borrowing, Congress used merely $254,000 as the initial capitalization for the Bank of North America in Philadelphia (1781), along with $85,000 subscribed privately. This was the first corporate bank in the United States, and its note issue was kept responsibly limited and redeemable in specie. (It became a Pennsylvania chartered bank in 1787, and was bypassed consciously by Hamilton in 1791.) These emergency arrangements could not suffice for long.

When the American Republic won military and political independence in the early 1780's its finances were a shambles. Congress tried to stabilize the currency by exchanging most of the depreciated "older" notes for "new" ones, but a sizeable discount below specie remained. The "national" debt was largely in arrears, tax receipts were negligible, and public land sales were the largest revenue. Clearly, for the nation to survive, money and finance had to be organized more soundly. This was the task achieved under Alexander Hamilton's leadership as first Secretary of the Treasury.

The Treasury Department was created in 1789, internal taxes were levied, the budget soon balanced, and the whole national debt (including state war loans) was funded in 1790 with long-term bonds (mostly at 6 percent). Regular borrowing authority remained, though, to supplement revenues, if necessary. In 1791 the first Bank of the U.S. was established, with $10 million capital (one-fifth from the federal government), and a substantially larger note issue potential. In 1792 the U.S. Mint was established on a bi-metallic basis (gold and silver), coining gold eagles ($10) at 247.5 grains, and silver dollars at 371.25 grains. In addition, the states chartered more banks to expand bank money even more. Bank notes issued by these state banks and the Bank of the U.S. soon became the larger part of the money supply, supplementing U.S. and foreign coins in circulation. On the whole, these measures were successful, and the credit of the new republic was established in the world market.

While opposition from state bank and agrarian interests prevented charter renewal for the first Bank of the U.S. in 1811, the War of 1812 promptly proved the need for a more reliable note issue and a strong method of federal government borrowing. Many state banks had become increasingly lax, and it was widely felt that specie redeemability should be enforced more systematically for bank notes. Accordingly, Congress created the second Bank of the U.S. in 1816. The new "national" bank was larger, with $35 million share capital (one-fifth from the federal government) and stronger powers. Congress also required all payments to the government to be made in specie, Treasury notes, or notes of the Bank of the U.S. At first, Bank leadership was lenient, allowed extensive loans, and accepted too many state bank notes for deposit without proper specie redemption, which encouraged a land speculation boom and a subsequent recession in 1819. Meanwhile, the Supreme Court sustained the constitutionality of the Bank in McCulloch v. Maryland (S.Ct.1819), and held its banknotes were immune from state taxation. Then a new Bank president, Langdon Cheves (1819–23), tightened up on lending practices, curtailed the note issue, collected state banknotes promptly, and floated a $2 million specie loan in Europe. These measures were not popular in agrarian states, but achieved the basic goals intended. Banknote issue for the country was tightened up, and made much more reliable.

The next Bank president, Nicholas Biddle (1823–36), had more ambitious objectives. Under his leadership the Bank of the U.S. expanded its branch network aggressively, and allowed the branches to issue their own notes in the form of "branch drafts", even though Congress refused to grant branch note issue authority. In this way, Biddle's Bank offered strong competition to state banks. Meanwhile, the Bank systematically presented state banknotes promptly for specie redemption, thus preventing looseness or "over expansion" from his state bank rivals. Biddle became rather arrogant and boastful, unfortunately, and was labeled, not surprisingly, as Tsar Nicholas, by his enemies. But the country enjoyed increasing prosperity in this period, with reasonably sound money, growing revenues from tariffs and public land sales, rapid immigration, and the spread of new settlements and population. While it would be wrong to say the Bank had evolved a modern Central Bank role as a money market regulator, the potential for such activity was established. If the second Bank of the U.S. had become a permanent institution, the economic history of the country might have been quite different, with a much earlier, stronger centralized influence on economic policy.

But Andrew Jackson's administration (1829–37) destroyed the Bank of the U.S., leaving decentralized, local banks as the dominant tradition in American banking history. [It took another full century before Franklin Roosevelt's New Deal (1933–35) achieved a comparable strengthening of "central bank" influence for the Federal Reserve system.] Jacksonians distrusted Eastern bankers, feared centralized authority, and wanted more latitude for state banks and local business interests. Perhaps, if Biddle had resigned, and allowed Jackson to reappoint another President of the Bank its survival might have been managed; actually the majority of Jackson's cabinet favored the Bank. But Biddle not only stayed on, he collaborated with Jackson's political opposition and his chief rival, Henry Clay. Upon Clay's nomination by the Whigs in December, 1831, they planned to drive Jackson from the White House over the bank issue, and they applied early (four years ahead of schedule) for charter renewal for the Bank of the U.S. Congress enacted the measure on July 3, 1832, but Jackson vetoed it. The controversy became a key issue in the 1832 campaign, but to the surprise and distress of the pro-

Bank forces, Clay was badly defeated. Relations between the Bank and Jackson were further embittered. Meanwhile, state banks were growing more rapidly, which encouraged land speculation, and Biddle attempted deflationary measures, still hoping to influence charter renewal. Jackson recommended an investigation of the Bank's solvency (actually in strong condition), which Congress refused. Then Jackson stopped further U.S. deposits in the Bank, and switched them into some 29 state "pet" banks. When the Whigs failed to elect enough Congressmen in 1834 to over-ride Jackson's veto, Biddle accepted his fate, paid off the federal government's stock for $7.9 million, and reorganized the Bank as a Pennsylvania state chartered bank. Thus ended the first era of "central bank" development in the U.S.

What could have become a strong institution, like the Bank of England, died in its youth. True central banking in the United States came much later. The Federal Reserve System, created in 1913, only gradually assumed greater powers with New Deal reforms (1933–35), and did not assume much independence until the Accord with Treasury in 1951. An important political lesson is illustrated, too. Central bank leaders and the Federal Reserve System must coordinate their activities, within reason, to the political realities and moods of their time. If conflict with powerful political leaders is pressed too far, a central bank's institutional independence and strength may be undermined. And yet, the disciplinary role of healthy central bank traditions, in enforcing sounder money, reducing inflationary pressure, and preventing loose practices, can be very helpful, if wisely sustained with realism and political prudence.

The Panic of 1837, and subsequent depression until 1842, illustrate the weakness of financial institutions without disciplines to enforce sound banking, and without a lender of last resort to limit a chain reaction of bank failures. Looser banking, excessive loans and state banknote issue had helped to sustain a speculative land boom in the 1830's. Liberal loans and investments from Europe added momentum. When Jackson's administration, alarmed at speculation and worried about government deposits in selected state banks, cracked down and enforced specie payments for public lands (instead of state banknotes), the bubble burst. A panic followed, with a rapidly spreading financial crisis. By May, 1837, most of the country's banks (now entirely state chartered) had suspended specie payments, and many failed. Foreign capital stopped flowing, many states defaulted on their debts for a while, and a few actually repudiated their obligations. Foreigners were distressed when the federal government offered no support to the states. But federal powers and responsibilities were felt to be limited in this period and it took years for the natural productivity of the country to rebuild prosperity.

2. DECENTRALIZED BANKING,
1837–1913

For the next generation (1837–62) state chartered banks were the sole form of banking activity in the United States of America. The nation muddled through the years before the Civil War with states rights pre-eminent. During most of this period, the federal government used an Independent Treasury system to collect, store and disburse specie for federal finance. Banking was left entirely to the states, with increasingly liberal chartering policies (the free-banking era) in most areas. This "system" had serious weaknesses. Specie circulation tended to be constricted. State banknote issue was unreliable (except in those states which enforced tougher reserve requirements, specie redemption, and regular examination). But the country enjoyed reasonably good fortune. New lands were rapidly opening up, production was expanding, immigrants and foreign capital kept flowing, railroads proliferated, and the California gold boom added specie resources. Federal funding requirements were generally modest, and the Mexican War (1847–48) was successfully brief, so that it could be conveniently financed—only $65 million—with short-term federal notes (later refinanced into long-term federal bonds). When the long boom ebbed, the vulnerability of banking facilities helped to exaggerate somewhat the Panic of 1857. But in this Panic the banks were left to fend for themselves, and after a period of widespread suspension in specie payments on bank notes, things slowly improved.

3. CIVIL WAR AND THE DUAL CHARTERING SYSTEM

The Civil War emergency greatly multiplied the financial needs of government. Federal expenditures grew from $67 million in 1861 to $1,297 million in 1865. The Union War effort was financed mainly with government borrowing and paper currency (Treasury notes or "greenbacks"), although tax revenues increased from $40 million in 1861 to $300 million in 1865. (Confederate finance was even more heavily dependent on paper currency, repudiated by the Union at the end of the war.) This vast expansion of the money supply (including roughly $400 million of federal greenbacks) produced a substantial inflation, though less than might have been expected. A large industrial expansion and surge of output was called forth by the war effort, especially in the Union states. (The federal debt mushroomed from only $65 million in 1860 to $2.8 billion at its peak in 1865, and was still $1.8 billion in 1898 before the Spanish American War. But the interest burden required to service the debt declined from one third of federal spending in 1869 to less than one tenth of the federal budget in 1898; this reflected expanded national income, along with reduced interest rates, as the debt was refinanced into longer-term obligations.)

The next major financial development was enactment of the National Bank Act in March, 1863. With 11 agrarian states out of the Congress, it was possible to take a substantial step toward federal coordination and strengthening of the banking system. Under this legislation banks were "encouraged" to recharter themselves as national banks, with the Comptroller of the Currency as the new agency for screening and supervision. Modest capitalization requirements were involved, although somewhat stronger reserves against deposits were mandated: (i) 25 percent for "reserve city" banks; (ii) 15 percent for "country" banks. However, reserve banks outside New York City could keep half their reserves in interest-bearing accounts in N.Y.C. banks; meanwhile, country banks could keep three-fifths of their reserves in interest bearing accounts in any reserve bank. Initially a small tax (½ percent annually) was placed on average banknote circulation for all banks. But when relatively few state banks converted to national bank charters, this annual tax was raised to 10 percent in 1866 for state banknotes. This onerous, prejudicial tax virtually ended state banknote circulation; it also forced the majority of state banks to switch into federal charters and become national banks. [The Supreme Court held this tax constitutional in Veazie Bank v. Fenno (S.Ct.1869).] This "national banking" reform did not really create a "central bank." But it did strengthen banking reserves, facilitate assistance from larger city banks, and encourage a stronger banking center for the nation in New York City.

But gradually the tendencies toward decentralized, state charter banking resumed their influence. As shown in Chapter I, page 13, supra, state banks grew in number from 475 in 1878, to 8,696 in 1900 and 17,440 in 1929. Meanwhile, national banks increased their numbers more slowly, from 2,056 in 1878, to 3,731 in 1900 and 7,530 in 1929. The share of deposits in state banks grew from 7 percent in 1868 to 18 percent in 1878, 43 percent in 1900, and reached 56 percent in 1929. Key factors were rapid development of checking accounts as a substitute for banknotes, which allowed state banks to compete effectively, together with more relaxed, liberal reserve requirements and easier chartering and entry for state banks. Eventually, national bank charter and reserve requirements were liberalized, too, so that national banks could compete more equally, and their numbers expanded very substantially. A final factor was the prohibition on branching for national banks in the National Bank Act of 1864. Branching for national banks was only partly liberalized, right before the Great Depression in the McFadden Act of 1927, which allowed branching for national banks to the same extent, in each state, as state banks. (Branching had begun, mainly in the 1920's, in some states; the states divided into three roughly equal camps—unit banking or no branches at all, limited branching [usually county-wide only], and statewide branching.) This restriction against branching had greatly encouraged new bank formation in cities and towns with growing population and increased prosperity. Thus, laws regulating market structure and allowing easy entry strongly sustained the decentralized banking tradition of the U.S. from the Civil War through the Great Depression, and even into the Post–World War II prosperity. National banks represented only a limited incursion of federal chartering into an industry that had become greatly decentralized, with liberal state standards setting the dominant style for the industry until the New Deal reforms of 1933–35.

Unfortunately, this decentralized banking system was vulnerable to financial panics. Three major panics and depressions occurred between 1865–1913. Each featured over-expanded credit, thin reserves, and vulnerability to a chain reaction of liquidation and bank failures. The Panic of 1873 and subsequent depression resulted from excessive credits after a long boom, weak bank reserves, collapse of many banks (including Jay Cooke's in N.Y.), and government help that was too small and late. Controversy about "excessive" greenbacks left outstanding from the Civil War crippled government policy, and it took years for renewed agricultural exports and revived industry to restore prosperity. A smaller panic and recession occurred in 1883–1884, but this decade was largely prosperous. The next setback came in the early 1890's, as the terms of trade shifted against the U.S., and a substantial gold outflow weakened confidence. Then the Panic of 1893 erupted, with insufficient bank reserves, substantial contraction of liquidity, and a serious recession. Many blamed renewed silver coinage after the Sherman Silver Purchase Act of 1890. But silver's impact on the money supply was modest, and over expansion of bank-money and fragility of the banking system was the important problem.

Although this depression affected the industrial economy, and caused populist pressure for easier money and "free silver" coinage, fear of strikes, radicalism and "unsound" money proved stronger in the 1896 election. By 1897 the economy revived, and another decade of renewed prosperity ensued, strengthened by expanded industry and new gold production. The last setback was the Panic of 1907. It involved another excessive accumulation of bank credit, insufficient reserves, and a run on the banks. The Treasury provided somewhat more aid to the banks this time, and this financial crisis was not so serious or lasting. A healthier balance of payments facilitated recovery, and prosperity soon resumed. But the limitations on bank reserves and potential fragility had finally become evident to conservative and sound money interests, and the appeal of silver and populist inflationism had abated.

4. FEDERAL RESERVE SYSTEM, 1913–32

a. Establishment of the Federal Reserve

The problem facing the National Monetary Commission of 1908–12 (and draftsmen of the Federal Reserve Act) was how to create stronger, centralized national reserves and discipline in a tradition of decentralized, easy entry banking institutions. Such a compromise was not easy, nor in retrospect, should we be surprised that achievements proved to be limited. A crucial conflict emerged between (i) banker views, favoring a National Reserve Association of Banks (voluntary membership) under control of bankers, with broad note issue authority, lending and discount authority, and reserve regulation, and (ii) the populist wing of the Democratic party, which wanted limited banker influence, government (greenback) currency issue, and strong government supervision. Due to the Pujo Committee investigations of the "money trust" and malpractices leading to the Panic of 1907, and Democratic control of the Congress, the Monetary Commission's bill (favoring the banker view) could not be enacted. But President Wilson supported compromise legislation which led to the Federal Reserve Act of 1913. Although some bankers complained of "socialistic" potential for government control, and some agrarians wanted more credit and increased currency along with less influence from bankers, the compromise was enacted by large majorities in both Senate and House.

The result was as far as the United States could go toward central bank regulation at that stage in its history. The new Federal Reserve Board comprised seven members, including the Secretary of Treasury, Comptroller of the Currency, and five other presidential appointees serving 10 year terms (at least two should have banking or financial experience). Federal Reserve District Banks would be established in every region with nine member boards (three banker representatives; three representing business, commerce or agriculture; and three public representatives). (Member banks would elect the first six directors and the Board would appoint the last three directors.) All national banks became members, and state banks could become members. Member banks had to purchase District Bank stock equal to six percent of their own capital and surplus accounts. This would capitalize the Reserve Banks. The Reserve Banks could issue "Federal reserve" notes secured 100 percent by commercial paper, and by 40 percent reserves in gold or gold certificates. Additional notes might be issued, but subject to a graduated tax that tended to limit such circulation. These federal reserve notes would be legal tender and serve as currency. This arrangement provided substantial gold backing for an enlarged currency issue, with some flexibility allowed the Reserve Banks to "meet the needs of trade." In addition, presumably, the Treasury could issue more of its own Treasury notes (or greenbacks) in emergency situations, or alter the gold backing percentage with Congressional approval.

The Federal Reserve Banks would carry on lending operations to member banks, rediscounting 90 day commercial paper or 6 month agricultural obligations. The discount rates for such lending would be a discipline on member banks. In addition, reserve requirements were specified for demand deposits in all the member banks: 18 percent for reserve city banks, 15 percent for city banks, and 12 percent for country banks. On time deposits all banks had to maintain 5 percent reserves. Along with this statutory power, the Federal Reserve Board received financial supervision authority, and the right to enforce special reports from all member and reserve banks, to suspend and remove officers, and to suspend District banks. The Board could also allow District banks to make loans to each other. Thus, financial integrity and emergency lending support would be assured to all member banks, in all Districts of the country.

To help the Treasury in government debt financing, each District bank was permitted to buy and sell government obligations under rules and regulations of the Federal Reserve Board. This provided a sound basis for emergency borrowing by the federal government through the banking system. This authority enabled also what later came to be known as "open market operations", designed to influence the size of bank reserves and money market conditions. Sales of government securities can absorb bank reserves and "tighten" credit markets, while purchases of government securities may increase bank reserves and "ease" credit and money market conditions. Open market operations work more delicately and sensitively to affect bank reserves on a daily basis, provided that a large volume of government debt is outstanding and extensively traded. Open market operations have become in later years the most frequently employed instrument of monetary control.

b. World War I and the Twenties

Early Federal Reserve operations before World War I were limited. Reserve requirements had been higher, on the average, for national banks than under the new Federal Reserve Act. Thus, "free" reserves were created at the outset for member banks. Because District banks did little lending to member banks, in these circumstances, their discount rates had little impact. The principal result, in fact, of the new legislation was to encourage more agricultural lending, and to allow easier credit for industrial activity in the World War I boom. Britain, France, and other allies required greatly increased raw materials and munitions imports for their war efforts. Gold exports to America increased rapidly during the war, and the U.S. quickly became a substantial net creditor nation. This further expanded the gold base for bank reserves in the Federal Reserve system, and sustained easy credit conditions.

When America entered the War in April, 1917, it faced major mobilization requirements. Taxes were increased substantially, but government borrowing at relatively low interest rates was the major source of war-time finance. Altogether $21.5 billion of new long-term bonds was issued, along with another $3.8 billion in short-term debt. (Federal debt in 1914 was merely $2.9 billion). The money supply and credit expanded rapidly. Some rationing was used for scarce materials, but consumer prices went up about 60 percent between 1914–1919. Treasury policies on war finance and borrowing left little scope for Federal Reserve action, especially since substantial excess bank reserves and rapidly expanding gold imports enabled monetary ease and ample credit.

Post-war conditions allowed somewhat more active Federal Reserve policy, and the discount rate was raised sharply in 1920, reaching a peak of 7 per cent in June, 1920. But demobilization and conversion from war industry had already caused a significant recession. This particular tight money policy aggravated the recession, and has been widely criticized by economists. But soon Federal Reserve policy eased, with lower discount rates, along with modest open market operations through purchases of government securities to increase bank reserves. In April, 1923, under Governor Strong's leadership at the New York Reserve Bank, an Open Market Investment Committee was set up to coordinate open market operations. (This was the fore-runner of the present FOMC.) In most of the 1920's money market conditions remained relatively easy. This is especially important in light of the increasing stock market speculation of the later 1920's. While some economists warned of speculative excess, the government and Federal Reserve authorities could not agree on strong measures. Modest increases in the discount rate, and "moral suasion" to discourage speculation were the main responses.

Meanwhile, easy entry into banking, low capitalization requirements, and sagging farm prices allowed a considerable number of bank failures, mostly among small rural banks. Some 5,700 banks "failed" between 1921–1929, and the aggregate number of banks declined from 30,500 to 25,300 in this period. Federal Reserve Act reforms, in other words, had not entirely eliminated the problem of banking "fragility" in the country.

c. The Great Depression

The stock market crash of October, 1929 and the Great Depression of the 1930's was a severe economic tragedy. It brought increased regulation of banking, financial institutions, and securities markets. Controversy followed over the causes of this derangement, which still divides conservative, moderate and Keynesian economists. But consensus exists on many aspects of the Depression. Most importantly, excess speculation, featuring over-valued stocks and highly leveraged margin accounts, was a prime difficulty. Once a rapid collapse in stock values occurred, it forced extensive losses upon many well-to-do and ordinary families, led to a spreading slump in sales, rapidly increasing unemployment, and eventually, a severe crisis of defaulting loans to banks and savings institutions. Unfortunately, neither the Federal Reserve, Congress, nor the President acted with sufficient aid or boldness to halt this slump quickly.

The Hoover administration urged that "public confidence" had to be restored, but not enough was done to limit the growing depression. Soon it became world-wide in scope, with aggravated difficulties brought on by European currency devaluations, and a substantial gold outflow. Relief efforts were controversial, and inhibited by budget deficits. Easier monetary policy from the Federal Reserve, including open market purchases of government securities (to increase bank reserves) and reduced discount rates had little impact. Alarmed at the gold drain and its threat to sufficient backing for the currency (federal reserve notes), emergency authority was enacted (in February, 1932) to use government obligations as currency backing. Finally, stronger open market operations were conducted in the spring and summer of 1932 to increase credit, but by this time the economy, employment, and the use of credit by business had sagged drastically. A more constructive step, the Reconstruction Finance Corporation, came late in January, 1932, but it only loaned $2.2 billion by March, 1933.

The Great Depression was the country's worst financial panic, with most tragic consequences. Gross national product dropped from $103.4 to $55.8 billion between 1929–33. The index of industrial production declined from 100 to 63. The money supply (currency and demand deposits) fell from $26.6 to $19.9 billion. Half the banks in the nation (mostly smaller banks) closed by the summer of 1933. Unemployment increased from 3.2 to 24.9 percent of the civilian labor force, and reached a total of 15 million workers. And prices declined substantially, especially for agricultural commodities (which hurt farmers badly, although some people still employed without loss in income may have benefitted).

5. NEW DEAL REFORMS AND THE FEDERAL RESERVE, 1933–41

Much of the banking, financial, and securities legislation of the New Deal era survives today. On the whole, it strengthened the financial system. But

it should be understood as a series of emergency
and other corrective measures designed to be helpful, rather than as a single master plan or ideologi-
cal program. The dominant theme was pragmatism,
and a feeling that government should act forcefully
to restore prosperity, if possible, and to prevent
another depression. (These "reforms" are summarized in Chapter I, and set forth in more detail with
respect to money and banking in Chapters II and
III, with respect to savings institutions in Chapter
IV, and securities markets in Chapter V infra.)

When Franklin Roosevelt took office in March,
1933, the most immediate problem was a nationwide banking crisis, i.e., a massive run on the
banks. Rapid gold withdrawals and outflows to other countries were undermining the gold base for the
currency. Almost all the commercial banks had
closed, expecting some form of relief by the new
administration. The new Treasury Secretary, William Woodin, helped orchestrate the following emergency action: (i) temporary closure of all banks; (ii)
financial aid on a much larger scale to the weaker
banks through "soft" RFC loans and Federal Reserve advances; (iii) authorizing banks to issue 6
percent preferred stock in return for RFC capital
loans; (iv) authorizing the Comptroller of the Currency to appoint conservators for closed banks with
powers to reopen or liquidate; and (v) strict prohibitions on any export of gold except under license by
the Treasury Secretary. Emergency legislation gave
the President broad powers to regulate transactions
in specie, and by Executive Order the United States

left the gold standard. The Federal Reserve issued $200 million in emergency reserve notes, substantial new loans were made to banks and the RFC purchased $1.3 billion in bank stocks to strengthen their capital structures. This latter injection of capital approached nearly half the equity or capital accounts in the banks surviving the depression. Thus, when large scale aid at last came to the banking system, it was sufficient to restore depleted bank capital and viability.

But more action quickly followed to ensure public confidence in money and banking. Most significant, for the long term, was the Banking Act of June 16, 1933. This law established the Federal Deposit Insurance Corporation. The FDIC expanded the old New York safety fund concept (1829–1837), and created a federal insurance guarantee system for bank deposits up to $2,500 (now $100,000) on each account. Its initial capital was provided by the Treasury and the surplus in Federal Reserve District Banks, and was replenished by modest insurance premiums on the insured banks. Virtually all banks joined the new system (whether national or state chartered), because most depositors wanted this protection for their bank deposits. Every normal commercial bank now maintains this insurance to stay in business. This provided much greater supervisory leverage for bank examination purposes. The FDIC staff, along with the Comptroller's staff for national banks, the Federal Reserve staff for state chartered member banks, and the various state banking commissioners have subsequently developed a much better, comprehensive surveillance system for commercial banks than existed before the Depression. For over 70 years since the FDIC system was established, bank runs have been largely eliminated. Only a few hundred American banks had failed between 1940–80, and the majority of these were salvaged in forced merger transactions in which all depositors were fully protected (even those not insured). [Unfortunately, bank and thrift institution failures became more common in the 1980's and early 1990's; about 1,500 banks and 1,000 thrifts became insolvent in this recent period. Much greater FDIC (and FSLIC) expenses were incurred recently as a result. In response, improved supervision, tougher capital requirements and risk oriented deposit insurance premiums have been implemented to overhaul the FDIC insurance system between 1989–92.]

Other provisions of the Banking Act of 1933 became more controversial: (i) Interest payments on demand deposits were outlawed to prevent "excessive" and cut-throat competition among banks that might weaken their financial strength. In the DIDMCA of 1980 this provision was finally rescinded for NOW accounts with any financial institution. (ii) Investment banking was separated from commercial banking, and some of the biggest commercial banks in New York divested their investment banking operations into separate companies. This provision, often described as the "Glass–Steagall Wall," operated into the 1980's, but was gradually relaxed, and largely eliminated in 1999. Many doubted the need for it today, especially since major brokerage and investment banking houses (like Merrill–Lynch) developed money market accounts and CMA's rather like checking accounts, and compete more directly with banks. But this provision did help to maintain more detachment in commercial bank lending and trust account management, with little cost to anyone in society. (iii) Another provision, credit control authority, was designed to prevent speculative excesses. It has been used occasionally to limit credit and restrict inflation in emergencies, and most recently, in the spring of 1980. (iv) Another aspect of qualitative credit control was power for the Federal Reserve Board to suspend a member bank if it made undue use of credit for speculative purposes. The broad purpose of these provisions in the Glass–Steagall compromise (the Banking Act of 1933) was to reduce risk for commercial banks, and allow regulators more power to prevent another depression. But, these "risk limiting" measures could be misused, especially if employed to limit healthy and desirable competition among financial institutions.

Other steps completed the abandonment of the gold standard. Congress declared "gold clauses" void in government and private obligations in June, 1933. In mid-summer, the International Monetary Conference in London broke up with a failure to agree on measures to restore the gold standard. Although U.S. devaluation brought some immediate "stimulus" to the economy (and slightly increased commodity prices, greatly desired by farmers), this "gain" was reversed by the late summer, as it gradually became apparent that floating exchange rates were stabilizing. By January, 1934 Congress stabilized the dollar's value in terms of gold at $35 per oz., a ratio that was to last until President Nixon's devaluation of August 15, 1971. Thus, the U.S. created a gold-exchange standard for international dealings, but used an irredeemable paper dollar for domestic trade.

In the Banking Act of 1935 Congress strengthened the powers of the Federal Reserve Board to act as a central bank. The Board received authority to regulate the discount rates of District Reserve Banks. The Board could set reserve requirements for demand deposits within a broader range, i.e., 13–26 percent for reserve city banks, 10–20 percent for city banks, and 7–14 percent for country banks. (This leeway was restricted recently by the DIDM-CA of 1980, which restored a more uniform reserve requirements policy, i.e., 12 percent for "transaction accounts" and 3 percent for time deposits, except for emergency periods when higher reserves could be required.) The Board's influence on open market operations was strengthened by restructuring the FOMC. Formerly an adjunct of the New York Federal Reserve Bank, the FOMC became an extension of the Federal Reserve Board (with the seven Board members on the FOMC, along with five District bank representatives). And the Board received authority to regulate interest on time deposits, which led to Regulation Q limits on interest rates for savings accounts. (This limitation on interest rates served to strengthen the Fed's disciplinary authority, but became controversial in the 1970's after Regulation Q limits restricted the competitiveness of passbook savings accounts in periods of high market interest rates, and caused substantial disintermediation from savings institutions and reduced the funds available for housing finance. The DIDMCA of 1980 scheduled a phased elimination of Reg. Q limits on interest rates by 1986.)

Finally, the Federal Reserve Board itself was restructured to increase its independence. Although the Board retained seven members, the Secretary of the Treasury and Comptroller of the Currency were eliminated. All seven simply became presidential appointees, but with lengthened terms, from 10 to 14 years. This led over the years to an increasing independence from political control, a result favored by most bankers, though controversial at times among political leaders.

Monetary policy during the New Deal years was designed to facilitate recovery. The system had substantial free reserves and surplus liquidity, interest rates remained low, and the discount rate was kept down too. However, after July, 1936, the Federal Reserve tightened reserve requirements substantially. They feared that accumulated deficits, excess reserves, and the gradual economic recovery could launch a surge of inflation. So reserve requirements were stepped up to the new maximum levels of 14, 20, and 26 percent by May, 1937. In this way, a large part of the *excess* reserves in the banking system were absorbed. Nonetheless, interest rates remained low and money markets reflected ease throughout the 1930's.

Fiscal policy was mostly stimulative, and considerable deficits were run throughout the 1930's. But in 1936–38, expecting a stronger, more rapid recovery, the federal government increased taxes (including new social security levies), slowed the growth in spending, and tried seriously to bring the budget into balance. But a significant recession developed in 1937–38, after which larger scale deficits resumed in 1939–41. Unemployment increased substantially from 6.4 to 9.8 million between 1937–38, and was still 8.8 million or 17.2 percent in 1939. Unemployment declined to 14.6 percent in 1940, 4.7 percent in 1942, and reached an all-time low of 1.2 percent in 1944. Clearly, the American economy only reached "full" employment during World War II, when much larger deficits were used in the national mobilization effort. This experience with the 1937–38 recession was significant for postwar Keynesian economics, for it led to the view that fiscal policy would be more important as stimulus for the economy than easy money market conditions. Thus, government deficits might be more important than low interest rates to achieve full employment.

6. WORLD WAR II AND POSTWAR ADJUSTMENTS, 1941–51

World War II brought forth the largest military and industrial mobilization effort in the nation's history. Between 1941–46 the war cost $330 billion in direct expenditures. Taxes increased from $6.6 to $46.5 billion between 1941 to 1945, while annual spending (civilian, military and foreign aid) grew from $13.8 to $100.4 billion in these years. The cumulative federal deficits were $210 billion. Fortunately, these deficits and patriotic enthusiasm virtually ended unemployment, and brought many new millions of women into the work force. At the peak of mobilization in 1944–45 the war absorbed half the national output. In World War I, by contrast, only one-fourth of the nation's production was diverted into the war. And yet, World War II was financed to a greater extent by taxes, with more extensive rationing and price-wage controls, and more comprehensive economic planning.

Economic policy was dominated by the war effort. The larger portion of military outlays was financed by government borrowing. The federal debt expanded from $49 billion in 1941 to $279 billion in 1946. This growing burden led the government to insist upon low interest rates to keep the carrying charges bearable, and to limit "excess" profits for financiers, when many families were sacrificing lives and crippling injuries. In the early part of the war, substantial slack, unemployment and excess capacity absorbed these deficits nicely. Later, the war called forth production and employment (with many more women), that went beyond previous national capacity. Inflation developed, especially in critical war materials, but controls and limited rationing kept increases in the cost of living to 25 percent between 1941–45. On the whole, World War II economic policy was successful.

Banking and monetary policy during the war was tailored to the support of government borrowing. Altogether $230 billion of new government debt was created to finance the war, or nearly twice the 1941 GNP of $125 billion. Although real economic growth was substantial during the war, the total debt of $279 billion in 1946 substantially exceeded that year's GNP of $210 billion. Even with low interest rates enforced by Treasury Department policy, this debt interest burden reached 3½ percent of the GNP. Higher interest rates would have increased greatly the government's carrying charges. This debt burden explains why the Treasury wanted to impose "pegged" low rates on government borrowing upon the Federal Reserve and money markets.

Postwar financial policy brought changes. The country promptly demanded demobilization, and an end to war-time controls. A strong surge of price inflation followed, caused by the buildup of savings and purchasing power during the war. The cost of living increased 33 percent between 1945–48. Many feared a major postwar depression, but the adjustment process proved relatively smooth. While the 1948–49 recession slowed the economy, inflation was halted. Unemployment only reached 5.9 percent in 1949, and declined to 2.9 percent by 1953. Strong prosperity with fuller employment proved a great blessing to the nation.

But some disagreements arose as to the postwar level of government spending, taxes, national defense, foreign aid, inflationary pressure, and the dangers of unemployment and recession. Clearly, military forces had to be reduced greatly from their war-time peak of nine million. But tensions with the Soviet Union and the vulnerability of Western Europe, Japan, and other parts of the world led to a stronger peacetime defense effort. The Cold War began, with defense and foreign aid accounting for 6–8 percent of GNP between 1947–50, and increasing to 9–10 percent between 1951–69. Veteran's benefits and interest on the national debt accounted initially for another 4–5 percent of GNP. Civilian and non-war related expenditures of the federal government were reduced, compared to the later New Deal years. Federal civilian outlays were only $2\frac{1}{2}$ percent of the GNP in the Truman years. By contrast such expenditures had been 6 percent of the GNP in 1939. A large part of the difference was explained by unemployment relief programs in the mid-late 1930's, which had accounted for 3 percent of GNP in 1939. After World War II such relief expenditures were relatively modest, because the economy was stronger and unemployment was reduced.

The Korean War provoked open conflict between the Treasury and the Federal Reserve over interest rates for increased federal debt. The Korean War emergency and stronger support for European rearmament (NATO) forced increased spending. Federal outlays went from $40 billion in 1949–50 to $60 billion in 1951. Defense expenditures grew from $13 billion in 1949 to $45–50 billion annually between 1951–65 (on the average). While taxes were increased promptly, and economic growth provided more revenue, the Treasury feared that substantial new debt had to be floated, and wanted low interest rates pegged (as in World War II and its immediate aftermath). But the Federal Reserve refused to go along this time. Instead, the Federal Reserve began (in September 1950) to sell short-term government obligations in open market operations at slightly higher interest rates (1.30 instead of 1.25 percent) to sop up credit. Later that fall and winter the Federal Reserve board members made it clear that they would no longer support low interest re-financing of the government's debt (then at 2 ½ percent for long-term obligations).

Gradually, banking and monetary policy in the post-war era settled down to a more stable, predictable pattern. Once the size of government and defense outlays had been established, with appropriate tax revenues to support them, more "normal" money market conditions could be restored. With stronger economic growth, fuller employment, and relatively low inflation, the Federal Reserve Board sought an end to "pegged" low interest rates for government debt.

This led to the famous "Accord of 1951" between the Treasury Department and the Federal Reserve Board. Public disagreement embarrassed the Administration and Congressional Committees threatened to launch investigations into the subject. On

March 4, 1951, the Treasury and the Board jointly announced "full accord with respect to debt management and monetary policies—[and] to minimize monetization of the public debt." Its immediate impact was to relax support of lower interest rates by the Federal Reserve, though it did not, as some bankers preferred, bring a strong switch in policy to higher interest rates. Fortunately, tax increases reduced the scale of budget deficits, so that less pressure was placed on debt markets and interest rates. Moderate increases in interest rates followed, with Treasury accommodation to the asserted independence of monetary policy. The long run impact has been to establish more firmly a general presumption, though not an absolute rule, in favor of Federal Reserve independence in monetary policy management.

Chart II-1

Monetary Policy Guidelines

Alternatives—	Monetary Targeting—	Federal Reserve Targeting Procedures (Evolution)—
1) Monetarist Thinking		
a) Chicago-St. Louis Strict M1 Growth Discipline with more or less strict fiscal discipline	M1 with contemporaneous reserve accounting	1920's—Money market conditions, leaning against breeze
b) European Monetarism [1] Fiscal Discipline and Monetary Restraint with competitive disciplines from world market	M1, 2 or credit and interest rates, with exchange rate constraints	Great Depression—Slack and easy money
2) Traditional Banker Views		
a) Conservative Monetary-Fiscal Discipline—"leaning against breeze"	M1, 2 or credit and interest rates, along with economic conditions	1942-51—Artifically low interest rates to support government borrowing
b) C.E.D. Style Fiscal and Monetary Stimulus except with inflation, "reasonable" restraints	M1, 2 or credit and interest rates, along with economic conditions	1950's—Money market conditions, reserves and leaning against breeze

1. European monetarism includes categories 1b, 2a, and 2b as alternatives to "socialists" using 3a, 3b, or 4.

Chart II-1

Monetary Targeting—	Federal Reserve Targeting Procedures (Evolution)—

Alternatives—

3) Keynesian Outlooks

a) Moderate

Full employment budgeting with monetary fiscal and wage-price restraint for inflation

Interest rates, macro goals-growth, unemployment, and inflation

1960's—Money markets, interest rates, and macro objectives . . . "fed funds" and money supply

b) More Extreme

Full employment budgeting with wage-price controls if necessary; non-restrictive monetary policy except nationalized banking might allow more selective restraints and credit allocation

Growth, unemployment, and inflation, plus equity

1970's—Federal funds rate, plus macro conditions and monetary aggregates

October '79—Summer '82—Monetary aggregates primary emphasis

4) Strongly Socialist

General government controls for significant prices, wages, capital allocation and interest rates

Growth, employment, and inflation, plus equity and government goals

After Fall 1982—Pragmatic easing, with unresolved controversy on targeting

After Fall 1985—Easing and restraint, with more concern for exchange rates, balance of payments, and general economic conditions

7. MONETARY AND ECONOMIC
POLICY, 1951–PRESENT

During the early postwar era, America's economy enjoyed expanded growth and prosperity. Money and banking policy reflected continuity, for the most part, and made its contribution to healthy economic conditions. Fiscal policy and modest government deficits came to be relied upon as the main response to recessions, slack and unemployment. The Federal Reserve leaned against the breeze, to some degree, tightening upon interest rates slightly in boom periods, and easing money market conditions when softness appeared in the economy. This policy worked reasonably well, so long as inflation remained low, and the overall growth trend was strongly upward in the 1950's and 1960's.

But in the late 1960's and 1970's the economy suffered greater inflation, which was soon followed by more unemployment and slack, i.e., what became known as "stagflation." Macro-economic coordination became more erratic, and the role for monetary policy became controversial in these later years. Inflationary momentum and expectations built up gradually, with intermittent surges of substantial deficit spending. More strain was placed on monetary policy in these circumstances, and restraint from the Federal Reserve became much more strict in late 1979 and most of the early 1980's. In this later period the Federal Reserve was the focus of increasing argument, although inflation slowed markedly in late 1981 and 1982 with substantially enlarged slack and unemployment. But government deficits increased, too, which brought upward pressure on interest rates through large public sector borrowing. This also sustained inflationary expectations to some degree, and weakened prospects for economic recovery. Disagreements emerged among politicians and conflicting schools of economic thought about tax burdens and government spending. It took 15 years to eliminate excess deficits, i.e., until the later 1990's. Better balanced budgets and sound monetary policy were needed together.

a. Truman–Eisenhower, 1951–60

Economic and monetary policy in these years featured nearly balanced budgets, except in recession periods, when deficits were run to offset slack and unemployment. The Korean War and NATO defense efforts brought military spending up to 9–10 percent of GNP, but taxes (including income tax bracket creep) kept revenues pretty much in line with expenditures. Moderate deficits were allowed in recessions, i.e., 1954, 1957, and 1960. But the deficits in these peak years never exceeded 2 percent of GNP, and averaged less than 1 percent overall. Inflation remained low, for the most part, except for wage-price pressures from powerful unions and in some concentrated industries, especially in 1957–59.

In this situation the strain on monetary policy was limited. The Federal Reserve leaned against mild breezes, and gradually tried to improve its economic indicators and targeting. The major criticism offered in the late 1950's came from liberals, populists and Keynesians. They complained that the Fed erred on the side of restrictiveness. They sought stronger wage-price discipline for concentrated industries and major unions, so that monetary policy and interest rates (and, perhaps even fiscal policy) might be eased and thus allow "fuller" employment. But conservatives were skeptical of such hopes, and some of them began also to argue for less discretion in monetary policy and more regular growth in the money supply as the best guideline for the Federal Reserve (later labeled the "monetarist" viewpoint).

b. Kennedy–Johnson, 1961–68

While the Kennedy administration implemented a limited policy of wage and price guidelines, its fiscal policy remained relatively conservative, and budget deficits were slightly lower (on the average) than the Eisenhower years. A moderate tax cut in 1963 roughly approximated, in fact, an adjustment for accumulated bracket creep. And economic growth improved, with low inflation between 1961–66. This put little strain on monetary policy, at least until the second half of 1966.

Meanwhile, the Federal Reserve's economic staff was strengthened, part of a general trend in government and business. This increase in professionalism and data gathering involved more attention to money supply statistics along with other economic indicators. During the period 1961 through early 1966

Federal Reserve policy was moderately accommodative, consistent with increased economic growth and reduced unemployment, yet inflation remained low.

But in 1966 the economy was approaching full employment (in most sectors), and the Vietnam War mobilization added further deficit pressure. At this stage the Federal Reserve tightened monetary policy considerably, and M1 growth was cut to zero for the second half of 1966 (as compared to nearly 5 percent for 1964 and 1965). Interest rates moved up substantially. And when Regulation Q limits on savings account interest rates were not raised appreciably, these accounts became less attractive, and the flow of funds into savings and loan associations was cut drastically. Because of these strains and the risk of recession, the Fed eased its braking action late in 1966. Meanwhile, growth slowed in 1967, and in 1968 the Vietnam War surtax came into effect, which balanced the federal budget. These circumstances led the Fed to moderate accommodation, and it allowed somewhat faster growth in the money supply, even though the wage-price guidelines had been increasingly abandoned in 1967–68 and the inflation rate was picking up.

c.   Nixon–Ford, 1969–76

The Federal Reserve tightened up more restrictively in 1969 and tried to break the inflationary spiral. A sustained boom in stock prices ended with a substantial retreat, and a moderate recession began later that year. Then in the summer of 1970 Penn Central filed bankruptcy, and nervousness spread in financial markets. The Fed eased fears by announcing that its discount window would open wider to accommodate squeezed borrowers, and it liberalized Regulation Q exemptions for larger CD's (certificates of deposit) so that banks and S & L's could buy the deposits needed for their lending. Reserve requirements were relaxed slightly. But interest rates remained reasonably firm.

In these circumstances the economy had slowed down, unemployment increased, yet inflation eased only slightly. The Nixon administration made its opposition to wage-price controls clear, and partly for this reason, the Democratic Congress enacted controls authority, intending to blame Nixon for not using a "more balanced" anti-inflation policy. Price and wage movements were not seriously inhibited in this environment, and the recession was not big enough to brake their spiral momentum.

Meanwhile, the balance of payments deficit had grown and a long accumulated buildup of dollar holdings abroad (as reserve currency) began to be cashed in for gold or harder currencies. Persisting inflation in the U.S. and a sizeable payments deficit was seen as a fundamental weakness for the dollar, and a speculative capital outflow anticipated devaluation—thus, exacerbating the payments deficit. In August, 1971, a run on the dollar began, this outflow started to hemorrhage, a rapid decline in gold reserves ensued, and a devaluation became unavoidable. (Other countries complained that the U.S. was "exporting inflation," and financing itself with cheapened dollars.) At this stage, fearing the political impact of a devaluation (the first since 1933–34), aggravated recession and unemployment, the Nixon administration decided upon a bold reversal of policies.

On August 15, 1971, price and wage controls were imposed, and convertibility of the dollar (at $35 per oz. for gold) ended, forcing the dollar to float against other currencies. This eased the capital outflow problem, and currencies could, presumably, find their own values. Phase I controls, a "hard freeze," lasted three months, and Phase II "controlled increases" 15 months. Budget stimulus was added to the mix, and the Federal Reserve accommodated with easier monetary policy and lower interest rates. This "game plan", as administration leaders labeled it, was designed to allow a more balanced, rapid economic recovery, with limited inflation pressure. These policies were closer to what Democratic opponents had been suggesting, so that wags called Nixon's shift the "NEP" (or New Economic Policy), referring to Lenin's NEP or partial switch to free market policies in the early 1920's for several years.

Short-term results of the NEP were successful. Inflation was substantially reduced, growth improved, and unemployment declined. Public support and confidence was strong, and Nixon won a landslide election victory against McGovern, the Democratic nominee. But the NEP package provoked controversy, and was criticised from both right and left. Conservatives opposed the use of controls, feared their distortions, and wanted them dismantled as soon as possible. Conservatives also believed inflation would have come down anyway, and some were concerned about excessive fiscal and monetary stimulus. Keynesians wanted even more stimulus, and challenged the durability of Nixon's commitment to wage and price guidelines.

During 1973 most controls were soon relaxed, and by the spring of 1974 were almost entirely eliminated. But this early release of wage-price discipline combined with bad harvests in Europe and Russia, the trebling of oil prices by the OPEC cartel, and scarcities in other raw materials markets, to cause 12 percent inflation in the U.S. Double-digit inflation spread quickly to the majority of industrial nations, along with many less developed countries.

Fiscal policy in the U.S. shifted toward balance in 1973–74, and the Federal Reserve's monetary policy tightened too. The prime bank rate climbed to a peak of 12 percent in July, 1974. The Federal Reserve continued restrictiveness during most of 1974, even though a major recession developed in 1974–75, with unemployment reaching a postwar peak of 9 percent.

But the severity of this recession provoked a large federal deficit, i.e., 4 percent of GNP in 1975, the biggest since World War II. Monetary policy shifted to relative ease. Nonetheless, this recession, along with a relaxation in scarcity inflation from the world market, brought inflation down to 5–6 percent in 1976. Unfortunately economists remained badly divided on the next steps with many Keynesians demanding sustained fiscal stimulus to reach full employment and, if necessary, wage-price controls to reduce inflation. Conservatives denounced controls as a "proven failure," and wanted more limited fiscal and monetary stimulus.

d. Carter, 1977–80

Carter won the 1976 election with a moderate campaign, emphasizing his success as a farmer, and claiming to be a "social liberal" and a "fiscal conservative." His economic policies reflected this compromise approach, and he slowly reduced the federal deficit between 1977–79. He also encouraged economic growth, and the Federal Reserve was moderately accommodative until the second half of 1978. Economic growth improved and 9 million new jobs were added in three years. But these policies did not adequately discipline the wage-price spiral, and Carter specifically denounced the use of controls.

As inflation gradually increased in the U.S. from 7 to 9 percent in 1977–78, inflation rates declined to much lower levels (1–3 percent) in Switzerland, West Germany and Japan. The strength of these export economies and their currencies encouraged a shift in international liquidity away from the dollar toward the Swiss franc, Deutschmark, and Yen. The dollar declined significantly against these currencies, and some others. This sag in the dollar increased American import costs and aggravated inflation for the short run (as U.S. exports responded much more slowly to reduced dollar values.) In the fall of 1978 this international trend reached crisis proportions, as another run on the dollar seemed imminent.

In November, 1978, Carter's administration was forced to make a substantial mid-course correction. They implemented "voluntary" wage-price guidelines, borrowed $30 billion in hard currencies abroad to defend the dollar, and insisted otherwise that their policies were correct. The foreign borrowing helped prop up the dollar for awhile, but the voluntary anti-inflation effort failed. Unhappily, the voluntary guidelines program, under "inflation Czar" A.E. Kahn, actually seemed to encourage anticipatory price-wage increases, and in 1979–80 the second round of OPEC oil price increases added further inflationary pressure. In late 1979 the inflation rate reached 13 percent, and briefly during early 1980, a monthly increase of 1.8 percent was recorded (or 20 percent a year).

During the late summer and early fall of 1979 the Federal Reserve and the Carter administration came under increasing attack from Monetarists and many bankers. The monetary aggregates were still increasing, and these critics felt a tougher monetary policy was essential to reduce inflation. The Federal Reserve had been "raising" interest rates gradually for many months, but it really cracked down in October, 1979, and even more severely in early 1980. Federal Reserve policy clearly moved in a monetarist direction. The prime rate went from 16 to 20 percent in the winter of 1979–80, and M1 growth was halted in these periods. But with record high interest rates, rapid growth of money market mutual funds (and high interest CD's), more liquidity shifted into quasi money accounts (M3, M4 and M5), which still grew considerably. After a sharp recession in the spring of 1980, the Federal Reserve relaxed its grip for awhile, allowed short term interest rates to drop substantially, and the monetary aggregates picked up somewhat.

Meanwhile, the inflation rate had not fallen very much in the spring 1980 recession, and the wage-price spiral seemed strongly entrenched with expectations of continued high inflation. Monthly increases in the cost of living resumed their upward trend, and by the November, 1980 election, the annual inflation rate of 12 percent showed little progress as compared to a year earlier. The Federal Reserve cracked down again in the later fall with tighter monetary restraint, and interest rates moved back toward the high levels of early 1980, i.e., 20 percent. In this situation, the economy and its troubles, along with the Iranian hostage mess, were important factors in converting a cliffhanger election into a 51–44 percent sweep for Reagan (independents got the remainder).

e. Reagan, 1981–88

Reagan's administration wanted to reduce the share of government spending in GNP, cut the tax load, and increase defense outlays. Their major legislative push was for a 25–30 percent reduction in personal income taxes (over three years) designed to eliminate accumulated bracket creep, and increase investment incentives. This, they felt, would strengthen the economy, and provide sustained leverage to cut "unnecessary" government expenditures quite substantially. Monetary policy, they believed, should provide complementary discipline to help break inflationary expectations. Wage-price monitoring (or guidelines) activity, which had existed in some form between 1961–68 and 1971–80, were abolished as "useless."

Implementing this policy proved more difficult. The income tax cuts were enacted, but log-rolling politics added substantially greater tax relief, especially for business interests. And spending cuts came more slowly, partly because a planned social security "solvency" study was delayed by the Democratic opposition. This delay, along with the 1982 elections, set back the schedule for social security reductions. This widened the gap between revenue and spending more than was expected and more than many economists believed appropriate. Government deficits projected grew from 1 percent of GNP in 1980 to 3 percent of GNP in 1982, and reached almost 5 percent of GNP annually between 1983–87. This increased load of government deficits strained monetary policy.

The Federal Reserve felt obliged to maintain firmness against inflation. The Fed wanted, this time, to avoid a premature relaxation. But, these high interest rates, i.e. winter of 1979–80, resuming again in the summer of 1980 through (at least) the fall of 1982, did impose substantial deflationary discipline. Unemployment increased from 7.5 percent to nearly 11 percent, and much of the economy remained sluggish, with little growth until later in 1983–84. Monthly inflation rates did come down substantially in the fall of 1981, and stayed lower from 1982 through the 1980's. Helpful factors in the world market were a growing oil glut, and increased world agricultural output, which lowered farm prices. However, the underlying inflation rate still seemed to be around 3 percent and was worrisome, and financial markets anticipated eventual inflationary pressure from government deficits. Interest rates were coming down, but only slowly, in a gradual saw-tooth pattern (until late 1991, when recession led the Fed to lower short-term rates more substantially for a while).

Toward the end of July, 1982, the Federal Reserve appeared to soften its monetary policy somewhat. The widely publicized failure of the Penn Square Bank in Oklahoma, and losses caused by bigger bank participations in some "high flying" energy loans, had caused unease in the financial press. The combination of a sluggish economy, increased deficits, weakening of the trade balance, worries about inflation, unemployment, and doubtful prospects for a strong recovery, seemed to accentuate risk factors.

Yet as U.S. economic growth resumed and unemployment declined in 1983–84, Republican fortunes improved (thanks, in part, to Volcker and the Federal Reserve). While some Administration and Congressional leaders sought substantially reduced deficits, this was difficult with enlarged defense outlays and Reagan's opposition to new taxes. Mondale, the 1984 Democratic nominee, tried to highlight deficit dangers and offered to raise taxes. President Reagan replied that the last thing he wanted was a tax increase (a popular line with voters). A landslide victory followed for Reagan, although little realignment occurred in Congress.

In 1985 Congress enacted the Gramm–Rudman Act compromise as an effort (spread over 5 years) to gradually reduce excess budget deficits. But the Supreme Court held unconstitutional a crucial element—the delegation of specific budget reduction amounts to the General Accounting Office. This weakened deficit reduction, because Congress was not willing to accept the Administration's OMB allocations for automatic percentage spending cuts. During 1986–87 Congress tried to comply with Gramm–Rudman's deficit reduction schedule, but did so only with the help of some sales of government assets (and extra revenues flowing from the 1986 Tax Reform Act). Prospects were not too encouraging, and it seemed likely that stronger budget discipline would be a task passed along to the next Presidential administration. Nonetheless, interest rates were eased, reaching a temporary low or trough between Sept. 1986–March 1987, though rising again some until the Fall of 1987.

Unfortunately, another development was greatly enlarged U.S. trade deficits, from $123 billion in 1984 to $148 billion in 1985, $160 billion in 1986, and $171 billion in 1987. Higher U.S. interest rates (needed to help offset big budget deficits) did bring in more foreign investment and borrowing, but soon made this country the world's largest debtor nation (approaching $400 billion by the end of 1987).* A seriously over-valued dollar (especially between 1983–86) had weakened U.S. exports, and fostered even greater imports. Although the dollar later slumped, the U.S. trade deficit improved only briefly. By the fall of 1987, widespread worries about the twin deficits—excess budget and trade deficits—finally weakened confidence in the U.S. stock market. A major retreat or correction ensued, spreading to other stock markets around the world, with the Dow Jones industrial average falling briefly from over 2700 (its all time peak) to below 1700. This helped to focus political attention on these problems for awhile.

All these events (of the later 1980's), demonstrated that international trade, capital flows, competing interest and exchange rates were increasingly influential. This suggested a need for better macroeconomic coordination in the world economy. It also revealed that U.S. monetary and fiscal policy were less independent of events abroad, and that greater budget discipline was required. While many smaller countries had learned these lessons earlier, the leadership, size, and strength of the U.S. economy in the post-World War II era had allowed Americans to believe they enjoyed more freedom from world market forces.

* According to some estimates, the net external debts (or capital position) of the U.S. reached $2,000 billion in 2000 and this external debt load totaled $3,500 billion by year end 2005.

Major, unresolved issues facing the next administration, Congress, and the Federal Reserve were how to implement further spending cuts in 1988–92, and/or raise taxes in some way to narrow the budget deficit. Awkward conflicts between defense expenditures, social security and health care, and other civilian government outlays were involved on the spending side, and tax increases would be hard to allocate among constituencies. Yet most economic observers believed reduced deficits would be needed to ease the strain on U.S. monetary policy, allow substantially lower interest rates, improve the trade balance, and facilitate a stronger economic recovery.

f.   Bush, 1989–92

President George H. W. Bush promised to carry on Reagan's policies, including a pledge, "Read my lips ... No New Taxes!"* But his initial economic problem was a need to recapitalize FSLIC—the FDIC counterpart for S & L's and savings banks. (For details, see Chapter IV–D *Thrifts in Transition,* at pp. 271–285.) During the later 1980s hundreds of thrifts became insolvent, with hundreds more in trouble. By winter 1988–89 a costly bailout of FSLIC and a massive cleanup operation was required. This led to the Financial Institutions Reform, Recovery, and Enforcement Act of 1989 (FIRREA), which absorbed FSLIC into the FDIC.

---

* The Democratic nominee in 1988, Massachusetts Gov. Michael Dukakis, proved a weak challenger on economic issues. He offered to close the budget deficit gap with another $100 billion in "uncollected" income taxes, which lacked credibility to many observers. Meanwhile, important trade, industrial, and financial controversies were largely neglected in a campaign that focused more on social questions and foreign policy credentials.

Meanwhile, the FHLBB was brought into the OCC as the Office of Thrift Supervision—(OTS), and FIRREA created the Resolution Trust Corporation (RTC) as a receivership agency for failed thrifts. The FSLIC bailout was expensive ($160 billion in costs by early 1993, and another $200–300 billion ultimate interest expense). But most of this outlay was handled *off-budget* through Treasury borrowing (at least for the first 5 years), as an unanticipated, non-recurring expense.

Then attention shifted to foreign affairs. A dramatic liberalization began in Eastern Europe and U.S.S.R. that brought down their Communist governments, with a transformation to more democratic, market oriented regimes between 1989 and the end of 1991. Meanwhile, Iraq's invasion of Kuwait in August, 1990, the U.S. led rescue, and 6 weeks war between January–February, 1991, led to a remarkable joint effort by many nations toward collective security. In these years, the European Community also moved toward greater unification through 1992 and beyond, which helped inspire and reinforce East bloc developments. Meanwhile, the Uruguay GATT round negotiations, started at Punta del Este in 1986, made some limited progress toward freer trade in these years. But thorny conflicts over agricultural subsidies, together with disputes over financial, investment, and services liberalization forced delays until 1993. In a parallel effort, the U.S. broadened trade talks on a regional basis, too, and worked toward a North American

Free Trade Area (NAFTA), involving the U.S., Mexico, and Canada, and a wider Enterprise for the Americas Initiative (EAI) to bring other hemisphere nations into closer economic relations.

Gradually, it seemed that a considerable "peace dividend" of reduced military outlays could be achieved. Accordingly, during September, 1990, a substantial budget deficit reduction agreement was worked out between the Bush Administration and Congressional leaders. Unfortunately, deficit reductions were limited, and mostly prospective. Conservatives strongly resisted any significant new taxes, while Liberal Democrats wanted no significant cuts in domestic spending. The result was mainly a moderate reduction in defense spending over the next 5 years. This left further deficit reduction, agreed by many to be desirable, for the 1992 election and its aftermath.

As the economy slowed further into recession in late 1991, the Federal Reserve eased money markets considerably, and brought down short-term interest rates quite substantially (to levels not seen since the later 1960s). Unfortunately, the slump also slowed government revenues, and brought federal budget deficits back up to $375 and $350 billion for 1992 and 1993, respectively. In these circumstances, only modest fiscal stimulus was proposed by the Administration, and Democratic Congressional leaders initially seemed to agree. A variety of tax "reform" measures were suggested, however, for the longer term to promote recovery and improved economic growth, but serious conflicts over capital gains relief, investment incentives, progressivity, and burden-sharing among the middle-class and wealthy greatly complicated matters. Increasingly expensive health care was also a problem, especially since a sizeable minority did not have adequate health care insurance coverage. At this stage, it might be difficult to get rapid and strong fiscal stimulus quickly.

In this overall context, Federal Reserve policy between 1989–92 had tried to contain inflationary pressures, and kept growth of the monetary aggregates in check. This, together with continued, large federal borrowing requirements to cover large deficits, continued somewhat elevated interest rates. Partly for these reasons, U.S. economic growth slowed somewhat, reflecting also increased strains on many banks, thrifts, and over-leveraged corporations (a legacy from the 1980s financial "boom" years, the tightening of lending policy by many institutions, and slowed industrial expansion). This slowdown hurt the prospects for Bush in the fall, 1992 election. But other circumstances, including strong campaigns by Clinton, Buchanan, and Perot, together with unease about the movement of jobs to lower wage nations, may have been more influential in the defeat of Bush.

But as the world marketplace had become more interdependent, U.S. economic recovery depended also on external developments. Both Germany and Japan had tightened up their credit markets in 1991, which helped cause a global slowdown among many industrial nations. Serious economic disruptions and reduced output in the former U.S.S.R. also influenced things. International economists were divided on remedies, but many insisted that increased global liquidity—a substantial part targeted on the East bloc countries and poorer developing nations—could be generally helpful for the U.S. and world economy altogether. With greater excess capacity in many nations the dangers of inflation did not seem so great for awhile. But the easing of subsequent monetary policies, which this allowed, was too late for the re-election of Bush.

g. Clinton, 1993–2000

When Clinton (43 percent) and Perot (19 percent) defeated Bush (38 percent) in the fall 1992 elections, many saw a mandate: (i) improved jobs growth; (ii) stronger trade policies and a more level playing field in world markets; (iii) health care reforms, cost containment, and broader coverage; and (iv) gradual budget deficit reduction, eased debt loads, and lower interest rates. The Clinton administration began with a modest deficit-reduction and tax increase package (enacted with only Democratic votes). But the recent Bush slowdown and new deficit reduction package allowed interest rates to come down somewhat. Economic activity was picking up with some jobs growth (although U.S. *manufacturing* jobs declined further).

On trade policy Clinton implemented the free trade initiatives of the Bush administration. NAFTA was signed by Clinton with modest Side Agreements (for import surges, environmental problems, and labor standards). Congress approved NAFTA in fall 1993 despite extensive Democratic and populist opposition. Shortly thereafter Clinton accepted the Uruguay Round GATT 1994 agreement (largely as negotiated by the Bush administration) with a new World Trade Organization. Multinational corporations were relieved, and more capital flowed from OECD nations to emerging nation markets. But some domestic U.S. interests complained that more should have been done to promote U.S. jobs and manufacturing.*

Meanwhile, Clinton developed a complex plan for broader health care coverage, increased oversight and cost disciplines, financed by employer mandates and additional taxes. Unfortunately, opposition developed from many directions, and Congress was unable to achieve consensus on funding sources, oversight, or cost disciplines. By fall 1994 this major health care reform effort, described by Clinton as a "centerpiece" of his administration, collapsed. This was an embarrassing political failure, since the Democrats had a majority in both houses of Congress during 1993–94.

In a sharp reaction, the November 1994 Congressional elections gave majorities to Republicans in both Senate and House. Led by Rep. Newt Gingrich of Georgia, House Speaker in 1995–96, Republicans offered a new "Contract with America." It featured

* Some trade experts also complained about key features in GATT 1994 and the WTO: (i) UN General Assembly-style voting (one country-one vote); (ii) U.S. concessions on dumping, safeguard remedies, and subsidies; and (iii) insufficient protection for U.S. intellectual property and service firm interests.

stronger budget discipline, a balanced-budget amendment to the Constitution, cost-saving welfare reforms, and reductions in the growth of medicare-medicaid entitlements. Financial markets reacted favorably to the prospect of U.S. fiscal restraint. But by fall 1995 a budgetary impasse resulted, with Clinton's administration and the Republicans determined to press their points through the 1996 election campaign. Partial shutdowns of federal services followed; but defense and spending cuts were patched together by Clinton and Congress before the next election. And, despite partisan bickering, this "progress" on deficit reduction enabled interest rates to be eased even more, which helped growth.

Interestingly, Clinton did better at "spin control" than Congressional Republicans in 1995–96. The press and polls gave him more credit for an improving economy, increased jobs, a rising stock market, lower interest rates, and minimal inflation. Actually, the progress on budgets, interest rates and growth came *at least as much* from the Republicans and Greenspan's Federal Reserve. Some welfare reform also helped to get more poor people working over the next few years. Normally, an improving economy aids an incumbent President's re-election. Clinton was able to beat Rep. Senate majority leader Dole fairly handily in the 1996 elections. Republicans held the Congress, however, although their margin in the House was thinned.

Then Presidential scandals (including the Monica Lewinsky affair) took center stage, and a big struggle over impeachment followed in 1997–98. Clinton ultimately survived, but public attention on the economy was distracted for awhile. Nonetheless, the economy continued to improve. Jobs grew, unemployment declined, and the stock market boomed. Further progress in deficit reduction came from economic growth. Republican resistance to new government spending was helpful, and a growing medium-term surplus was generated in social security reserves.

The social security surplus (a medium-term phenomenon) was caused by demographics and delays in retirements. There were fewer depression era babies born between 1930–42, and not so many were retiring in the late 1990's-until say 2010. Also, more people were working longer—until 70 or more. Meanwhile, the baby boomer bulge (people born 1943–1963) was still working and earning more; payroll taxes were generating a large medium-term social security surplus. This good fortune would be reversed, however, from 2010–2030, as baby boomers retired in larger numbers. Unfortunately, this "surplus" gave politicians a temptation (big tax cuts and/or spending increases could be carried on between 2000–2010. (See Chapter VII, Part D, infra).

Yet, an important worry troubled international economists. U.S. trade and current account deficits were growing again, with sizeable net deficits accumulating. Between 1981–99 U.S. trade deficits totaled $2,500 billion; U.S. current account deficits totaled nearly $2,000 billion. The Americans were living beyond their means in world markets. Foreign capital was flowing steadily into the U.S., with a rising net debt load for the U.S. The rest of the world was giving the U.S. (with its dollar as the world's dominant reserve currency) a free ride. The U.S. was being allowed to live substantially beyond its means.*

Few experts thought this could go on indefinitely, as an "over-priced" U.S. stock market and dollar currency seemed vulnerable to many observers, and threatened a large downslide and/or dollar devaluation. Clearly, a large part of this net "lending or investment" into the U.S. was placed by speculation to exploit the U.S. stock market boom (or "bubble"). A big question was whether corrective adjustments could come gradually, with little disruption, or more harshly.

In this context, Europe's movement toward a European Monetary Union (EMU) and a single currency, the "Euro", was significant. If the Europeans successfully implement the EMU, *with sufficient fiscal, monetary and trade discipline*, the Euro (for a larger trading area) could challenge the dollar's place as the world's leading reserve currency.

* No other country was allowed to run large and chronic trade-current account deficits so long. For all other nations such deficits would have brought rapid and substantial devaluation of their currencies. Why the difference? Since the early 1980's when Reagan/Volcker restored confidence in the dollar, U.S. capital markets were bigger, more liquid and attractive. The dollar became more reliable again "as a parking place" for medium-term investments than other currencies. Meanwhile, recurrent confidence problems afflicted many other countries, causing capital flight and portfolio diversification into the U.S. and the dollar. The U.S. stock market boom also attracted large foreign investments, at least for awhile.

The U.S. could be put under pressure to reduce large trade-current account deficits; otherwise the dollar would weaken substantially in value. This would bring other external disciplines and reduced living standards for Americans until U.S. industry and exports improved their competitiveness. Thus, a problem for Americans is to restore the more fully balanced, coherent macro-economic policies of the later 1940's through 1960's. In those earlier years, U.S. economic growth was stronger, budget deficits were modest, interest rates lower, with a solid industrial base, healthy exports, and no significant balance of payments problems. One way or another, the U.S. should restore realistic economic policies; the nation must learn again to live within its means in terms of domestic finance and external accounts.

But, the U.S. stock market boom surged into "bubble" stage of speculative exuberance. Between 1993–2000 the Dow Jones average more than tripled; the S & P grew comparably, and the NASDAQ went up six fold. PE ratios escallated for many U.S. stocks. Had computerization and the internet really multiplied the real net worth of America's economy that much in just seven years? Could this surge of prosperity be sustained through the 2000 elections and beyond?

In the 2000 presidential election both parties used "rosy" scenarios of increased economic growth, along with tax cuts and spending increases. The Republicans and Bush campaign emphasized tax cuts, while Democrats and Gore offered somewhat larger spending. The election was close, with

disputed returns in Florida and a recount controversy resolved by the U.S. Supreme Court. George
W. Bush won a narrow victory in the electoral
college.

h. Bush, 2001–2004

Most economists predicted a slump or recession
following the 1994–2000 boom. A major stock market downslide followed, especially in "tech" stocks
and the NASDAQ. The Federal Reserve responded
by easing credit and lowering interest rates to prevent panic and facilitate recovery. The Bush administration and Congress also implemented substantial tax relief as stimulus for recovery. Inflation
remained low, so this fiscal-monetary stimulus did
not worry the Federal Reserve. Many countries
slumped, although China, India, and some other
Asian countries managed to preserve strong growth.
At issue was how quickly the U.S. and global economy could recover more broadly.

Then on 9/11/01 Al Qaeda terrorists high-jacked
U.S. airliners for suicide bomber attacks. The World
Trade Center in New York City was destroyed by
two planes, and a third crashed into the Pentagon
(U.S. Dept. of Defense) in Washington, D.C. This
disruptive event aggravated economic uncertainty,
and the Federal Reserve eased credit further. Meanwhile, the Bush administration launched retaliatory
strikes against Al Qaeda terrorists in Afghanistan,
and gave extensive support to Northern Alliance
rebels against the Taliban. Within a few months the
Taliban that hosted Al Qaeda terrorists in Afghani-

stan were overthrown, with wide international support for U.S. efforts.

During the fall and winter of 2002–2003 the Bush administration next decided to overthrow Saddam Hussein's regime in Iraq. Sanctions against Saddam's WMD programs seemed to be collapsing. With increased Iraqi oil revenues Saddam could soon get nuclear weapons, and he threatened to undermine moderate Arab regimes and get more influence over Persian Gulf oil supplies. Although most Arab Gulf states allowed U.S. forces to deploy for intervention in Iraq, European allies (except for Tony Blair's Britain) were reluctant to join the operation. Another round of WMD inspections was suggested, but the Bush people felt it essential to begin military operations promptly. France and Germany strongly opposed the action, and the U.S. and Britain could not obtain a Security Council majority in support.[1]

From an economic standpoint the Iraq intervention accentuated fiscal stimulus in the U.S. as war outlays increased. This encouraged broader economic recovery. But increased "outsourcing" of manufacturing and service jobs to low wage countries also

1. Although U.S. and coalition forces quickly toppled Saddam's regime, it proved more difficult to establish a viable successor regime. Controversy and recriminations followed. Was the intervention force sufficient to provide adequate security? Should more of the regime's military and bureaucracy have been retained? Was the hand-off to Iraqi's too leisurely? Should the makeover have been less ambitious? Could casualties and resistance have been limited more effectively? In retrospect did the U.S. intervention make sense? The U.S. election campaign in Fall, 2004 reviewed these issues.

reduced the employment gains from recovery. This was a structural implication of wider globalization, in which the U.S. was leading the way (since the late 1980's, through the 1990's, and into the 21st century).[2] Energy markets were stressed with Mid–East conflict uncertainties, but also by broad economic growth in China, India, other parts of Asia, Latin America, and much of Europe. The Federal Reserve began to tighten credit and interest rates increased somewhat in the summer of 2004.

In November 2004 the U.S. faced another contentious election. The Iraq war was controversial. Bush people insisted the removal of Saddam Hussein was needed and righteous. But Democratic candidate Kerry challenged the timing, execution, and management of intervention and reconstruction. Kerry wanted more allied support and promised to withdraw U.S. forces within another four years. Bush emphasized the broadening recovery, while Kerry criticized the slower improvement in jobs. Bush and Kerry also divided on fiscal policy. Bush wanted more tax relief and reform, with more discipline on

2. International finance and trade economists disagreed over the extent to which the benefits of globalization were shared, and which countries were "winners" and "losers." Disagreements emerged over "asymmetry" problems. The U.S. and Europe were more open and less "protected" than most new industrial countries (NIC's). Many NIC's (including China, India, and Russia) were neo-mercantilist, and insisted upon greater import restrictions while demanding more rich country openness in WTO negotiations. Meanwhile, The U.S. was suffering (or "benefiting" from) greatly increased U.S. trade and current account deficits in the range of $500 to $600 billion annually between 2002–2005 (or roughly 5 percent of U.S. GNP). Most agreed such large trade imbalances for the U.S. were "unsustainable," but there was no consensus on appropriate trade-finance remedies.

spending. Kerry wanted higher taxes on the "rich", more health and other government spending.

Meanwhile, populists from the right and left were harshly critical of the Iraq intervention, and wanted tougher trade policy and U.S. withdrawal from the WTO. Ralph Nader ran again as an independent candidate for President to highlight his challenges on the "capture" of both Republican and Democratic parties by multinational corporate (MNC) and financial lobbies. Pat Buchanan, the conservative populist, condemned Bush on these issues. Although populists Nader and Buchanan largely agreed on trade, Iraq intervention, and MNC's they disagreed on budgets, taxes, and some social issues.

For Republican winners of the 2004 elections for President, Senate, and House of Representatives, there are big challenges. National security, terrorism, nuclear proliferation, Iraq and other problems impose costs. Allied support should be increased from the U.S. standpoint, but outlooks differ around the world. Many nations are content to be free riders and concentrate upon expanding their own growth, exports and jobs. Big U.S. budget deficits resumed in 2002–2005. Reduced economic growth, enlarged spending, and tax cuts are to blame. More fiscal discipline is needed, and boom level growth of the later 1990's is probably unrealistic.

The U.S. has been living beyond its means in recent years and has become a large net debtor country. At end 2005 the U.S. net capital position was nearly $–3,500 billion on a GNP of $11,600 billion. Continued U.S. current account deficits in the range of $–500 to $–600 billion annually are unsustainable. Another four years of such large net trading deficits would increase net U.S. external debts to $–5,500 or $–6,000 billion. It's quite unlikely that foreign investors (governments, central banks, corporations, and wealthy families) would continue lending or investing into the U.S. at these very high levels much longer.

So U.S. dollar devaluation pressures are increasing. Neither the U.S. President, Treasury Secretary, nor the Federal Reserve can afford politically to urge a U.S. dollar devaluation. The U.S. public is relatively naïve in these matters; so is the U.S. business and professional class. The U.S. dollar has been the dominant world currency since World War II (some might claim since World War I). Somehow the U.S. will be forced by world markets to cut imports, increase exports, and largely eliminate "unsustainable" current account deficits and big capital inflows.

Crucial issues are what disruptive side effects may occur. Will lost exports to the U.S. impose global recession? To what extent will U.S. living standards and world influence decline? Can growth in Asia, Europe, and elsewhere sustain broad global prosperity? With less reliance on U.S. economic leadership? Could U.S. banks and MNC's suffer from rapid dollar devaluation? Or from gradual currency realignment? How can "softer" landings be achieved?

Gridlock over spending priorities, entitlements, and tax allocations is a renewed national problem. This left a crucial role for Federal Reserve policy in applying offsetting monetary restraint. But large deficits, higher interest rates and debt service burdens, over the long run, are not sound economic policy. The U.S. was simply living beyond its means in terms of both domestic finance and the balance of payments.

h.   Lessons for Policy

It should be evident from this brief review that monetary policy and Federal Reserve decisions, although taken "independently", cannot be understood apart from overall economic policy and trends, and the world market. The Federal Reserve always operates in a political context, where Presidential and Congressional influence, along with forthcoming elections, have considerable weight. Budget developments, expenditure levels, tax loads, and the deficit have great impact on monetary policy, money market conditions and interest rates. And yet, the Federal Reserve has real leverage to shape, within some degree, the growth path of money supply, interest rates, and the demand for credit and liquidity. The precise evolution at each stage is a fairly complicated blend of politics, the fiscal situation, and world market realities.

Some lessons can be drawn from this experience. First, monetary and fiscal policy should be closely coordinated. Thus, for example, national economic performance tends to suffer when budget deficits and monetary restraint conflict with each other as investment, growth, and employment are weakened. Stagflation can be encouraged, and perpetuated in these circumstances. Second, it is desirable to mesh monetary and fiscal stimulus together to encourage economic growth and full employment. Too much reliance on one or the other leads to imbalance, conflict and possible inflationary pressure. Third, there are limits to the degree of stimulus which an economy can absorb without inflationary pressure and the danger of building up sustained inflationary momentum. This can be hard for politicians to accept, since their outlook is to help people, interest groups, and encourage national accomplishments. But these aspirations must be constrained, at each stage, to the resources available, including a healthy flow of saving and investment to sustain productivity and appropriate economic growth. And, more than many realize, a more open global economy cannot be fully coordinated with national policy measures alone. The world market offers opportunities, within limits, but it also constrains what nations can do by themselves.

Controversy, within limits, is unavoidable in these matters. In the OECD industrial democracies four major viewpoints or tendencies of thought have emerged in the post-World War II era. The first outlook might be labeled as "Traditional Banker" thinking. It has been shaped by accumulated experience in banking, and the interest of this industry. Bankers believe sound economic growth is best encouraged by mostly balanced government budgets, no more than moderate tax loads, and strong incentives. Within this framework government deficits are appropriate in emergencies, and to some degree in recessions. Hopefully, central bank discretion can keep recessions and inflation minimized by skillful intervention to ease money market conditions in economic slack, or to tighten them as booms or full employment develops. Provided that strong, self-sustained economic prosperity can be maintained, the strain on monetary policy is limited. But the central bank, along with the government treasury should stand ready to act as "lender of last resort," and to help guarantee sound economic conditions.

The second viewpoint is the Keynesian, which developed as a reaction to the Great depression and fears of excessive unemployment. This outlook encourages budgetary and fiscal stimulus, with deficits, if necessary, as the means toward fuller employment. The years of stagflation in the 1970's have tempered their boldness, however, and made them more mindful of the dangers of inflation. But Neo–Keynesians still believe under-employment is costly and unfair, and emphasize the shortcomings of monetary restraint and recession, by themselves, as anti-inflation policies. A vigorous Keynesian policy often employs wage-price discipline with monitoring agencies and wage-price guidelines. These efforts, however, can be hard to implement in countries where significant inflationary momentum has developed. Monetary policy should assist in these efforts, and not interfere. Thus, to Keynesians, budgetary and wage-price policy assume a more central role, with monetary policy merely needed to avoid "excessive" restraint or stimulus.

A third viewpoint is the Monetarist, according to which monetary policy plays the crucial disciplinary role. Money supply growth, i.e., the monetary aggregates (M1, M2 and/or M3) should be confined to a relatively stable upward growth path, consistent with long term economic growth needs. Short term fluctuations in interest rates, capital flows, business activity and employment are to be accepted. Fiscal policy should be supportive and avoid excessive deficits, though moderate short-term fluctuations in deficits (or surpluses) can have their impact minimized by central bank policy. This view differs most drastically from the Neo–Keynesian, but significant departures from more traditional banker thinking are evident, too. Monetarists are willing to allow substantially more variation in interest rates, and associated risks than many bankers believe desirable.

A fourth viewpoint, Trade Balance and Exchange Rate oriented thinking, has emerged from the practice of many countries in the last generation, especially those with open and/or export-dependent economies. Nations like Switzerland, Germany, Japan, Korea, Taiwan or Singapore learned that a crucial target of macro-economic and monetary policy must be a realistic currency exchange rate that allows successful exports and a healthy balance of payments.* This means, at least, overall balance in

* National exchange rate policies have become more important since the early 1970's, when the Bretton Woods fixed exchange

their current accounts for most years, if not frequent surplus. Nations that suffer chronic trade and current account deficits, by contrast, tend to have unreliable and depreciating currencies, weakened confidence, and often capital flight. Troubled economies and currencies reflect underlying difficulties for their business, industrial, and export sectors. Accordingly, central banks and international economists increasingly focus upon the "mix" of national (and trading bloc) policies that yield realistic exchange rates, stronger competitiveness in world markets, economic growth, low inflation, and healthy employment performance. (Traditional Bankers, Keynesians, and Monetarists all tend to be more concerned now with exchange rates and external accounts, from their various perspectives.) As more countries become involved to a greater extent in the global marketplace, international trade and external accounts must receive greater attention.

Targeting procedures for monetary policy are different in each of the four major viewpoints. Traditional bankers have emphasized interest rates in the general context of money market conditions, and observe overall economic performance. Keynesians are similar in their range of target variables, but emphasize macro-economic performance, and especially growth, employment and inflation. Only Monetarists place a crucial reliance upon money supply targeting as the key indicator of successful

rate system broke down. Subsequently, floating exchange rates have been used by most countries, which can be significantly influenced by monetary and trade policies, along with domestic spending, taxes and industrial development measures.

economic policy. Trade Balance oriented economists must focus upon exchange rates, but their fiscal, monetary, and other economic policies stress the overall productivity, growth, and competitiveness of a country. Naturally, the Federal Reserve's public statements, targeting procedures, FOMC reports, and their contribution to economic policy (like those of every central bank) are controversial in this climate of sincere, but substantial disagreement. No wonder that monetary policy has become the focus of debate in the financial press, and among politicians and journalists as well.

This leaves a very interesting, but awkward problem for banking law and administration. To what extent should banking law and institutions try to circumscribe the policy choices available to the Federal Reserve and other national monetary authorities? Reporting requirements are built into present law which now force the Federal Reserve, the President, and even Congress itself, to account for current developments in the money supply, money market conditions, interest rates, industrial and business activity, employment, unemployment, inflation, and economic growth. But the choice of policy emphasis thus far, at least, has been left to the incumbents in office at each stage, reacting to contemporary market conditions, the most recent elections, and desired economic objectives.

B. GUIDELINES AND CONSTRAINTS

The legal authority for money and banking policy is the accumulated legacy of legislation (supported by constitutional powers) in effect today. As this historical review demonstrates, such a complex, pragmatic accumulation of law-making and regulatory practice does not reflect any single viewpoint or interpretation. Its thrust, rather, is a framework of authority, powers, and general responsibilities. This framework has been regularly adjusted, often enlarged, and tailored to evolving national policies and current economic objectives. And, to some degree, overall standards, or goals, have been provided by Congress. But for the most part, money and banking policy have been allowed considerable latitude for discretion, partly because Congress, bankers, and economists have not achieved complete agreement on these matters, and because important questions remain to be specified in contingent circumstances—involving economic growth, employment, capacity utilization, prices, exchange rates, and varied money market conditions.

Some find this state of affairs unsettling. Those favoring particular economic strategies, such as the Neo–Keynesian or Monetarist, have attempted to enact more restrictive legislation implementing their outlooks. But Congress has generally softened and weakened these formulations, leaving, in fact, ample scope for discretion to the monetary authorities, along with the executive leaders and Congress at any given time. But the accumulation of such guideline enactments and reporting responsibilities does provide an important standard for discussion and debate in our Federal democracy. It is through these requirements for disclosure and justification that central bank and government economic policies are assessed. In this way, hopefully, public controversy and politics helps enforce performance for money, banking, and financial policy, and leads to occasional adjustments in the legislative framework and guidelines.

1. INSTRUMENTS OF MONETARY AND BANKING POLICY

The monetary authorities (Federal Reserve System and the Treasury) do not "control" the money supply, the demand for liquidity, or market interest rates in any direct or comprehensive sense. Instead, the Federal Reserve strongly influences bank reserves, lending potential, and affects interest rates, mainly through the *supply* of bank liquidity (under domestic regulatory jurisdiction), and also through the discount rate for loans to the banking system. The Treasury and the Federal Reserve together affect the *demand* for liquidity and interest rates through management of government debt (federal liabilities), deficits, and borrowing policies, which can impact on money markets very substantially. Meanwhile, Congress and the Executive branch influence money markets and the entire economy with spending programs, taxes and their allocation, and government deficits, borrowing requirements or surpluses.

Chart II–2

Monetary Instruments, Targets and Policy Goals

Monetary Instruments	Channels of Impact (Proximate Targets)	Market Targets	Policy Goals
Open-Market Operations	Bank Reserves and Monetary Base	Money Supply	National Incomes and Output
Reserve Requirements		Credit Supply	Prices and Interest Rates
		Interest Rates	
	Interest Rates		Employ-ment and Productivity
Discount Rates		Demand for Money and Credit	Exchange Rates, Int'l Trade and Investment Flows
Credit Regulations	Credit Demand		
Government Debt Policies and Deficits		Exchange Rates	Balance of Payments

The most important instruments of monetary "control" or policy have been open-market operations, reserve requirements, and the discount rate. Credit regulations have been employed as well. And, though not always considered a part of monetary policy in the narrow sense, government debt and deficit policies have had, at times, a powerful, even over-riding impact upon money and credit markets.

a. Open Market Operations

The Federal Open Market Committee directives to the account manager at the New York Federal Reserve Bank (called the "Desk") regulate the

"Fed's" *purchases or sales* of government securities (which tend to influence banks reserves). This authority has existed for the FOMC since 1935; previous open market operations were carried out informally by the New York Federal Reserve Bank since the early 1920's. The discretion of the Desk is limited to achieving such target objectives or results as are established by the FOMC.

Alternative targets used by the FOMC in the past have included standards like "ease," "active ease," "tightness," or "moderate restraint" in terms of general money market conditions. More specific emphasis has often been placed on bank reserves, unused or "free" reserves, unborrowed reserves, or total reserves (including those borrowed from the "Fed"). The market price for free bank reserves traded among banks, i.e., the "federal funds rate," has been used as a key targeting variable, too. Money supply measures or the "monetary aggregates" often have been used as targeting variables. Among the most widely used measures are M1 (currency and narrowly defined demand deposits), M2 (M1 and most time deposits), and M3 (M2 plus other liquid deposits). Changing regulations for deposit accounts and innovations by financial institutions have led to frequent revisions in money supply definitions, or the "monetary aggregates," reflecting the growth of NOW accounts, certificates of deposit [CD's], repurchase agreements ["repos"], money market mutual fund shares, banker's acceptances, and Eurocurrency deposits.

Controversy developed over the best blend and emphasis for target variables. In earlier years, with less inflationary momentum, the main targeting procedure employed was to watch money market conditions, interest rates, and bank reserves carefully for indications of "ease" or "tightness." More recently, as better money supply measures were developed, and Monetarist-oriented economists placed more emphasis upon them, the monetary "aggregates" received greater attention. Formal guidelines expressed by the FOMC often were expressed in primary target ranges for M1, M2 and M3, along with a desired range for the federal funds rate. This shift in emphasis was welcomed by many economists, partly in response to increased inflationary momentum and the need for more credibility in resisting inflation with an unambiguous, firm targeting procedure. And yet, other economists challenge "excessive" stress upon any single indicator, and prefer more flexibility and latitude for the central bank. Clearly, the monetary aggregate approach and/or interest rates have been more influential in monetary policy. And although many economists and central bank leaders still believe that all indicators must be watched together, bank reserves and the aggregates are now given special concern in most countries subject, perhaps, to interest rate or exchange rate constraints.

In any event, open market operations are generally believed to be the superior instrument for affecting bank reserves, money supply growth, or even interest rates on an incremental basis for countries

like the U.S., with a large market of outstanding
government securities. Because banks hold a large
part of their liquid assets in government debt securities, (and these bank holdings play a big role in
government securities markets), the Federal Reserve's substantial purchases (or sales) of these
instruments tend to increase (or decrease) reserves
held in banks. The great advantage of open market
operations over changes in reserve requirements is
that much smaller, incremental impacts can be
achieved in outstanding bank reserves. Thus, banks
can adjust much more gradually, with less disruption to themselves or their loan customers depending on bank credit, than if large movements in
reserves through altered reserve percentages were
imposed on the banking system.

b.   Reserve Requirements

Legal reserve requirements have been specified
since the Federal Reserve Act of 1913 in terms of a
range of alternative reserve ratios, rather than a
single fixed percentage. This allows the Federal
Reserve Board to vary reserve requirements somewhat for most larger banks (national banks and all
state chartered member banks). This provides a
powerful, but relatively crude method by which big
reductions in bank reserves and bank loans can be
enforced. (Most banks normally carry a narrow
margin of excess reserves so that they can obtain a
maximum volume of interest on assets to achieve
the greatest yield available). Bank reserves can be
expanded in large increments the same way

through reserve requirements, but additional bank loans take time to develop and ordinarily follow more slowly as a stimulative result. Thus, changing reserve requirements is mainly a quick discipline against excess money supply or credit creation under inflationary pressures. Enlarged reserve requirements work more slowly as a device for expanding the economy, as we have learned in many recessions, and the Great Depression.

Reserve requirements do serve an important protective function, however, in forcing banks to hold enough cash and/or liquid securities as a prudential safeguard against the risk of runs on banks. Higher reserves are required for demand or transactional accounts than for time deposits. The reason is that demand deposit withdrawals tend to occur more quickly, and before banks can borrow enough extra reserves from other banks, the Federal Reserve or other government agencies. Under the Federal Reserve Act of 1913 the range of allowable reserve was originally 12–18 percent for demand deposits, and 5 percent for time deposits. The Banking Act of 1935 broadened these allowable percentages on demand deposits to 13–26 percent for reserve city banks, 10–20 percent for city banks, and 7–14 percent on country banks, along with 0–6 percent on time deposits. And most recently, the DIDMCA of 1980 phased in new, "standardized" reserve requirements of 12 percent for "transactions" deposits (including NOW accounts), and up to 3 percent for non-personal time deposits, subject to substantial emergency increase authority. Thus, the Federal

Reserve still retains "central bank" authority to tighten money, credit, and economic activity in emergency situations.

c. Discount Rates

Discount rates also became an instrument of monetary control in the Federal Reserve Act of 1913. Britain's well known success with the Bank of England, its lending to banks, and use of the bank rate to regulate credit activity was part of this legislative history. But for a number of reasons the discount rate has proved less important, over the longer run, than open market operations in the United States.

First, the American banks did not become very dependent on borrowing from the Federal Reserve. In the "Fed's" first 16 years (including World War I and the 1920's), banks did not need to use the discount window very heavily, though the rate was used consciously as a discipline in the 1920's. Second, during the New Deal years monetary policy was generally "easy," with surplus reserves and little need for discounting by the Fed. During 1941–51 the Fed had to support cheap war debt borrowing, and "relative ease" also prevailed. Finally, when some monetary restraint was resumed in the 1950's, a large market in government securities had been developed, which allowed open market operations to be the superior instrument for affecting bank reserves, as compared to the less direct and weaker leverage of the discount rate on selective, not so frequent lending by the Federal Reserve.

Meanwhile, the private market for free reserves among banks, i.e., for "federal funds," had become the more routine source of borrowing for additional bank reserves. Thus, open market operations were more directly influential on this channel for expanding (or reducing) bank reserves, and upon the more significant and more flexible federal funds rate.

Nonetheless, the discount rates charged by the Fed as lender of last resort for emergency credits, or more routine credits for seasonal borrowing or very short-term credits, do have some significance. The Fed's official discount rates, in fact, tend to *follow* market interest rates, including the overall trend of the "fed funds" rate. If the discount rate were much below market for any sustained period, a subsidy to favored banks results that is hard to allocate on a non-discriminatory basis. On the other hand, if the discount rate moves much above market, it becomes a penalty rate in conflict with the lender of last resort function to aid troubled banks.

But even though discount rates follow market rates, they are more visible than open market operations, and often reveal, in fact, new directions and trends in FOMC policy. Thus, a trend of reductions in discount rates normally shows an easing of monetary restraint, whereas increased discount rates tend to reflect tightening of money markets. Financial reporting on monetary policy and open-market operations has become so sophisticated, however, in recent years, that this "educational" role for discount rates is somewhat less significant now than it used to be.

d. Credit Controls

Direct credit controls and allocations (or limits on the uses of credit, or interest rates available) are another dimension of monetary policy. The potential for credit restrictions is very large, including many forms of preferential and limited lending (or borrowing). But in capitalist countries with free market traditions this avenue for controls is normally avoided except in wartime or other serious national emergencies. Business and banking interests find such controls onerous, and complain of unreasonable discrimination, distortions, and the danger of corrupt administration. Thus, while the potential for credit regulation is enormous, for the most part U.S. law has employed these techniques in a very limited way, and often cautiously within this modest area of impact. (Exchange controls can be considered another dimension of money and credit restriction, i.e., those portions involving international flows of currency, financing or payments in any form.)*

War-time controls on foreign exchange and credit transactions were initially authorized by Congress as part of the Trading with Enemy Act in 1917. This authority for "qualitative" restrictions on

* Socialist and developing countries, however, have been more aggressive in using credit and exchange controls to direct and limit the flows of saving, lending, investment and trade in accord with national policy priorities. Strong preferences are often imposed for approved investment activity, while credits or financing for consumption—especially for "luxuries," automobiles, or some types of real estate—may be discouraged, or even prohibited. In capitalist countries like the U.S. such encouragements take the milder, and sometimes more complicated form of tax subsidies and incentives.

credit was broadened by Congress in 1933, as part of the first wave New Deal Emergency banking legislation. (Collateral legislation, previously explained, limited interest rates on demand deposits, and prohibited interest on checking accounts.) Further exchange and credit control authority was enacted in 1941, and the Federal Reserve restricted consumer credit significantly through Regulation W in World War II and the Korean War.

Stronger legislative authority for credit controls came in 1966, and especially, with the Credit Control Act of December 23, 1969. This last legislation empowered the President to declare an inflation emergency, which would put into effect broad authority for the Federal Reserve Board to regulate all kinds of credit. Its stated purpose was to allow less restrictive monetary policy and lower interest rates, to alleviate disintermediation problems, and ease the strains of fighting inflation. This rather drastic credit control authority was employed by the President and the "Fed" in the spring of 1980 to limit the volume of new credit consumer loans, and even new money market fund deposits (legality was challenged by the MMMF's). But after a few months these emergency controls were lifted. This Credit Control Act of 1969 "expired" in the summer of 1982, leaving much less residual authority for emergency controls. (Meanwhile, the "national emergency" authority of the President under the old Trading with the Enemy Act had been substantially narrowed in 1977.) A bill to renew the 1969 Act and broaden its Presidential "triggering" authority to reduce unemployment or combat recession was approved once by the House Banking Committee, but further action does not seem likely soon.

Proponents of credit controls seek to ease the strains of high interest rates, and the burdens resulting to some elements of the economy. In war emergencies with limited duration, such relief has broader support, especially when it might allow larger war production and reduce profiteering. In briefer inflation emergencies, this logic may have some appeal as well. But in the more extended stagflation of the late 1970's-early 1980's, the distortions resulting from Regulation Q controls created painful burdens of their own, and significant disintermediation from savings accounts. The prospects for even greater distortions helped persuade the "Fed" to abandon the spring, 1980 controls quickly, after its dramatic restraint and high interest rates brought a recession and eased credit demand significantly, with declining interest rates.

2. GOVERNMENT DEBT POLICIES, DEFICITS, AND WORLD MARKETS

The management of government debt, its financing, and the size of deficits relative to national income, savings and investment have great impact on money markets. Government borrowing competes with private credit demand, and may raise interest rates significantly—unless the Treasury, Federal Reserve and banks increase the money supply enough to offset this additional pressure. If the money and credit supply increases substantially, this may add to aggregate demand and enlarge the inflation rate appreciably, unless there is general slack and unemployment in the economy.

The Treasury could finance government deficits simply by printing treasury note currency, but this would increase the monetary base (currency and demand deposits) and tend to increase initial bank deposits that serve as the multiple for fractional reserve expansion of the bank money and credit supply. Alternatively, the Federal Reserve could finance the deficit by printing more federal reserve notes (with the collaboration of the Treasury), with similar consequences. To the extent increased federal government debt is monetized this way, "inflation," at least in the technical sense of expanding the money supply, is unavoidable. Whether or not significant price increases result depends largely on the degree of slack in labor and product markets, i.e., the extent of unemployment and excess capacity.

On the other hand, government debt securities can be sold to cover the deficits, with less of an immediate increase in money supplies. This may, however, tend to bid up the price of credit and increase interest rates, to some degree. Furthermore, the additional spending of government (beyond its revenues) may increase the price level for goods and services, to the extent additional production capacity is not available at existing price levels. Increased interest rates, reflecting a "crowding out" in some degree of private demand, also inhibit investment, reduce consumer purchasers (dependent on credit), and weaken industrial activity. Greater slack and unemployment may result.

Everything depends on the relative size of government borrowing relative to saving, investment, and national output. If relatively modest, i.e., say only ½ to 1 percent of GNP (or 5–10 percent of savings and investment), the crowding pressure and inflation pressure will be limited. But if the deficits and PSBR (public sector borrowing requirement) are substantially bigger, say 4–5 percent of GNP (or 40–50 percent of saving and investment), the crowding, inflation, and other distortion effects can be greatly increased—unless the extent of unemployment, excess capacity, and slack is quite large, too. Obviously, such reserve production potential could be rather quickly mobilized or used up, thus limiting the period in which large deficits could be run (e.g. the late 1930's-early 1940's). Or more sadly, perhaps, the slack and unemployment may be concentrated more lopsidedly in a few sick industries, depressed regions, or among badly educated, minority or immigrant workers not easily absorbed into the economy. In the later circumstances, large deficits may bring less benefit, and cause inflation more rapidly.

Once again, it should be clear that a direct "monetization" of government debt (either through Treasury notes or Federal Reserve currency, or some combination) has larger and more immediate inflationary consequences, given the same deficits. With fractional reserve banking, this money supply tends to be more "high powered" or multiplied in its impact. Thus, direct monetization tends to be avoided, unless there is really substantial and widespread slack in the economy that can safely absorb such a powerful injection of liquidity.

With sizeable international capital movements, the problems of debt management, deficits, and monetary policy become more complicated. In the 1980's, for example, as U.S. budget deficits increased, the Federal Reserve felt obliged to offset inflation risks by maintaining somewhat higher interest rates than Japan, Switzerland, and West Germany. Many economists feared crowding in capital markets that could limit U.S. recovery. But increased foreign investment and lending (partly capital flight) managed to cover a growing U.S. current account deficit (especially between 1983–87). Unfortunately, a significant misalignment of currencies resulted, which increased imports and weakened exports for the U.S. Although foreign capital inflows covered the deficits for some years, it was unlikely that this could continue indefinitely. Also in the mid–1980's the U.S. was switching from a creditor to a sizeable debtor nation. The dollar began to decline substantially in relative value after the Spring of 1985. Eventually, as all nations that run extensive deficits learn, foreign borrowing would no longer be available. Either its currency declines even further, and/or foreign creditors and investors become less generous. Ultimately, every country must live within its own means. This requires an overall limitation of imports (in the longer run) to what can be earned by exports of goods and services.

Special circumstances allowed the American economy foreign borrowing and investment leeway in the 1980's, the 1990's, and recent years. Insecurities abroad, a tradition of respect for private investments, and the great size of the U.S. economy were important factors. But growing concern, including worries about the boom in the U.S. stock market and its industrial health, suggested this grace would not last forever. Most other nations, meanwhile, have been forced to live under more immediate discipline from world capital markets if they run excessive budget and/or trading deficits. Foreign credit often runs out more quickly, currencies depreciate, inflation follows, and confidence weakens. Capital flight frequently occurs, while economic growth and industrial progress suffer.

For these reasons, government deficits, debt management, and borrowing policy can have great impact on the economy, and upon the conduct of central bank or Federal Reserve policies. Government deficits and borrowing, if at all substantial relative to GNP, become a powerful force—sometimes the over-riding influence—in monetary and banking affairs.

It is not surprising, therefore, that law and/or guidelines be considered for budget deficits, debt limits, etc. But there has been a lag, in some respects, in fashioning the most suitable deficit disciplines for a "post-Keynesian" era of budgetary momentum, and habitual deficits.

Some states have approved a balanced budget amendment to the U.S. Constitution, through a call for a constitutional convention for this purpose. Many national politicians have suggested an amendment to the Constitution as well, subject to the major loophole of a three-fifths vote of Congress approving unbalanced budgets. Conservatives and Republicans moved in this direction. Many observers of Congress worry that fiscal discipline is harder to maintain in an era of weakened political parties, with special interests that strongly resist spending cuts or new taxes that affect them. In frustration, some experts on government now support some kind of balanced budget amendment for the U.S. today.

Nonetheless, many still object to this constraint on government fiscal policy, especially those favoring Keynesian policies or stimulative finance to overcome unemployment. Others object to the "needless" rigidity of such an amendment. From this latter perspective, the problems with deficits come with excessive size *relative to GNP*, not in the bare fact of their existence (even if small or insignificant as a percentage). The most inflationary budget deficits are "large" relative to the GNP, taking into account the level of general unemployment and excess capacity in the economy. Thus, sustained deficits of 3–5 percent of GNP will probably become inflationary, except where a major recession and large unemployment affects the economy. On the other hand, deficits of 1–2 percent of GNP might not be inflationary, with moderate slack. Yet as the economy approaches full employment, even 1–2 percent deficits as a share of GNP may become inflationary. Conceivably, a balanced budget amendment could be framed in terms that focused upon the percentage of deficits as a share of GNP, and took account of unemployment, excess capacity, inflation, world trade and international capital flows. But whether pluralistic politics and Congress could achieve agreement on suitable language remains an open question. And yet, countries that fail to maintain reasonable budget discipline, over the longer run, tend to be less successful. Greater inflation, reduced saving and investment, and slower growth are typical penalties for a sustained lack of fiscal responsibility.*

* NOTE—Substantial Congressional efforts were mounted on and off in the Reagan, Bush, and Clinton presidencies to formulate and pass a balanced budget amendment to the U.S. constitution. But crucial disagreements on the details made the project difficult. Conservatives wanted a strong limitation on new taxes, while many liberals felt that sizeable tax increases should be *combined with* spending limits and reductions. This extended conflict on taxes and spending was largely to blame for excess deficits, greatly enlarged debt, and increased debt service burdens.

European Union (EU) counties fashioned a workable budget deficit guideline in recent years, i.e., the Stability and Growth Pact. It was successful in promoting more fiscal discipline in the later 1990's. More recently, however, big French and German deficits raised questions on the enforceability of this budget discipline.

CHAPTER III

BANKING MARKET REGULATION

Commercial banking is extensively regulated for potential entrants, chartered bank corporations, and bank holding companies. Banks are subject to financial supervision and regular examination, with substantial corrective authority for dangerous practices. Reserve requirements are enforced for banks, and their capital adequacy is an important concern of the regulatory authorities. The growth of banks, along with their branching, diversification and merger activity has been regulated. Significant limitations also apply to other bank activities, including lending limits, insider lending, some restrictions on investments and certain types of deposit liabilities. Interest rate ceilings were placed on some deposits, and interest on demand deposits had been prohibited (between 1933–80). There are disclosure requirements and privacy safeguards for borrowers and depositors. Although about 7,700 banks and 1,360 savings institutions exist in the United States, with substantial competition over many aspects of their activity, this rivalry had been softened and made less severe by protectionist regulation.* To under-

* In addition, 9,500 credit unions offer partial competition with banks and savings institutions.

stand these dimensions of banking law, we shift our focus from the entire banking system, the central bank and national economic policy, and consider the role of individual banks and particular banking markets.

Chart III—1

Agency Supervision and Examination Authority (partly over-lapping jurisdiction)

Regulatory Agency	Number of Banks	Assets (billions)	
Comptroller of the Currency (Treasury Department)	2,000	(National charters)	$3,834
Federal Reserve Board	951	(State charter Federal Reserve members)	$1,400
Federal Deposit Insurance Corporation	2,000	(National banks)	$3,834
(BIF insured)	951	(State charter Federal Reserve members)	$1,400
(BIF insured)	4,762	(State charter non-members)	$1,434
(BIF insured)	418	(Savings Banks— Mutual and Stock)	$354
State Banking Departments	951	(State charter Federal Reserve members)	$1,400
	4,762	(State charter non-members FDIC Insured)	$1,434
FDIC, OTS, and/or State Banking Depts (SAIF insured)	944	(S & L's and Savings Banks)	$1,073

SOURCE: See Tables II–1 and IV–1, and sources cited.

Three federal banking agencies, the Federal Reserve Board, Office of the Comptroller of Currency, and Federal Deposit Insurance Corporation, along with the State Banking Departments or Commissioners, are the major regulatory agencies for bank market regulation. At the federal level, the Comptroller of the Currency is the oldest agency, which has served since 1863 as the chartering authority for national banks, and their primary agency for the supervision and examination process. The Federal Deposit Insurance corporation became a collateral supervising agency in 1933 for all national banks, and virtually all state banks (those seeking FDIC insurance protection for their depositors.) The State Banking Departments are the chartering authority for all state banks, and remain responsible for their supervision and examination, too. The Federal Reserve Board, created in 1913, also has supervision and examination authority for state chartered member banks, and has become increasingly important as the most general regulatory agency for banking under many recent enactments (covering mergers, bank holding companies, truth-in-lending, fair credit reporting, and certain aspects of interstate and multinational banking.) In addition, the Federal Financial Institutions Examination Council (FFIEC) received regulatory or supervisory authority for certain aspects of banking and other financial institutions.[1]

1. The Federal Financial Institutions Examination Council now comprises the Federal Reserve and FDIC Chairs, the Comp-

A. CHARTERING AND ENTRY REQUIREMENTS

Entry into banking was easier when the National Bank of the United States did not exercise disciplinary and restraining influence, i.e., between 1781–91, 1811–16 and 1837–63. In these important years state charters were the exclusive method for creating banking corporations. In particular, the long generation before the Civil War, the "free banking era", firmly established the predominant pattern for ease of entry which lasted until the Great Depression of 1929–33. Whenever entrepreneurs could meet minimum capitalization standards to set up a bank, they normally could obtain a bank charter, in the great majority of states, between the 1830's and through the 1920's. (See Table II–1, Growth of U.S. Commercial Banking, 1792–2003). By 1921, the peak year for bank population, there were 30,000 United States banks.

But since the Great Depression, when more than 10,000 banks failed, entry into banking became more difficult. Standards for new charters were raised substantially, and entrepreneurs have been less eager for banking. More demanding criteria were established, including tougher requirements for capitalization and management, the "convenience and needs" of the community involved, along with competitive circumstances. These additional factors have been interpreted frequently to require

troller, the Office of Thrift Supervision Director, and the National Credit Union Administrator.

a showing that there is room for another bank. In other words, new entrants often have to demonstrate not only financial resources and managerial competence but show also that the market in question (a city or rural area) could accommodate another banking institution. This means, in practice, that a substantial limitation on the flow of new entry may be asserted by the existing banks in an area as Protestants against additional rivals. Whether or not this resistance will be effective depends on how these factors are evaluated, in the discretion of federal and state chartering authorities.

Table III–1

NEW BANK CHARTERS, 1935–2003*

Year	Nat'l Banks	State Banks) (member) Fed. Reserve)	State Banks) (non-member) Fed. Reserve)	Total
1935	12	0	33	45
1936	6	1	25	32
1937	7	1	38	46
1938	1	0	21	22
1939	3	1	22	26
1940	4	4	24	28
1941	6	1	30	37
1942	0	2	13	15
1943	3	4	29	36
1944	8	5	43	56
1945	17	8	76	101
1946	21	11	98	130
1947	19	19	61	99
1948	14	6	41	63
1949	12	6	40	58
1950	6	8	44	58
1951	9	2	40	51
1952	15	4	42	61
1953	12	10	37	59
1954	18	6	42	66

* Does not include Savings Banks or S & L's. (See Chapter IV, *infra.*)

Year	Nat'l Banks	State Banks) (member) Fed. Reserve)	State Banks) (non-member) Fed. Reserve)	Total
1955	28	4	71	103
1956	29	6	72	109
1957	20	3	50	73
1958	18	2	63	83
1959	23	4	75	102
1960	32	4	75	101
1961	26	2	70	98
1962	63	4	100	167
1963	163	3	115	281
1964	200	3	120	323
1965	88	4	90	182
1966	25	4	70	99
1967	18	3	73	94
1968	15	1	65	91
1969	16	7	92	105
1970	40	8	130	178
1971	37	9	150	196
1972	55	13	167	235
1973	90	26	216	332
1974	97	35	232	364
1975	75	13	158	246
1976	65	11	85	161
1977	39	17	101	157
1978	37	17	94	148
1979	42	31	131	204
1980	61	28	116	205
1981	100	25	74	199
1982	198	41	87	326
1983	260	39	62	361
1984	227	37	81	345
1985	207	50	98	355
	2,587	549	3,982	7,118

Year	Nat'l Banks	State Banks	Total
1986	107	137	244
1987	55	155	310
1988	65	159	224
1989	73	123	196
1990	58	107	165
1991	30	76	106
1992	37	35	72
1993	17	42	59
1994	20	30	50
1995	27	74	101
1996	52	96	148
1997	61	146	207
1998	48	145	193
1999	53	184	237
2000	38	154	192
2001	34	98	132

Year	Nat'l Banks	State Banks	Total
2002	29	32	81
2003	14	102	116
	3,407	6,107	9,512

Source: FDIC, *Annual Reports*, 1935–1994; Golembe and Holland, *Federal Regulation of Banking 1986–87*, Golembe Associates, Wash., D.C., 1987; Federal Reserve data, 2000, 2004.

Applicants for a bank charter must file a formal "application" with extensive supporting data. The organizers must outline their plan of operations, describe earning prospects, provide details on management capabilities (involving bank executives with appropriate experience, under contract or part of the organizing group), show adequate capitalization and soundness, and offer reasonable service to their community. In addition, the Comptroller's Office (OCC) and State Bank Departments require information on market circumstances, i.e., size and growth potential, and competition from existing banks and related financial institutions. Notice of the application must be published, which allows other interested parties (normally competing institutions already in the market) to file protests and relevant data. This provides ample basis for determining whether a particular charter might meet the convenience and needs of its community, taking into account competitive circumstances. Occasionally, hearings are organized to take additional evidence.

Obviously, the economic attractiveness of a banking enterprise, growth and income trends of an area, and the strength and branching networks of existing competitors will determine whether organizers materialize in the first place. Little new chartering activity occurred in the 1930's or in World War II. It picked up a bit right after the war, but not too much until 1962–65, when the OCC's attitude became more liberal under Comptroller Saxon, and as a longer term trend of improved prosperity began to be evident. This surge of liberality by the OCC induced a more relaxed attitude in many state banking departments. Gradually, a shift in thinking and emphasis developed, allowing soundly financed groups to enter banking markets more freely, and which is reflected by recent policy statements of the OCC. For example, in October, 1980, the Comptroller stated:

"This shift in emphasis reflects the OCC's experience that a strong organizing group with solid financial backing and a well-conceived and developed operating plan generally is able to establish and operate a successful bank even in the most economically distressed areas or most highly competitive markets."

Somewhat comparable thinking developed in many state banking departments, partly reacting to a danger they perceived in letting national banks become more numerous. Another factor is present in many states, though less evident in OCC chartering, i.e., the importance of "political" influence from leading state politicians. Thus, influential figures in state politics often get involved in bank charter activities, along with their friends and substantial campaign contributors. In any event, there was considerably greater bank chartering activity from the early 1960's until the late 1980's than for the period 1933–60. (See Table III–1). But recently, with increased branching and interstate banking allowed, new charter entries have declined greatly in the 1990's and beyond.

Charter applicants may obtain the appropriate forms and current guidelines for national charters from the OCC in Washington, D.C., or the Regional Administrator of National Banks in the area, and for state charters from the State Banking Department or Commissioner. Applicants may be able to obtain confidential treatment for portions of their submission data when requested. State charter applicants also should realize that an application to the FDIC for deposit insurance is required for this protection. FDIC insurance applications cover the same ground, i.e., financial history and condition, capital adequacy, earnings prospects, management and character, together with convenience and needs of the community. Capital and financial requirements for the FDIC may be somewhat more strict than state law or state authorities demand. (Federal Reserve membership requirements are comparable to those for national banks, and tend to be more demanding than state charters or FDIC insurance. Hence, brand new state banks normally do not become Federal Reserve members at the outset.)

It must be emphasized that statutory minimum capital requirements are generally low, and have not been updated to reflect inflation. Present federal statutes theoretically allow minimum capital to be as low as $50,000 for towns of 6000 or less, and no more than $200,000 in cities with 50,000 or more population. States may even be slightly more liberal. All this reflects the statutory history of "free banking" and actual practice up to the Great Depression. But, practically speaking, the OCC requires at least $1 million of initial capital for a national charter. The Federal Reserve requires the same for membership. The FDIC also now requires $1 million of capital for a new insured bank or savings institution. But these threshold capital requirements should not be understood as sufficient for a growing bank. In fact, "capital adequacy" tends to be looked at now in terms of continued financial soundness, and as a ratio or percentage of total assets (or liabilities).

The average bank in the United States normally had a capital account (shareholders' equity and retained earnings) of around 6–7 percent of total assets (or liabilities). But the largest banks in the late 1970's-early 1980's had less, often only 4–5 percent of capital compared to their total assets. Banks involved in a bailout absorption for a troubled bank, may even have part of their capital in long term debt (or notes owed to the FDIC or Federal Reserve). But most banks would be considered to have unsound management practices if their equity capital went much below these normal ranges. A "weak" capital position, in this more subjective, less definite sense, would raise questions, and perhaps invite a special examination or investigation as a possible "problem bank", particularly if other danger signs materialized, such as a significant growth of substandard loans, declining deposits, or unprofitable (loss) operations. (See, for Example, the Capital Adequacy Guidelines of December 17, 1981, issued by the Federal Reserve Board and the Office of the Comptroller of the Currency.) These guidelines set *minimum* standards of capital adequacy, i.e., 5 percent for regional banks and 6 percent, generally speaking, for community banks, with desirable ranges above 6.5 and 7 percent, respectively. Below 5.5 and 6.0 percent, respectively banks were then presumed to be undercapitalized and require continuous supervision. Major international banks, it was understood, had somewhat lower capitalization, but the Federal Reserve and Comptroller encouraged these banks to improve their capital positions.

In 1984–85 federal banking regulators promulgated new capital standards, i.e., 5.5 percent for "primary capital" and 6 percent for total capital/assets, for all banks (regardless of size). (Statutory authority for minimum capital adequacy had been strengthened with the International Lending Supervision Act of 1983.) Then in 1987 Central Banks and regulators for 12 major banking nations (U.S., Canada, Japan, U.K., W. Germany, Switzerland, France, Italy, Netherlands, Belgium, Luxembourg, and Sweden) agreed jointly to harmonize and strengthen bank capital requirements to 7.25 percent of total "risk assets" by 1990, and to 8 percent of total "risk assets" by 1992.

But "risk assets" were defined in the new G–12 framework a special way: (i) cash and guaranteed obligations of central banks and governments (e.g., U.S. T-bills and bonds) are zero risk, along with FDIC and FSLIC securities issued to recapitalize troubled institutions; (ii) securities issued by development banks or quasi-government corporations might carry 20 to 50 percent risk, depending on national policies; (iii) residential mortgage loans carry 50 percent risk, provided that realistic appraisals support collateral values; and (iv) normal risk applies to most commercial lending, commercial real estate loans, and even standby guarantees (except those related to particular transactions, e.g., performance or bid bonds, warranties, or letters of credit related to particular transactions, which might carry 50 percent risk). In this way, 60–80 percent of typical bank balance sheet assets would carry normal risk, and thus require overall capital of 6–7 percent (within the "traditional" range for modern banking).

On the other hand, capital was defined somewhat more liberally in the G–12 framework. "Core capital" (Tier 1) includes common stock equity and retained earnings, *plus* noncumulative preferred stock (but not, in most circumstances, "good will"). Only half the required capital has to be Tier 1. "Supplementary capital" (Tier 2) could include hybrid (debt/equity) securities, subordinated capital debt, general loan loss reserves or provisioning for contingent (possible) losses, or "undisclosed reserves" (hidden retained earnings or assets not marked up to current market values). But by the end of 1992 no more than half the supplementary

(Tier 2) capital could be in subordinated debt, and no more than 1.25 percent of total risk assets should be in general loan loss reserves (in other than exceptional and temporary circumstances). In this way, most U.S. banks could qualify as adequately capitalized, although the largest banks, which can more readily market hybrid securities and subordinated debt, might carry a substantial part of their "capital" in supplementary form, i.e., as "debt" serving the function of capital and taking equity-like risks.* So long as purchasers of such bank securities understood this capital risk, and received an appropriate premium in the marketplace, no fundamental change was involved (except a restructuring of the capital accounts and risks within larger banks). [Soon after these G-12 "risk based capital" requirements were promulgated in the U.S., the OCC announced in 1989 a slight

* NOTE—A few leading U.S. banks averaged only 3.5–4 percent capital on assets in 1981–82, which they claimed was reasonable for multinational risk diversification. Many believed this insufficient capital coverage, however, especially for country risk exposure. But regulators found it hard to complain publicly in the early 1980's in the midst of rescheduling for international debts. An awkward rescheduling situation, requiring collaboration among many countries and international banks, would be more difficult if worries spread over capital adequacy in major multinational banks. Leading banks in some other major banking countries had even lower capital ratios, which reflected more explicit government or central bank support (or some degree of nationalized banking). Hence, the Federal Reserve and Comptroller worked to encourage improved capitalization. Between December, 1981, and June, 1987, the average "primary capital" ratio for the 12 largest U.S. multinational banks was strengthened from 3.66 to 6.86 percent, through the issue of $4 billion common stock, $9.96 billion preferred stock, and almost $20 billion of convertible securities and provisional loan loss reserves allowed to serve as "primary capital".

liberalization for Tier 1 capital, i.e., a new "leverage ratio" minimum of 3 percent equity (including retained earnings)/total assets. This allowed, in effect, "roughly" 1 percent of Tier 1 capital to be noncumulative preferred stock.]

More recently, because of heavy losses experienced by FSLIC in the mid-late 1980's (many institutions were undercapitalized, and some were allowed to operate although insolvent), banking regulators became somewhat more concerned with capital adequacy. The FIRREA of 1989 tightened up on loose accounting and capital standards (see Chapter IV–D *Thrifts in Transition*) for thrift institutions. Most experts agreed that somewhat earlier corrective intervention for capital "weak" institutions was generally desirable, i.e., a major lesson from the S & L debacle. When Congress voted $70 billion of additional borrowing to recapitalize the FDIC (also suffering bigger losses 1988–92) in the FDIC Improvement Act of 1991, they tried to impose more stringent minimum capital standards, and restrict regulatory discretion in the supervision process.

A key feature of the 1991 FDICIA was a new "critical capital level" of 2 percent equity/total assets. Regulators continue to set the normal "minimums", i.e., the "leverage" (3 percent equity/total assets) capital requirement and "risk-based" (8 percent [Tier 1 and 2] capital/risk-assets) capital requirement, and corrective action is authorized for institutions falling significantly below these minimums (e.g. changes in management, removal of officers and directors, restrictions on growth, suspension of dividends, and/or a plan to increase capital). But when an institution falls below the "critical capital level," regulators should take control (by appointing a conservator) or seize and close the institution (by appointing a receiver), *unless* other action would better protect the deposit insurance fund. If an institution stays below the "critical capital level" for more than a year, closure and receivership should follow in most cases, *unless* the regulators certified the institution was viable and making progress in a capital restoration plan. [Meanwhile, regulators were mandated under the 1991 legislation to adjust risk-based capital standards within 18 months to take account of risks associated with fluctuations in interest rates, concentration of loans, and non-traditional activities.]

In the last few years, however, the G–12 Capital Requirements were criticized by some of the largest banks as being too restrictive. Accordingly, Basle II Improvements have been worked out to allow somewhat relaxed capital minimums. Where big banks can mitigate their risks with collateralization, hedging, securitization, and derivative securities, somewhat lower capital may be sufficient. But substantial oversight will still be needed by bank regulators. U.S. banking regulators expect to implement this alternate framework in 2005–2006. Thus far, it is contemplated that only the largest 12–25 U.S. multinational banks will fall into the new, relaxed requirements category, at least initially. The EU banking authorities seem willing to move in this direction, too. But some question these relaxations, particularly if major exchange rate disruptions should develop among many countries. Systemic risk factors still exist in global financial markets.

B. BANK INSURANCE AND SUPERVISION

A fundamental goal of modern United States banking law is to prevent another Great Depression, with massive runs on banks, and heavy costs to society. Clearly the looseness of previous banking practices—with too many weak and undercapitalized banks, and inadequate lender of last resort assistance to limit a spreading panic—are considered major reasons for excessive frequency of bank failures in the past. The United States economy suffered too many panics and depressions in its earlier history, a burden now considered unacceptable when most people are employed in highly interdependent industry, services and trade, and family farms no longer provide a widespread cushion of livelihoods to absorb heavy unemployment.

Four policies supported a more secure and panic resistant banking system. (1) Our system of Federal deposit insurance for bank accounts (FDIC), savings institutions accounts (FSLIC), and credit union accounts (NCUSIF). The Federal Deposit Insurance Corporation is the most important, which set the pattern on insurance and risk pooling for other institutions. (2) Greatly expanded credit backing from the Federal Reserve and FDIC, along with Congressional commitments to further aid in emergencies. (3) Consensus among policy-makers reflected in the Employment Act of 1946 and subsequent measures, that government fiscal and monetary policy should be managed to support the level of production, employment, and business activity, and help maintain the soundness of our financial credit system. (4) Stronger examination and supervision for commercial banks and related financial institutions, which enforces a higher level of responsible bank management, and tries to correct situations before too much damage can be done to depositors, business confidence and activity, and their communities. In this latter effort, the FDIC, the Federal Reserve, State Banking Departments, and comparable authorities for savings institutions, have been willing and able to change leadership, halt serious malpractices, and force absorption mergers in a great many situations involving troubled banks or savings institutions.

Table III–2

Bank Failures, FDIC Payoffs and Assumptions, 1934–2003

FDIC Insured Bank Failures

Year	Total No. of Bank Failures	Payoff Cases		Assumption Cases*	
		No. of Banks	Deposits ($m)	No. of Banks	Deposits ($m)
1934	61	9	2.0	—	—
1935	32	24	9.0	1	4.2
1936	72	42	11.2	27	16.3
1937	84	50	15.0	25	18.4

Year	Total No. of Bank Failures	Payoff Cases No. of Banks	Deposits ($m)	Assumption Cases* No. of Banks	Deposits ($m)
1938	81	50	10.3	24	49.4
1939	72	32	32.7	28	125.0
1940	48	19	5.6	24	137.0
1941	17	8	14.7	7	15.0
1942	23	6	2.0	14	17.3
1943	5	4	6.6	1	5.8
1944	2	1	.4	1	1.5
1945	—	—	—	1	5.6
1946	2	—	—	1	.3
1947	6	—	—	5	7.0
1948	3	—	—	3	10.6
1949	9	—	—	4	5.4
1950	5	—	—	4	5.5
1951	5	—	—	2	3.4
1952	4	—	—	3	3.1
1953	5	—	—	2	18.2
1954	4	—	—	2	1.0
1955	5	4	6.5	1	5.4
1956	3	1	4.7	1	6.6
1957	3	1	1.1	—	—
1958	9	3	4.1	1	4.0
1959	3	3	2.6	—	—
1960	2	1	7.0	—	—
1961	9	5	9.0	—	—
1962	3	—	—	—	—
1963	2	2	—	—	—
1964	8	7	23.4	—	—
1965	9	3	43.0	2	1.0
1966	8	1	0.7	6	103.0
1967	4	4	11.0	—	—
1968	3	—	—	3	22.5
1969	9	—	9.0	5	31.0
1970	8	4	33.5	3	49.3
1971	6	5	74.5	1	57.5
1972	3	1	20.4	—	—
1973	6	3	25.7	3	945.5
1974	4	—	—	3	1,576.0
1975	14	3	40.0	10	300.0
1976	17	3	18.8	13	846.0
1977	6	—	—	6	205
1978	7	1	1.3	6	852.8
1979	10	3	12.6	7	98.0
1980	10	3	16.4	7	200.0
Totals	722	312	$546m.	266	$9,504m.

* Total of bank failures includes a considerable number of non-insured banks in the early years.

Year	No. of Failures	FDIC Insured Bank Failures, Payoffs, Assumptions, and Deposit Transfers (Deposits involved—$m)
1981	10	$ 3,826.0
1982	42	9,908.4
1983	48	5,441.6
1984	79*	2,883.2*
1985	120	8,059.4
1986	138	6,471.1
1987	203	8,568
1988	221	37,215
1989	207	24,097
1990	169	14,500
1991	114	53,800
1992	116	41,200
1993	96	3,100
1994	27	1,200
1995	5	767
1996	5	208
1997	1	27
1998	3	338
1999	7	1,296
2000	7	364
2001	3	58
2002	10	2,370
2003	3	909
Totals	1,634	$235,588

Sources: FDIC *Annual Reports,* 1981–94; Associated Press report, January 6, 1988; *Statistical Abstract of the U.S. 1991, and 1995,* U.S. Census Bureau, 1991 and 1995; FDIC, 2000–2004.

NOTE. Does not include the Continental–Illinois Bank "failure", bailout, and recapitalization. (At its peak size Continental–Illinois Bank had $42 billion assets and $29 billion deposits).

These policies have been successful in reducing the number of runs on banks and failures. In the 1920's an average of 600 banks suspended operations each year. Between 1930–33, another 10,000 banks were closed. But after emergency measures in the spring of 1933, including the new FDIC and emergency bank lending on a large scale, the rate of bank closings was lowered dramatically. Some 470 banks closed between 1934–40, or not quite 70 a year, which still reflected residual weakness from the depression crisis. (Of these 470 bank failures, 112 were uninsured.) In subsequent years, between 1941–80, only 242 banks failed (only 24 not insured), or an average of merely six a year. In other words, comparing the 1920's to the years 1941–80, the incidence of bank failures was cut roughly one hundred-fold. This was truly an impressive achievement. (See Table III–2)

Unfortunately, bank failures increased greatly in numbers during the 1980's (with 1,500 between 1981–92). And the deposits involved in bank failures totaled at least $200 billion between 1981–92, compared to $10 billion for 1941–80 (a period nearly 4 times longer). In addition, some 1000 savings institutions failed between 1981–92, with ultimate costs of resolution perhaps $250–300 billion (including interest). See Chapter IV–D. *Thrifts in Transition*. [If the Continental–Illinois Bank failure-bailout in 1984 is included, more than $230 billion in deposits were involved in failures between 1981–92.] Why did bank failures (and the deposits involved) increase so drastically? Three explanations make sense: First, the 1970's inflation was greatly reduced by strong restraint, deflation, and financial stresses in the 1980's for many businesses in much of the world. This weakened loan asset quality for most U.S. multinational banks, together with some regional and community banks (especially for Latin American lending, the grain belt, oil patch, and many real estate markets). Second, more banks became aggressive, sought higher earnings, and accepted greater risks. Third, bank regulators may have relaxed somewhat (at least with hindsight's wisdom) at the end of the 1970's—and into the 1980's. In any event, these events serve as a useful warning and lesson. We need continued vigilance, talent, and independent responsibility for the Federal Reserve, FDIC, OCC, and other regulators and their staffwork.

The size of bank accounts protected by FDIC–FSLIC insurance has been increased substantially to allow for increased prosperity and inflation. Original coverage was $2,500 per account. Today accounts of $100,000 are insured. Deposit insurance, however, protects the *same* depositor only up to a single limit, i.e., $100,000 currently. If the same depositor, for example, has 4 accounts of $50,000 each in his or her own name, then the insurance limit is only $100,000. But if these accounts are for *different* legal interests, e.g., one for himself, and three separate trust accounts for different people or organizations, then the $100,000 limit applies to each account. Thus, so long as depositors keep no more than $100,000 (the current limit) in accounts with the same legal interest in any one bank, their deposit accounts can be fully insured.

In all the 568 insured bank failures between 1934–80, the FDIC paid off its insured accounts virtually 100 percent; non-insured accounts (exceeding coverage limits) are normally protected when absorption merger partners assume the deposits of a failing bank, and non-insured accounts (exceeding insurance coverage limits) still received partial recoveries even in those bank failures involving closure and liquidation. Nearly 4 million depositors have received $6.2 billion in all of these payoffs. But the FDIC recovered the bulk of these disbursements from assets left in the liquidating banks, or from the assumptions of deposit liabilities by successor banks. Between 1934–80, the FDIC lost only $301 million in all of these bank failures. In contrast, interest earnings for the FDIC on its reserve funds in 1980 alone were $868 million for that single year.

Most earlier bank failures involved smaller and less strongly capitalized banks. Overall, 97 percent of the failed banks between 1934–80 (or at least those allowed to fail by the banking agencies) had less than $50 million in deposits. This reflects their greater vulnerability, and a conscious policy to "save" larger banks with merger bailout transactions (often with FDIC assistance.) Allowing larger banks to fail would greatly increase FDIC payout expenses, and bring more disruptive effects on business confidence and activity in the communities affected. Nonetheless, between 1970–80 ten banks with more than $100 million deposits failed, and three banks with more than $500 million. During 1981–92 bank failures became even more frequent, including Continental–Illinois, the 7th largest U.S. commercial bank in 1983–84 (with $42 billion in assets).*

This reflected a new development, i.e., greater risk for banks with more aggressive "liability man-

---

* Technically, Continental–Illinois Bank was not allowed to fail. It was a direct assistance "bailout" by the FDIC and other Federal authorities.

agement,'' seeking higher rates of return in a business environment with greater fluctuations in interest rates. Continued success for the FDIC (and the Federal Reserve) will depend on preventing large bank failures. This requires that troubled banks with large deposits be merged into other big banks, and, in any event, that the incidence of bad practices and failures be kept to a minimum among bigger banking institutions.

Chart III–2

Balance Sheets for Banking Institutions

ASSETS

Reserves—(10–12% typical on demand deposits)

Cash (Specie and currency)

Accounts in "Reserve" Banks

Other "Reserve" Assets [1] (if allowed)—

Federal bills, notes, bonds

State bills, notes, bonds

Municipal notes, bonds

Bank accounts earning interest (correspondent banks)

Liquid Assets—

Government Securities (all types)

Corporate Securities

Physical Assets and Miscellaneous—

Buildings, equipment, supplies, leases, etc.

Loans—(60% typical)

Loan obligations readily marketable—

Loan obligations not readily marketable—

Satisfactory quality—

Adversely classified—

Substandard (Delinquent or risky)

Doubtful (normally written down 50 percent)

Loss (normally written to zero)

LIABILITIES

Demand Deposits—

Checking Accounts

Savings Accounts (active turnover)

Savings Accounts (passive turnover) with higher interest rates

Time Deposits—

Repurchase Agreement Accounts (very short-term)

Short-Term Deposit Accts.

Medium-Term Deposit Accts.

Debts—

To Government, Central Bank, or other Financial Support (e.g., FDIC, Fed) for borrowing

To other banks for borrowing (e.g., borrowed reserves)

Capital—(6–7% typical) *

Shareholder Equity

Surplus (retained earnings)

Reserve for Contingent Liabilities

Capital Loans—

(Special loans to bridge need for subsequent sale of additional shareholder stock to increase capital resources)

---

* See also, pp. 129–136, supra.

[1] State chartered banks traditionally earned interest on some of their reserve assets. Federal Reserve may allow interest on required reserves (under some proposals).

NOTE. DIDMCA of 1980 requires all depository institutions to hold 12% reserves on "transactional accounts" (except for initial $40m only 3%); up to 3% reserves on non-personal time deposits.

Chart III–3

Income Statements (Cash Flow Accounts) for Banking Institutions

CURRENT INCOME

Reserves—

Income, if any, from reserves and reserve assets

Liquid Assets—

Income from government and corporate securities

Loan Accounts—

Income from loans, less any losses or collection expenses—
business lending
real estate loans
consumer loans

Fees—

Syndication or underwriting fees, commissions, participations, credit cards, etc.

Physical and Other Assets—

Any income from physical assets, equipment, or other services (including trustee earnings, card systems)

Total Income

Net Income—(.6–1.3% typical on total assets)

Income taxes
Income after taxes—
Profits paid to shareholders
Retained earnings (for surplus account)

CURRENT EXPENSES

Demand Deposits—

Net interest, if any, payable on checking accounts
Interest payable on savings accounts

Time Deposits—

Interest payable on time deposits

Debts—

Interest payable on debts—to government, central bank, support agencies, other banks

Expenses for Buildings, Staff and Other Services—

Outlays for buildings, rent, equipment, supplies, personnel, executives, fees for services (e.g., card systems, computers)

Total Expenses

C. BANK SUPERVISION AND PREVENTING FAILURE

The tradition of bank examination and supervision in the United States goes back into the 19th century. More successful bank supervision and examination effort followed in the wake of New Deal reforms and the FDIC in 1933. Comprehensive reporting responsibilities have been established, including regular "call" and financial condition reports (quarterly for larger banks, and at least semiannually for smaller banks), and regular examinations (annual for larger banks, and at least every 18 months for smaller banks.) Special reports and examinations are imposed by the banking authorities for "problem banks", and almost continuous monitoring for banks facing imminent or likely failure. Because of this supervision regime, made increasingly easy, in some respects, by electronic data processing and computer techniques, most bank failures can be detected early enough to allow a possible absorption merger, and often in time to allow corrective remedies that eliminate the financial vulnerability of troubled banks.

Under the Uniform Interagency Bank Rating System (formalized in 1978) six elements are emphasized: (i) Capital adequacy; (ii) Asset quality; (iii) Management ability; (iv) Earnings performance; (v) Liquidity, and (vi) Sensitivity to market risk. [Summarized by the acronym "CAMELS".] Banks are rated in terms of each element on a scale of 1 through 5. The highest rating of 1 applies to a bank sound in almost every respect. A rating of 2 reflects fundamental soundness that may have modest, correctable weaknesses. The three lower categories involve descending levels of "problem banks." A rating of 3 shows a combination of weaknesses, moderately severe to unsatisfactory, and only nominally resistant to adverse business conditions. A rating of 4 represents an immoderate volume of asset weakness (usually a "soft" loan portfolio, with too large a proportion of "substandard", "doubtful" or "loss" loans), or less than a satisfactory combination of other elements, with a potential for failure (though not pronounced). A rating of 5 involves an immediate or near term likelihood of failure, with urgent action and constant supervisory attention essential. In terms of previously articulated standards, a rating of 3 reflects a "problem bank", a rating of 4 a "serious problem" bank, and a rating of 5 a "likely failure" with probable FDIC deposit payoff (unless an assumption of deposits could be worked out with acquisition partners).

Banks rated 3 normally provoke some special surveillance, and may invite corrective initiatives. Banks rated 4 require more strict supervision, and more urgent remedies if they are feasible. Banks with a 5 rating might be saved in some circumstances with drastic remedies, but failure is likely, and the regulators ordinarily canvass merger or assumption partners at the same time emergency corrective actions are reviewed.

Realize that legal "insolvency" is not required for corrective action, or even a forced merger transaction, if the regulatory authorities (and any court involved) find that a bank is likely to fail. [Liquidity insolvency arises when a bank cannot meet current obligations, including deposit withdrawals, with liquid assets and cash. Balance sheet insolvency arises when liabilities exceed assets, or net capital sinks below zero.] Even though regulatory agencies must justify a need for drastic intervention, i.e., a forced merger or a closure and receivership, reviewing courts face great difficulty in opposing their recommendations when a bank is facing imminent failure.

A run on the bank is likely in these circumstances, if not already in progress, with a drastic decline in deposits, the danger of liquidity insolvency, a further decline in net capital, and probable balance sheet insolvency. Thus, the modern tradition of bank regulation normally intervenes before legal insolvency, with corrective remedies, forced merger or even closure and receivership, in order to prevent the larger losses to depositors associated with a "completed" run and actual insolvency.

Typical problems in troubled banks arise from taking undue risks in lending or borrowing activity; lax supervision of department managers by top officers and/or directors; unduly concentrated lending portfolios without enough diversification; losses from changing interest rates; bad luck in foreign exchange or international operations (caused by insufficient care to minimize risks); overly aggressive growth and profit maximizing strategies that involve excessive risk; self-dealing transactions or loans to friends, relations, or businesses owned by bank insiders; embezzlement, theft or fraudulent misappropriation of funds; even losses on bad checks, wire transfers, endorsements or guarantees. The strength of banks is power over spending, investments and business growth potential. Their vulnerability stems from losses or misuse of funds, whether through external forces, serious errors, negligence, selfish and irresponsible greed, or dishonest diversion of bank funds to illegitimate or unsound purposes.

Corrective options available to the regulatory authorities include: (i) expanding the capital available, through bringing in additional investors, levies on existing shareholders, or, conceivably, capital loans or assistance from the FDIC or Federal Reserve; (ii) changes in management practices, including tougher loan standards, avoiding areas of loan investment that have been unsuccessful or risky, reduced borrowing risks, along with cutbacks on growth, personnel, branching or other overhead expenses; (iii) suspension or removal of key management personnel, officers and directors, even when they might be substantial stockholders in the bank. Such actions may be difficult to impose upon a stubborn management, especially when the latter might lose community standing or economic advantages, or fear stockholder suits for "recognized" mismanagement. Loan portfolios may not be improved quickly, particularly when "tar baby" loan investments are involved—that may need extended rescheduling to improve prospects of eventual repayment. Errors in management policies may be identified with considerable precision afterwards, but turning them around may take some time. For these reasons, generally speaking, the FDIC avoids loan assistance to an existing bad management, and normally confines its capital loans to new management or an absorbing bank in a bailout merger situation. Federal Reserve discount borrowing, and even emergency loans are the more normal source of financial aid for a troubled bank management's effort to save itself. But Federal Reserve lending will cease to be available when community confidence has eroded, and the regulators believe a run on the bank is impending or has begun. Even if a management might still turn things around by changing its policies, when depositor confidence has been undermined, the only solution may be a new management and an absorption merger (or a closure and liquidation).

Legal authority for preventing bank failure is strongly established among the regulatory agencies, although good teamwork is needed for rapid combined effort. The most important leverage came in 1933 from FDIC authority to terminate insurance coverage, the threat of which could force substantial concessions from a bank management in serious trouble. Most modern banks could not sustain depositor confidence without FDIC membership, and its sudden loss probably would precipitate a run of panicky depositors. (Removal from Federal Reserve membership would have comparable effects now, and normally leads to loss of FDIC insurance coverage.) Charter revocation by the OCC or State authorities had been available earlier, but was hard to employ with enough speed or discretion in troubled bank cases. Much stronger justification and court action was needed for earlier charter revocation, whereas FDIC insurance coverage is an administrative determination that can be made more informally and discretely. Preliminary action by the FDIC frequently took the form of a proposed order to show cause why insurance should be terminated, sent confidentially to the troubled bank's management, which normally provoked negotiations to correct malpractices. The bank's management would fear public disclosure and embarrassment, a possible run, or suits by minority shareholders for breach of fiduciary duty for having caused the bank's difficulties. This gave the FDIC and other supervising agencies powerful leverage.

Financial assistance could be provided, as a possible sweetener for corrective action, but the Federal Reserve is the main source of credit (as explained previously). The FDIC, having limited reserves for assistance compared to the Federal Reserve Banks, largely confines itself to assisting absorption mergers with loan guarantees and capital loans to the bank or banks that assume a failing bank's deposits.

The Financial Institutions Supervisory Act of 1966 strengthened federal regulatory authority by adding intermediate and less drastic remedies, i.e., the issuance of cease and desist orders and the suspension or removal of officers, directors, or other key figures in a bank organization. This allowed more explicit intervention to correct unsound bank practices before a bank's situation had become too serious. The Financial Institutions Regulatory and Rate Control Act of 1978 (FIRA) (sometimes called the "Bert Lance bill") extended these powers to bank holding companies, their non-bank subsidiaries, Edge Act corporations, and provided more supervision for inter-bank stock ownership holdings. Cease and desist order authority was broadened to cover individuals along with banks. And civil money penalties were added to the corrective remedy authority.

Cease and desist order proceedings may now involve a temporary stay or injunctive effect upon bank conduct and management until a formal hearing. To set aside such "freeze" action, a bank's management must go into federal district court and get a judge to intervene on its behalf. The regulatory authorities have broad authority and discretion to stop activities likely to cause insolvency, dissipation of assets or earnings, weaken a bank, or seriously prejudice the interest of depositors.* This reflects the logic of preventing bank failure and runs, i.e., the need for speed, discretion, and powerful sanctions against a bank management's possible flight with the depositor's assets, and the imperatives for maintaining community and depositor confidence.

Bank managements may fear *ex parte* action and precipitate constraints on their behavior. But a soundly managed bank with adequate capital, quality assets, healthy earnings and reasonable liquidity has no cause for alarm. The banks that worry about corrective intervention are those with soft assets, or weakened capital, earnings or illiquidity. For weaker banks, public policy since the Great Depression has placed a priority upon protecting depositors, preventing runs and failure, and sustaining busi-

* The FIRREA of 1989 and the FDIC Improvement Act of 1991 further strengthened the authority, corrective remedies, restitution for fraud, civil and criminal penalties available to bank regulators in protecting the safety and soundness of insured banks and other depository institutions.

ness confidence in the communities involved. Bank management, therefore, is held to a special standard of quasi trusteeship or fiduciary responsibility that goes beyond normal business leadership, because it is the peculiar role of banks (and similar deposit institutions) to receive and hold money for safekeeping by the people and businesses of their area. Special profit opportunities and prestige are associated with playing the role of banker. Accordingly, the law and regulatory practice governing United States banks properly imposes a high standard of care in discharging this trust safely and prudently.

Successful collaboration and teamwork among the OCC, FDIC and Federal Reserve, and the State Banking Departments or Commissioners has developed over the last 70 years. Overlapping jurisdiction of two chartering authorities (OCC or the states), a separate insurance agency (FDIC), and the Federal Reserve (central bank and lender of last resort) may seem complex, and could have become cumbersome and unworkable. But fortunately, these agencies have worked well together. In fact, their overlapping mesh has been an advantage in limiting the risks of corrupt and irresponsible bank regulation. Because two or three different regulatory agencies may have access to the call reports, bank examination data, and other related information, it is more difficult for the staff or leadership in these agencies to be bribed or influenced by bank management, or their political friends. Improved integrity can be a by-product of multiple responsibility for bank supervision. This should be kept in mind when considering possible regulatory consolidation measures.

For the most part, bank supervision in the United States has been successful since the Great Depression. Hopefully this record will continue. Concerns have been voiced, however, in recent years. Some complained of relaxed bank and thrift supervision in the early-mid 1980's, especially with regard to weakened capitalization, aggressive growth, and risky lending policies for many institutions. Since 1,500 banks and 1,000 thrifts failed between 1981–92, many believe weaker supervision played a role. But other factors contributed, too. As interest rate ceilings on deposits were removed, increased rivalry brought pressure on margins. Eroded boundaries and interpenetration of markets added risks. Interest rate rises in the late 1970's, and volatility on into the 1980's, brought more risks for many financial institutions. Still another influence was a slowed industrial economy, with less manufacturing at home, which encouraged lending in other areas. Because of profits for financial dealmakers (including some banks), it became fashionable for many corporations to carry greater debt, leading to over-leveraging and strains thereafter for both borrowers and creditors. Tax policies fostered commercial real estate investment and sheltering, particularly after the Economic Recovery Tax Act of 1981 (ERTA), but then cut back heavily on real estate investment incentives in the Tax Reform Act of 1986 (TRA), as loopholes were sharply reduced.

An overriding problem in the 1980's was the impact of deflationary pressures that followed the excessive inflation trend of the 1970's; sustained tight money policies, and elevated interest rates, were needed to erode inflationary expectations in the 1980's. Unfortunately, this increased borrowing costs throughout much of the economy; many corporations, farmers, and real estate projects took on more debt service than they could really afford, which weakened loan asset quality for banks and thrifts in many areas.

From another direction, complaints from some free market enthusiasts question the need for FDIC insurance, wondering whether sound banks aren't subsidizing the more adventurous institutions. According to this reasoning, there is a potential vulnerability to banking because the FDIC and Federal Reserve are taking away the "normal and natural" risk of bank failure. Thus, higher risk and dangerous loan practices may be encouraged, leading to reduced capitalization (or declining net capital as a percentage of total assets and liabilities). A logical response to this criticism is that bank regulators need not allow such malpractices to spread. But the idea of completely eliminating FDIC insurance, or relying solely upon private insurance, lost ground badly after widespread bank failures in the later 1980's and early 1990's.

Instead, a strong consensus developed for risk related insurance premium charges by the FDIC for deposit insurance protection. In principle, it makes sense to charge "sound" banks less for FDIC insur-

ance than "unsound" banks. Whether or not the
bank regulators can make such distinctions publicly, however, without damaging the reputations and
deposit business of banks involved is a practical
question. But FIRREA in 1989 mandated serious
study of risk-related deposit insurance premiums,
and the FDIC Improvement Act of 1991 now requires this agency to implement them. Risk-based
assessments can be related to capital levels, the mix
of bank assets, activities, foreign deposits, and the
structure of rates and maturities for assets and
deposits. In addition, the FDIC is required to bring
bank insurance deposits back up to 1.25 percent of
aggregate insured deposits (over a 15 year period).

Another important controversy surrounds the
phenomenon that some of the largest banks seem
"too big to fail." Strictly speaking, however, this is
not exactly banking regulatory policy. When larger
banks become insolvent, their leadership and top
managers are typically removed, and their shareholders are largely (*if not totally*) wiped out in a
FDIC assisted recapitalization for a rejuvenated
bank (like *Continental-Illinois* in 1984), or in the
more common "purchase and assumption" (P & A)
deal. In a P & A transaction, a failing bank has its
deposits and "clean assets" assumed by a larger,
healthy, and properly capitalized bank (or banks).
The assuming bank normally pays a modest "good-
will" premium to the FDIC, appropriate to the
customers and branches in the assumed deposits
and assets. The "unclean" assets, i.e., bad or questionable loans, normally remain with the FDIC (or

FSLIC), which collects on them as receiver to the extent possible (salvage value). Only if the assumed bank is *not quite* insolvent would the failing bank shareholders receive something after all other creditors are paid (including subordinated debt or hybrid-security holders serving the capital function). If the assumed failing bank was more or less insolvent (i.e., with negative capitalization), then all its capital ownership would be wiped out, and the FDIC (or FSLIC) suffers net losses in the process of collecting on the bad assets.

In the normal "P & A" transactions (or the rare FDIC assisted recapitalization of a very large institution), *all* depositors are typically protected—the uninsured depositors (over $100,000) as well as the insured depositors. Why? This result minimizes the disruptive effects on local, regional, or national commerce (depending on the institution's size), and bank runs are prevented. By contrast, allowing *uninsured* depositors to suffer substantial losses would make commercial banking relationships more nervous, insecure, and weaken substantially the attractiveness of U.S. banks in competition for world deposits and international borrowing. Private depositors would find it hard to monitor bank managements efficiently because relevant information is closely held and hard to acquire.* But this means that the largest banks or institutions *do need* a P & A or recapitalization when they fail or become insolvent, in order to minimize disruptive impacts on

* Some scholars suggest the desirability of partial losses or "haircuts" for uninsured deposits, but there has been little support in Congress, banking, or industry generally.

commerce and losses to uninsured depositors. On the other hand, small institutions usually have no sizeable volume of uninsured deposits, so that a simple closure and payoff is often feasible and appropriate for the FDIC (although some discrimination against smaller institutions results). Thus, small banks should be prudent.

But heavy losses were suffered by FSLIC (and the FDIC) in the late 1980's, mainly due to a failure to enforce timely corrective actions and/or "resolutions" (i.e., P & A's, closure and payoff, or the rare assisted recapitalization for a very large institution). Because of this experience, Congress in the FDIC Improvement Act of 1991 tried to prevent any reoccurrences: (1) Stronger capitalization, earlier intervention, and "critical capital level" requirements are designed to minimize excessive forbearance; and (2) Least cost resolution is now required, which mean *earlier* P & A's or closures and payoffs (*before* significant insolvencies). Losses to *uninsured* depositors are allowed (if this is the least cost solution). But under narrow circumstances of "systemic risk", i.e., involving the largest institutions, banking regulators can protect *all* uninsured depositors, provided, however, that special assessments against total assets held by banks (*including overseas deposits*) are levied to pay these extra costs. In this way, presumably, Congress tried to restrict "too big to fail" relief to the very largest banks, and for that infrequent relief *special assessments* against total banking system assets (including overseas deposits) should share the premium insurance burden.

Finally, the overall success of modern United States bank supervision raises an important question in another direction. Could bank-like supervision and examination routines be extended more generally to cover insurance companies, mutual funds, and pension fund fiduciaries?* Certainly electronic data processing and computer techniques have enlarged the potential for accountability very substantially. The Securities and Exchange Commission already enforces extensive disclosure of financial data for publicly held companies. Other financial information, together with production, shipments, sales, and profits data for corporate performance is regularly collected by the Commerce Department, and by the Federal Trade Commission. It is published in summary tabulations, with confidential treatment for most individual company reports. More information is collected and tabulated by the Internal Revenue Service from confidential tax returns, with limited summaries published as statistical data. An enormous amount of additional data is regularly generated by business in the normal course of operations, much of which might be standardized with more uniform accounting, records and reporting disciplines.

But it should be understood that broader accountability for corporate enterprises outside the finan-

* Actually, substantially improved capital requirements have been developed in recent years by the National Association of Insurance Commissioners (NAIC). See Chapter VI, *infra*.

cial institutions sector might be more difficult, with much greater divergencies in capitalization, investment planning, production and sales operations, research and development, management strategies, overhead, financing, insurance, and even tax avoidance among firms in so many different industries. More uniformity might be imposed than exists now, but greatly varied patterns remain unavoidable. Problems of trade secrets and confidentiality treatment could be awkward. Aside from the public utilities sector, which already tries to achieve some uniformity in their accounts, such as for railroads, power companies, etc., we see only modest government accounting efforts along these lines. More might be attempted over the years, but recent attitudes favoring some momentum toward "de-regulation" suggest that expanded corporate accountability does not seem to be a strong trend at present. This could change, however, with a Presidential administration that favored a more active supervisory role for international investments, and/or stronger accountability for corporate pensions, profit-sharing, and employee stock ownership plans (ESOP's).

D. SPECIFIC LIMITATIONS ON BANKING ACTIVITIES

In addition to general banking market supervision, there are important special limitations placed on bank operations. Four major goals are reflected in these specific limitations: (i) Sound banking, reliable financial institutions, and reduced risk of irresponsibility; (ii) Competition, efficiency, and decentralization within financial and capital markets; (iii) Fairness for depositors, borrowers, and other customers of banks and financial institutions; and (iv) Adequate flows of credit to business, industry, housing and consumer markets.

1.   LENDING LIMITS

The main purpose of lending limits is to enforce diversification of loan account risks, and to prevent banks from putting too many depositor eggs into any one basket of loan investments. For national banks, the most general limitation is 12 U.S. Code Section 84, which provided for many years that total obligations or loans extended on behalf of any person, co-partnership, association, or corporation shall not exceed 10 percent of the bank's unimpaired capital stock and surplus. Since the capital stock and surplus accounts of a bank normally represent about 6–7 percent of total liabilities or total assets, this meant that no more than .6 or .7 percent of a national bank's assets could be invested in any single loan account relationship. However, the Depository Institutions Act of 1982 significantly increased this lending limit to 15 percent of capital and surplus for unsecured loans, and an additional 10 percent for loans fully secured by readily marketable collateral. This means now that a national bank may loan, roughly, up to 1.5–1.8 percent of their total assets to their biggest customers, provided that at least 40 percent of these amounts are secured by readily marketable collateral. But diversification discipline is still maintained, and courts have enforced strict Section 84 liability upon officers and directors for knowing violation of this rule without need for proof of negligence. Thus, bank managements are held accountable for compliance with the lending limits.

This general limit of Section 84 is subject to some further exceptions, based upon the reliability, strength of collateral, and liquidity of the loan obligations involved. But for most ordinary loan accounts, Section 84 limits the extent to which loans can be made to particular customers. These lending limits force smaller and medium-sized banks to bring other banks into participation loans for large corporate borrowing, and even the bigger banks are forced into multi-bank loan participations for their largest corporate or international customers.

Another restriction on national banks applied to real estate loans. Generally, 12 U.S.C.A. § 371 required that first mortgage loans on real estate should not exceed the total of capital stock and surplus, or time and savings deposits, whichever might be larger. But this explicit restriction has been replaced in the Depositary Institutions Act of 1982 by general regulatory authority of the Comptroller of the Currency. These regulations were relaxed to allow more competition by banks against savings institutions with respect to real estate mortgage lending.

State chartered banks (including those which are members of the Federal Reserve) must comply with comparable, though slightly different, state lending limits laws. Many states have employed the general limitation of 10 percent on capital and surplus, others 15 percent, and still others 20 percent. (Liberalization up to the new federal limit of 25 percent may follow.) Exceptions had been somewhat more generous in state statutes, especially in the rural states, where more latitude was desired for smaller town and country banks, which do not have many big loan customers, businesses, factories, farms or ranches in their market areas.

2.   BANK AFFILIATE TRANSACTIONS

Transactions between affiliated banks and related companies involve dangers of financial abuse and threats to the integrity of banking, along with possible advantages of mutual support, cost saving and convenience. Such transactions were regulated by the Banking Act of 1933 for member banks, Section 23(A) and (B) Federal Reserve Act, with amended regulation extended to all FDIC insured banks in 1966. These "firewall" restrictions have been alleviated, in part, and strengthened, in other respects, by the Banking Affiliates Act of 1982 (a portion of the Depositary Institutions Act of 1982).

This legislation, 12 U.S.C.A. § 371(c) (and § 371(c)–1) as amended, imposes two major disciplines, i.e., quantitative limitations and collateral requirements. In general, banks are not allowed to loan more than 10 percent of their capital stock and surplus to a single affiliate, or more than 20 percent of their capital stock and surplus to the aggregate of all affiliates. The required collateral used to be stocks, bonds, debentures, or paper eligible for rediscount by Federal Reserve. Now a broader list of debt instruments is allowed, including receivables, leases, real and personal property, with appropriate increases in value for collateral. Thus, the required collateral value for receivables is 120 percent of the loan, and for real and personal property 130 percent of the loan. This liberalization facilitates bank loans to mortgage, finance, leasing and factoring company affiliates, by allowing more realistic collateral to be employed. However, low quality assets such as substandard, doubtful or loss loan obligations are not acceptable collateral.

As a further safeguard, the 1982 amendments required that all bank transactions with affiliates be on terms and conditions that are consistent with safe and sound banking practices. This allows a second line of defense against adverse transactions with affiliates, consistent with prior regulatory policies. More recently, for bank holding companies that became seriously troubled, federal banking regulators implemented tougher requirements and guarantees among holding company "family members" (parents and affiliates), i.e., the so-called "source of strength" doctrine. See 12 C.F.R. § 225.4(a)(1) (1991). This can be interpreted as an obligation to use their combined capital, and save the FDIC from undue losses as far as possible. The

FDIC has gone further in some recent assistance cases (MCorp. of Texas, Republic Bank of Texas, and NE Bancorp), where cross-guarantee obligations were imposed on BHC's and affiliates as a precondition for receiving "open bank assistance", i.e., an assisted recapitalization.

This problem of inter-affiliate responsibilities and mutual vulnerability is also known as the "firewalls controversy." When bank holding companies are connected to corporate interests outside of banking, additional difficulties arise. Frequently banks were abused or endangered by holding company leaders who issued excess loans or loan guarantees in favor of corporate affiliates from the holding company group. The C. Arnholt Smith real estate enterprises were a classic example of this in the failure of U.S. National Bank of San Diego in 1973, one of the largest bank failures before the later 1980's. Another recent example of holding company abuses was the collapse of Bank of Commerce and Credit International (BCCI). These experiences suggest that as financial holding companies become more extensive and international, that greater "firewalls" supervision by the Federal Reserve and other Central Banks will be required.

3. INSIDER LENDING

Insider lending and "sweetheart" loans are subject to special restrictions and reporting requirements, which were strengthened by the Financial Institutions Regulatory and Interest Rate Control

Act of 1978 (FIRA). Federal Reserve Board regulations implement these requirements. Insider lending transactions have been a common reflection of mismanagement, and often the source of bank failures. Consequently, no bank (whether national or FDIC insured), can make loans to executive officers, directors, affiliates, or to stockholders owning more than 10 percent of voting stock, unless such loans are on substantially equal terms to those granted outsiders. Board of directors approval also is required within the bank for such loans, when the amounts are significant.

In addition, there were limitations on the amounts allowed for certain specific loans, most recently $60,000 for home mortgage loans, $20,000 for education loans, and $10,000 in other loans. Because of inflation, however, these specific limits became unrealistic, and the Depositary Institutions Act of 1982 repealed them, and simply replaced the loan limitations with a grant of regulatory authority to set appropriate limits.

Federal law also prohibits any preferential lending by Federal Reserve member banks to officers, directors, attorneys or employees. 12 U.S.C.A. § 376. This provision had been added to the Federal Reserve Act in 1918.

4. BORROWING LIMITS

Every national bank had been prohibited since 1863 from borrowing funds, becoming indebted, or becoming in any way liable beyond the level of its paid in capital stock, together with the total of all their deposits and banknote circulation. This provision was designed to minimize the risk of overborrowing, and to enforce balance sheet solvency upon national banks. It was codified as 12 U.S.C.A. § 82. Further exceptions were added for liabilities to the Federal Reserve Banks, the Federal Deposit Insurance Corporation, and Reconstruction Finance Corporation, which allowed "lender of last resort" borrowing beyond this level. A further liberalization followed in 1959, which permitted additional borrowing up to the level of 50 percent of a national bank's unimpaired surplus.

However, the Depositary Institutions Act of 1982 repealed 12 U.S.C.A. § 82. In an explanatory bulletin, the Comptroller of the Currency stated: "This deregulatory action places more responsibility on bank chief executives for sound asset and liability management. As the variety and volume of nondeposit liabilities increase, the job of maintaining net interest margins and adequate liquidity will become more difficult and complex. As always, bank asset and liability management policies and practices will be closely scrutinized by national bank examiners." If excessive bank borrowing becomes a serious problem in future years, regulation in this area may be restored to some degree.

Obviously, the interest rates payable to depositors (a liability of banks) are a cost of funds somewhat equivalent to "borrowing" in the narrower sense of earlier banking law. Between 1933–80 excessive deposit interest payments were prevented under Regulation Q. But between 1983–90 some institutions, particularly the more aggressive S & L's, were paying more for deposits than was prudent (especially those dependent on deposit brokers). Accordingly, the FDIC Improvement Act of 1991 has restricted above market interest payments through deposit brokers, by greatly limiting this practice for undercapitalized institutions.

5.   BRIBERY, FRAUD, AND EXTORTION

Criminal penalties are imposed on FDIC insured bank officers, directors, employees, agents, or attorneys who receive or consent to bribes, commissions, fees or gifts in connection with bank loans, extensions of credit, or acceptance of any paper, note, draft, check or bill of exchange. (18 U.S.C.A. § 215). The offer of such inducements is likewise unlawful with respect to Federal Reserve banks. (18 U.S.C.A. § 214.) In addition, criminal penalties apply to FDIC insured bank examiners or assistant examiners who receive gratuities or loans from any bank or organization examined by them. (18 U.S.C.A. § 212.) Imprisonment for not more than one year and/or up to $5000 fines are the penalties provided.

FIRREA of 1989 greatly increased the maximum penalties for false bank reports, entries, and unauthorized transactions by bank officers, directors, agents, or employees (18 U.S.C.A. § 1005) from $5,000 and/or 5 years to $1,000,000 and/or 20 years imprisonment. FIRREA also created a new bank fraud crime (18 U.S.C.A. § 1344) with penalties of up to $1,000,000 and/or 20 years. Subsequent amendments in 1990 increased maximum sentences to 30 years for both crimes.

Extortionate credit transactions are prohibited, with extortion defined as involving the use of "violence or other criminal means to cause harm to the person, reputation, or property of any person." (18 U.S.C.A. §§ 891–896.) Knowing participation in any such transaction, or the collection of such debts, justifies imprisonment of up to 20 years, and/or substantial fines.

Whoever knowingly makes false statements or reports to obtain loans, extensions of loans, discounts, or release of security is criminally liable for imprisonment of up to 30 years, or up to $1,000,000 in fines. (18 U.S.C.A. § 1014.)

6.   SECURITIES MARKETING AND COMMERCIAL BANKING

The stock market Crash of 1929 led to a legal separation in 1933 of investment banking, securities marketing, and the stock and bond trade from commercial banking. In previous years, some large New York banks had securities affiliates, were major underwriters of new securities issues, and helped market stocks and bonds on a big scale. Similar links among regional banks and securities firms were permitted, but were less significant outside the Wall Street money market center. Most commercial banks only got involved in securities through holding part of their liquid assets this way (mostly high grade bonds or preferred "blue chip" stocks), and in the management of trust account securities for many customers. But with the Crash and its tragic losses, a factor in restoring confidence in "commercial" banks was to insulate them from the securities business. The whole experience left people suspicious of securities, brokers and underwriters. Some commercial banks, including leaders on Wall Street, were accused of dumping less successful issues, and even portions of their own securities with declining prices, into the trust accounts of unfortunate customers. Such transactions reflected conflicting interests, and often involved breach of fiduciary duties as trustees. In this context, it is understandable that the emergency banking legislation of 1933 should separate commercial banking from the securities business and underwriting activity.

Sections 16, 20, 21 and 32 of the Banking Act of 1933 became known as the Glass–Steagall Wall, because they prevented banks from underwriting, selling, or distributing securities, while securities firms and brokerage organizations were prohibited from receiving deposits like commercial banks. (See 12 U.S.C.A. §§ 24, 78, 377, 378(a), and 335 and 221.) Thus, commercial banks and investment banks were prevented generally from entering each other's territory. But this Glass–Steagall wall became increasingly controversial in the 1980's–90's; finally, in 1999 the Gramm–Leach Financial Modernization Act largely eliminated this wall.

More and more, over the 1980's, the Glass Steagall Wall was criticized as outmoded. Traditional
bank loan business to bigger corporations was declining. Big companies increasingly issued commercial paper (notes)to the public, rather than get loans
from banks. This led larger banks into securities
marketing, so that their loan business could be
recovered. Major loopholes grew. Banks were allowed to underwrite and deal in government obligations (federal, state and local subdivisions), provided the full faith and credit of the issuer supports
them. Many types of state and local revenue bonds
could be underwritten by banks. On the other hand,
banks were excluded from marketing mutual funds
until the mid–1980's. *Investment Co. Institute v.
Camp* (S.Ct.1971). For many years only a limited
opportunity for combined trust accounts, and closed
end investment company sponsorship was allowed
to commercial banks, along with investment advisor
roles for bank affiliates. But since the mid–1980's
increasingly extensive securities transactions for individual customers were allowed to banks by banking regulators.

Money market mutual funds (MMMF's) grew rapidly in the late 1970's when savings institutions and
commercial banks sought to keep Regulation Q limits on passbook deposit rates low. But large denomination certificates of deposit were issued by banks
and large savings institutions at higher rates to
corporate and institutional investors. Specialized
mutual funds began to invest in highly liquid portfolios of such jumbo CD deposit accounts, along

with Eurocurrency bank deposits and some corporate commercial paper. Limited check writing privileges were added by MMMF's to encourage money market accounts, and initial deposit requirements were reduced to broaden their appeal for the public. Ultimately, cash management accounts (CMA's) evolved from these MMMF's, which are close to commercial bank checking accounts in many respects.

The Depositary Institutions Act of 1982 allowed banks and savings institutions to respond with new money market accounts at comparable interest rates. Under recent regulations FDIC (and FSLIC) insured "money market deposit accounts" may be established by banks (and savings institutions) with the following characteristics: (i) initial deposits of $2500; (ii) average balance requirements of $2500; (iii) no minimum maturity or holding period; (iv) at least seven days notice for withdrawals; (v) no interest rate ceilings on deposits that meet initial and average balance requirements; and (vii) availability to all depositors. But without this external rivalry from the securities brokerage industry and MMMF's, it is doubtful that banks (and savings institutions) would have increased interest paid to depositors, and their cost of funds from depositor accounts to the same extent.

Another big break by banks into securities marketing occurred in 1982–84 with Bank of America's acquisition of Charles Schwab & Co., the leading discount brokerage operation. When regulators and the courts approved, it opened the door for many large banks to offer similar services (by contractual relationship or otherwise). Bank "lobbies" sought further securities powers, with emphasis on the underwriting of commercial paper, mortgage-backed securities, and revenue bonds, along with the marketing of mutual funds. Some large banks demanded full repeal of Glass–Steagall, but much of the securities industry challenged the need for that much change.

Although Congress refused for 15 years to repeal completely the Glass–Steagall Wall (despite lobbying pressure from many large banks, and the Reagan, Bush, and Clinton administrations), major erosion occurred between 1987–96 with respect to the larger BHC's. In a series of regulatory decisions by the Federal Reserve Board and the OCC, many large banks were allowed to underwrite commercial paper, securitized mortgage backed instruments, and even many corporate bonds and stocks, along with lending to support private placements of securities. However, most of this underwriting was carried on in affiliates where the new activities were not a large part of their business (so as to not violate a prohibition against being "principally engaged" in underwriting corporate securities). [However, overseas underwriting by big U.S. banks was already exempt, and had become a large loophole since the 1970's.] Some of the biggest U.S. banks (e.g. Citicorp, Morgan, and Banker's Trust) already became serious players in U.S. domestic underwriting by 1989, and were even stronger abroad. Some large regional banks also sought underwriting access, but most smaller banks could never play an appreciable role in underwriting. Congress again refused to enact general underwriting authority for most BHC's in 1991, although the Bush administration proposed to authorize full line financial conglomerate holding companies (for banking, insurance, and securities).

Some favored broad holding companies (along the lines of German-style "universal banking"), but resistance was still substantial. Many insisted that stronger "firewalls" supervision—like Section 23(A) and (B) of the Federal Reserve Act, would be needed as a safeguard measure in the event that broad financial service holding companies would be authorized by Congress.* Those opposing Glass–Steagall repeal believed feared that firewalls were inherently difficult to maintain and supervise, especially for troubled institutions that could borrow heavily from their subsidiaries, and leave disproportionate losses for the FDIC, SIPC, PBGC, and/or insurance guaranty insolvency funds.

Finally, the Gramm–Leach Financial Services Modernization Act of 1999 resolved the conflict by allowing new Financial Holding Companies (FHC's). But FHC's are confined mainly to banking, securities, or insurance activities. (A limited exemption for other commercial activities was allowed

* In 1996 the Fed raised the limit on bank securities activities to 25 percent of revenue in their securities affiliates from 10 percent previously allowed. Only 23 U.S. and 15 foreign BHC's used such "Section 20 affiliates" by mid–1996. By 2003, 630 FHC's had been established; 57 of these FHC's were dealing or under-writing in securities.

mainly as a transition rule to ease hardships. The central theme of Gramm–Leach is to continue separate regulation for FHC's of banks by banking regulators, of most securities by the SEC, and of insurance by the state insurance departments and commissioners. However, the loophole already established for bank affiliate subsidiaries (Section 20 affiliates) is widened to 45 percent of parent bank assets, or $50 billion, whichever is smaller. In this way banks with Section 20 affiliates are given broader leeway and are not compelled to transform themselves into Financial Holding Companies (FHC's).

7.   TRUST ACCOUNTS AND DEPARTMENTS

Trust accounts have become important for bank deposits and as a vehicle for securities investment since the late 19th century. State banks and trust companies (often consolidated, but with many independent trust companies) took the lead. National banks joined in this activity after the Federal Reserve Act of 1913 authorized them under Federal Reserve Board regulations (promulgated in 1915). Early regulations required separation of each trust account and its securities. But since the later 1920's common or "pooled" trust accounts also had become widely used for smaller trusts and fiduciary accounts, provided that settlors, testators, and others with appropriate powers have specified this treatment and signed the correct forms.

For many years the Federal Reserve supervised national bank trust account activity under Regulation F, but in 1962 Congress transferred this authority to the Comptroller of the Currency (OCC). The current law and OCC regulations allow national banks as much latitude for fiduciary activities as enjoyed by state banks and trust companies. Bank trustees must keep their fiduciary records separate from all other records, with full information for each account (including any pending litigation). Annual audits of the trust department are required. Investments must be in accord with the instrument establishing the fiduciary relationship and state law. Self-dealing by the bank, its directors, officers, or employees generally is prohibited, except as it might be allowed under state law. Trust account investments shall be kept separate from other banks assets, and responsible trust officers must be adequately bonded. The bank may charge reasonable compensation for services as allowed by local law.

Under this fiduciary authority commercial banks hold a considerable part of the assets they manage. Thus, commercial bank organizations are among the sizeable institutional investors in the securities markets. Bank trust departments compete with pension funds, insurance companies, mutual funds and other investment companies as institutional investors and securities traders. (In fact, many banks act as trustees for pension funds, along with other fiduciary accounts.) In this role, however, commercial banks are not underwriting or marketing securities as are the brokerage firms. The Glass–Steagall Act was drawn carefully to separate bank trust department activities from the securities marketing and "investment" banking business. (For more on this distinction, see the preceding section on Securities Marketing and Commercial Banking, and Chapter V, Securities Market Regulation, especially Investment Companies and Mutual Funds.)

8.   REGULATION OF INTEREST ON DEPOSIT ACCOUNTS

Control of interest rates on deposit accounts entered banking law in the 1930's. Its goal was to limit "excessive" competition among banks, and was implemented by the Federal Reserve Board's Regulation Q. But between 1933–65 Regulation Q ceilings were set either above or closely aligned with market rates of interest. Therefore, little "disintermediation" pressure was evident, i.e., there was no appreciable outflow of savings and time deposits into other forms of investment activity.

Disintermediation problems developed in the later 1960's, 1973–74, and most significantly, between 1978–82. In these three periods, and especially the last, the gap between higher market rates of interest and the lower deposit rates on most forms of smaller bank accounts (and thrift institutions deposits since 1966, when Regulation Q was extended to them) was so large, that major shifts in consumer deposit activity occurred, benefiting particularly the new money market mutual funds.

Rates under Regulation Q had been gradually raised during the later 1950's, 1960's and 1970's, but not enough recently to keep pace with market interest rates. Thus, protection against "excessive" bank and savings institution interest rates to depositors became, in recent years, a stop-gap, unsuccessful attempt to hold down the cost of funds for these institutions, and thereby "slow" the rising tide of increased interest rates.

But this Regulation Q policy was abandoned in the DIDMCA of 1980, with the phased elimination of interest rate ceilings by March 31, 1986. This gradual phase-out was accelerated by the Depositary Institutions Act of October 15, 1982, which mandated higher interest rate "money market accounts", and speeded up the expiration of differentials favoring thrift institutions to January 1, 1984. Thus, money market accounts have narrowed the interest rate gap between MMMF's, on the one hand, and bank or savings institutions accounts on the other. (However, a gap remains in many areas.)

9. PROHIBITION OF INTEREST ON DEMAND DEPOSITS

Banks generally set interest rates on deposit accounts to meet competition and attract funds. This sometimes worked out so that interest would be paid on larger checking accounts, and interest normally was paid on all savings and time deposits. But in the crisis of banking in the Great Depression, many bankers felt interest on checking accounts had been excessive, and led to cutthroat competition. Accordingly, the Banking Act of 1933 outlawed interest on demand deposits (checking accounts). This prohibition lasted until 1980, when the DIDM-CA allowed nationwide NOW (negotiable order of withdrawal) accounts that paid interest on these demand deposits.

NOW accounts were initiated by mutual savings banks in the early 1970's within Massachusetts and New Hampshire. This started to break the ice on interest rates, and NOW accounts spread to all of New England in 1976, New York 1978, and New Jersey 1979. (Rising interest rates and the growth of money market funds also supported this trend.) The DIDMCA extended NOW accounts nationally the following year, and effectively ended the prohibition of interest on demand deposits.

In 1982 the Depositary Institutions Deregulation Committee (DIDC) authorized Super–NOW accounts with more generous interest rates. This brought banking practices back to the pre–1933 era, so that interest might be paid, according to local market competition, on the larger checking and NOW accounts. For smaller checking accounts service charges generally exceed any interest payable, and these customers have to pay for the cost of check writing and maintaining accounts.

10.   TRUTH–IN–LENDING

In 1968 Congress required standard form disclosures for almost all types of consumer credit lending, so that citizens could be better informed, and supposedly, bargain more effectively for fair treatment in credit finance. The Federal Reserve Board developed Regulation Z to specify the details of disclosure. Enforcement by the Federal Trade Commission was provided through administrative remedies, along with private rights of action (with attorneys fees) for twice the finance charges involved, or at least $100 up to $2000 for each disclosure violation. Criminal penalties apply for willful violations. Class actions were encouraged under the initial legislation, although scope for this enforcement procedure has been narrowed subsequently to the lesser of $500,000 or one percent of the creditor's net worth. Most importantly, subsequent amendments limit civil liability to disclosures which might be of material importance in credit shopping. These amendments were provoked by considerable nuisance litigation from attorneys seeking to exploit "technical" violations of disclosure regulations. Standard form language approved by regulators also helped to reduce nuisance complaints and litigation.

Although loan shark operators, high pressure sellers, and low grade finance companies were the principal targets of this consumer protection regulation, it applies also to commercial banks, savings institutions, credit unions, consumer finance companies, and all other sellers of goods and services who extend credit to consumers. Transactions exceeding $25,000 are unregulated, except for purchases of homes, which are now covered by TILA. (Bear in mind parallel disclosure requirements of the Real Estate Settlement Procedures Act [RES-PA] of 1974.)

Required disclosures are designed to show interest and finance charges, direct or indirect, in consumer loan, mortgage, or revolving credit account transactions in terms of the annual percentage rate of interest. Credit life insurance charges must be explicitly revealed and accepted by consumers. Exclusions are narrowly defined, and include title examinations and insurance, escrow accounts for future payment of taxes, insurance, water, sewer or land rents, notary fees, and fees for appraisals and credit reports, and not much else.

11. CREDIT CARDS AND ELECTRONIC BANKING

The growth of credit card and bankcard use greatly affects financial institutions and banking. It allows speedier, less expensive transactions, with some vulnerability to mistakes and irresponsibility like any other "human" mechanism. Liability of credit card holders has been limited to accepted cards, and no more than $50 of charges before notification that a card was lost or stolen (through amendments to TILA). Billing procedures for credit cards are regulated by the Fair Credit Billing Act of 1974 (FCBA) as amended. Full disclosure of terms, interest rates, and penalties are provided, along with a 14 day period between mailing of bills and their due dates. In addition, this legislation limits tying arrangements whereby card issuers might require merchants to maintain deposits with the issuer or subscribe to other services as a condition for participating in the card issuer's payment system.

Bankcards are regulated by the Electronic Funds Transfer Act of 1978 (EFTA), actually Title XX of FIRA (1978). Cardholder liability is limited to $50 only if a customer notifies the financial institution within 2 business days after learning of the loss or theft of the card or its access code. Liability expands to $500 when more than 2 business days is taken for notification. And if a cardholder should fail to report unauthorized transfers on the monthly statement within 60 days after the statement is mailed, they risk unlimited losses of the entire account (including maximum overdrafts). The act requires notification to customers of bankcard transactions, but more than 60 days delay in response after the statement is mailed may waive rights of objection to erroneous transfers. EFT or bankcards must be accepted by the customer or holder before they become effective to create liability.

12. FAIR CREDIT REPORTING AND PRIVACY

Banks and savings institutions have been vital sources of credit information on their depositors and borrowers, which they tend to share with other related institutions and potential creditors. The Fair Credit Reporting Act of 1970 (FCRA) gives some protection to individuals injured by obsolete or inaccurate information in reports circulated by credit rating agencies, when their access to credit, insurance or employment may be affected. The act does *not* apply, however, to reports used for business, commercial or insurance purposes. The FCRA provides individual access to report information (except investigative sources and medical data), and creates some rights to replace incomplete or obsolete data with more accurate material, and the right to file brief explanatory statements. Civil actions for actual damages with attorneys fees may be brought when the credit reporting agency is shown to be negligent regarding non-compliance with the Act. This statute tends to make financial institutions more careful in providing credit information, and reinforces, hopefully, a tendency to be reasonably discreet and cautious in these matters.

The Right to Financial Privacy Act of 1978 (Title XI of FIRA) generally provides individual notice of government agency requests for their bank or financial institution records (within U.S. jurisdiction). Such requests normally require proper subpoenas, summons, or search warrants when relevant to legitimate law enforcement. Individuals seeking to resist such disclosure may oppose them by motions in court or special challenge procedures. Customers may authorize such disclosures by signing written and dated waivers to this effect. However, search warrants may be issued under the Federal Rules of Criminal Procedure to obtain customer account information confidentially, and without the special notice required by this act. (Subsequent disclosure to the individual normally would be required unless a court orders delay in such notification.) Individuals enforcing their rights under this act have access to injunctive relief, where appropriate, along with costs and attorneys fees in the court's discretion.

Some countries, notably Switzerland, have gone further with customer account privacy for banking institutions. Swiss customs on bank privacy were strengthened in 1934 by special legislation responding to Nazi Germany's brutal methods of investigation, often involving intimidation and torture, with respect to refugees, or people suspected of flight or removal of assets. Under present Swiss law violations of bank secrecy are a serious criminal offense, and this applies to anyone inducing such breach of secrecy as well as the bank officials involved. Only in situations of criminal misconduct of conspiracy under Swiss law (normally held not to include tax avoidance) would Swiss authorities collaborate with foreign governments in obtaining bank account information. This means that Swiss bankers, who normally enjoy strong reputations for financial integrity, accept accounts created, in part, to avoid taxes or exchange controls in other countries. These practices are controversial in countries suffering significant capital flight, but Switzerland firmly insists upon its traditions of respect for the rights of refugees and foreign investors.

Many other nations have tried to emulate Swiss bank secrecy practices (including numbered accounts that restrict knowledge of owners to a few bank officials.) But few countries rival the Swiss in a long tradition of respect and integrity in handling foreigner accounts, so their secrecy laws have had a special importance in attracting this type of investment to Switzerland. This tradition is rooted in a long history of liberalism, private property, neutrality and religious tolerance.

13. DISCRIMINATION IN CREDIT

Traditional banking practices have allocated credit according to the strength of collateral, earnings, and risk of default, with interest rates and fees reflecting these differentials and some bargaining between borrowers and lenders. The greatest protection for borrowers has been adequate competition among lenders, which helps ensure adequate alternatives in bargaining for loans and interest rates. Hence, the antitrust laws, bank merger and holding company legislation, and other regulations limiting excessive concentration play an important role in preventing unreasonable discrimination or exploitation with respect to terms and conditions of credit.

In addition, however, recent federal law prohibits discrimination in granting credit with respect to sex, marital status, race, color, religion, national origin, age (provided the applicant has the capacity to contract), receipt of public assistance benefits, or exercise of rights under some consumer credit laws. An important law on discrimination is the Equal Credit Opportunity Act of 1975 (ECOA), implemented by Regulation B of the Federal Reserve

Board. A major purpose of this legislation was improved access to credit for women, married and unmarried, and those involved in matrimonial litigation, divorce or separation proceedings. Amendments extended its scope to include other forms of discrimination.

The ECOA and Regulation B limit the scope of questions that may be asked about sources of income, including alimony, child support, or separate maintenance payments, or plans with respect to children. Checklists of factors that may be legitimately considered by financial institutions are provided in Regulation B. Some information on reasons for denying credit can be demanded by applicants, but considerable latitude remains in the use of multiple factor standards and scoring systems. Enforcement actions may be brought under this legislation by the Federal Trade Commission, Justice Department, and bank regulatory agencies. More importantly, perhaps, private remedies are provided for actual damages (including, conceivably, embarrassment, humiliation, and mental distress), declaratory or injunctive relief, and punitive damages for willful violations. Class actions are allowed, with ceilings of $500,000 or one percent of net worth (like Truth-in-Lending). Attorneys fees and costs may be awarded in a court's discretion. These remedies were designed to change credit granting practices in conformity with the law.

Anti-redlining legislation is another effort of recent years to suppress discriminatory practices in credit transactions. Redlining is the systematic refusal to extend home mortgage loans by banks and savings institutions in certain areas, usually run-down neighborhoods with lots of poverty, and largely inhabited by low-income minorities or changing in that direction. The term "redlining" refers to the actual marking of real estate maps by financial institutions to exclude such areas from consideration. More subtle forms of discrimination involve less favorable terms, higher interest rates, greater difficulty in approval, and perhaps, the shifting of deposit funds from "bad" neighborhoods to more promising areas and suburban tract housing through loan allocations. Redlining activity can be an aspect of urban decay, reflecting blight, and to some degree tending to reinforce it.

An important law on redlining and discrimination was the Home Mortgage Disclosure Act (HMDA) of 1975, followed by the Community Reinvestment Act (CRA) of 1977. The HMDA required depository institutions with assets of $10 million or more in standard metropolitan statistical areas to disclose their mortgage loans and maintain records for 5 years so that "redlining" patterns could be identified. The Community Reinvestment Act (and other related legislation) provides a rather general mandate to the federal financial regulatory agencies to investigate and discourage discriminatory practices. Policies implemented by these agencies have led to banks and savings institutions making extra efforts to solicit loans in minority neighborhoods, and the location of branches so that all sections of a city can be effectively served. Between 1993–96 the Clinton administration tried to strengthen CRA enforcement with tougher regulations and supervision, including limits on merger and expansion activity by institutions lacking good compliance records. But complaints erupted over paperwork burdens and ambiguous mandates. Most large BHC's with extensive branching accepted "some" responsibilities in this direction, but smaller and niche market institutions wanted relaxed obligations, insisting that serious inequities and disproportionate burdens affected them. Meanwhile, exemptions for mortgage and finance companies were particularly controversial. Thus far, enforcement has been held up by delays in rule-making and Congressional efforts to limit burdens on financial institutions.

E.   CONSTRAINTS UPON BRANCHING, HOLDING COMPANIES AND MERGERS

Banking laws in the United States set constraints on the growth of banks and bank holding companies. The legislation reflected a strong tradition of federalism and decentralized banking. The major policies were chartering and branching limits, bank holding company restrictions, and merger regulation. As a result the U.S. banking system still has more banks, about 7,700, than most other countries relative to population. This fosters competition and broadened economic opportunity in American society.

But U.S. branching, merger, and holding company restrictions were greatly relaxed over the last 25 years. As a result, U.S. banking concentration increased greatly between 1980–2003, which reflected the growth of large and expansionist U.S. multinational and regional banks. Between 1980–2003 the 10 largest U.S. banks grew from 18 to 41 percent of U.S. bank deposits, the top 25 from 29 to 55 percent, and the top 100 from 46 to 72 percent of U.S. bank deposits. This is a massive consolidation. (Concentration is appreciably higher if foreign deposits are included.)

In recent years, this area of law—branching, holding companies and mergers—has become controversial. It represents a battleground of conflicting interests among financial institutions. Public policy should encourage healthy competition, efficient savings and investment flows, minimize distortions, foster reasonably decentralized enterprise and social mobility, and prevent undue concentration of economic and political power in the banking and related financial industries. But, increased automation, data processing, and electronic flows of information and funds transfer offer real cost-savings. Economies of integration and scale have become more important, and yet, reasonable access and pricing of new technology for smaller firms still allow considerable decentralized, competitive rivalry to continue. Much will depend on the evolution of law and oversight with respect to branching, holding companies and mergers, along with access, pricing and sharing of automated and EFT systems.

1. BRANCHING LAWS

When the Bank of the United States (a multi-state branching organization) was terminated in 1836, the states were left as the exclusive chartering authorities for banks. Single-site banks or "unit banking" became the overwhelming pattern in the free banking era that followed. This practice was extended to the new nationally chartered banks shortly after Congress authorized them in 1864, and national banks were prohibited from having any branches. This policy tended to keep most banks relatively small by confining their deposit collecting areas to a single town or city. Only bigger banks in a few major cities, especially New York and its emerging Wall Street money market center, collected substantial deposits over broad areas from large corporations, smaller correspondent banks, and wealthy business interests. As a practical matter, few state banks developed branching networks until around World War I and the 1920's.

But a growth of branch banking in the prosperous 1920's forced a change upon Congress for national banks. For many years, the states divided into roughly three major camps insofar as branching laws were concerned: (i) unit banking, i.e., no branches allowed; (ii) county-wide branching; or (iii) state-wide branching permitted. As branching proliferated for some state banks, the national banks demanded more latitude. The McFadden Act of 1927 gave national banks the same leeway in branching as their state chartered rivals enjoyed under the law of each state. Thus, the problem of branching, with its conflict between urban and rural interests, was resolved separately in each state's legislature (until the Riegle–Neal Act of 1994 allowed widespread interstate banking and branching.)*

With the rise of Electronic Funds Transfer technology in recent years, and particularly Automated Teller machines (ATM's) that dispense cash, accept deposits, and provide balances to customers, additional questions on branching policy have had to be resolved. Generally, ATM units were considered branches under the McFadden Act, so that state laws regulated the scope for such ATM expansion activities along with the normal "brick and mortar" branch buildings. See, for example, Independent Bankers Association of America v. Smith (D.C.Cir. 1976). Most states have enacted specific compromise legislation that allocates opportunities for ATM's for banks and savings institutions. But the growing use of bankcards from many different banks (or other institutions) among integrated, multi-institution EFT networks is not considered branching activity. Thus, the law allows collaborative networks of bankcard use that link member institutions even across state lines. But the banks (or other financial institutions) that participate in such

* The Riegle Neal Interstate Banking and Branching Efficiency Act of 1994 followed a widespread trend of state enactments (often with reciprocity requirements) that allowed interstate bank holding company acquisitions into their states (especially in the mid-late 1980's).

networks are allowed ATM's within their market areas only according to each state's branching law (including specific legislation on ATM's).

Meanwhile, however, bank holding companies became increasingly important in the 1970's as a route by which restrictive branching laws were evaded *within* many states. Although the Bank Holding Company Act of 1956 was intended to curtail the anticompetitive excesses of chain banking, more liberal interpretations by the Supreme Court and Federal Reserve Board in recent years allowed bigger statewide banking chains or holding companies. See, especially, United States v. Marine Bancorporation (S.Ct.1974). Unless a state enacted separately its own limitation on bank holding company expansion, most large banks now face little difficulty in extending their operations within each state by acquisition of independent banks through the holding company device.

But for many years (1956–94), *interstate* "branching" through bank holding companies had been almost entirely prohibited by the "Douglas Amendment" to the Bank Holding Company Act of 1956 [§ 3(d) of the BHCA, i.e., 12 U.S.C.A. § 1843(d)]. This law prevented any approval by the Federal Reserve Board of bank holding company acquisitions in other states, unless the state in which the acquired bank is located explicitly authorized acquisitions by out of state banks. For many years no state allowed such acquisitions. Aside from a few interstate bank holding companies that were grandfathered before the 1956 Douglas amendment, this meant that interstate bank holding companies had been prevented generally from making bank acquisitions across state lines.

Recently, however, the majority of states allowed interstate bank holding company acquisitions on a reciprocal basis, and some without reciprocity requirements. Maine was first in 1975, followed later by Alaska and South Dakota. Each of these states wanted to attract new banking capital for development and more jobs. New York enacted such a law in 1982, but its purpose was to facilitate large N.Y. city bank acquisitions in other states. Massachusetts responded the same year with a more restrictive law that allowed reciprocal bank acquisitions only in New England, and prevented leapfrogging into Massachusetts thru Maine or any other state. The Massachusetts plan was to encourage a New England banking region that limited entry by the big New York banks. Although Citicorp challenged the constitutionality of New England regional interstate banking, the Supreme Court upheld such statutes. Northeast Bancorp, Inc. v. Board of Governors (S.Ct.1985). Soon afterwards a majority of Southern states enacted at least regional interstate banking, along with a majority of North Eastern, North Central, and Southwestern states. Resisting this trend were many Plains and Mountain states, with strong community and independent bank traditions.

But once most states allowed interstate BHC's to acquire banks within their territories (at least to some extent), the stage was set for the "Riegle–Neal Act" in 1994. This new legislation, the Interstate

Banking and Branching Efficiency Act of 1994, allowed interstate BHC's to make bank acquisitions in all states after 1996. But states were permitted to set limits on acquisitions of "de novo" banks (less than 5 years old), and to restrict *branching* activity by out-of-state BHC's to a substantial extent. Caps on banking concentration also were specified, but at relatively "high" levels. Thus, acquisitions of banks were prohibited only if the resulting bank controlled more than 10 percent of all U.S. insured depository institution deposits, or 30 percent or more of such deposits in any state. This law could allow a "massive" consolidation movement for U.S. banking and depository institutions, i.e., thru "chain store banking."

Nonetheless, some kinds of banking activity already were allowed across state lines. Lending had long been a nationwide market for the larger corporate borrowers. Loan production offices were generally permitted throughout the country. And Edge Act subsidiaries were allowed in other states since 1919 to service international banking operations, including loans, investment, export-import finance, and even non-domestic deposit gathering. Nationwide advertising for deposit customers had been considered proper, and is increasingly employed by major multinational banks (including "800" toll free telephone numbers). What remained localized, however, was most ordinary deposit activity and smaller loans to households and regional business enterprise.

The full implications of the Riegle–Neal Act could become controversial, if in fact, a great increase in U.S. banking concentration does occur in the coming years. A special feature of the U.S. banking industry has been widespread decentralization, with strong regional and community banks in all the states and most sizable cities. By contrast, almost every other country has a highly concentrated banking system—in most instances with more government influence over its oligopoly of nationwide banks. Effective banking competition for small business and consumers is usually weaker in other countries. Americans have been blessed by their banking history, a big country, ample banking competition, and a tradition of decentralized federalism in banking and capital markets. This heritage and broad access to capital and borrowing has been a crucial advantage in U.S. economic development, and a powerful contribution to decentralized democracy. It remains to be seen whether Riegle–Neal leads, in fact, to a dramatic increase in U.S. banking consolidation; if so, antitrust and federalism concerns should invite serious reappraisal of Riegle–Neal and its impact.

2.   BANK HOLDING COMPANIES

Under the Bank Holding Company Act of 1956 as amended, the Federal Reserve Board is the principal regulatory authority. Bank holding companies are subject to the Board's jurisdiction, require its approval for their creation, and there is Board su-

pervision for some activities. Bank holding companies (BHC's) are defined as those that "own or
control" one or more banks. Ownership or control
of 25 percent of the voting shares is enough for this
purpose, and somewhat less if the Board finds a
controlling influence is exercised. A presumption of
no control operates if the BHC owns less than 5
percent. Federal Reserve Board approval is needed:
(i) to become a BHC; (ii) for a bank to become a
subsidiary of a BHC; (iii) for a BHC to acquire more
than 5 percent of the stock in a bank; (iv) for a
BHC to acquire the assets of a bank, or (v) for a
merger of BHC's. The holding company framework
has become extremely popular for larger banks.
BHC's already owned most of the commercial bank
assets by the late 1980's, and there were more than
6,000 BHC's.* This left only a fringe of small banks,
mostly smaller ones, that were independent of
BHC's. Hence, supervision of BHC's governs the
great bulk of banking resources in the country.

The principal criteria for Board review of BHC
transactions are convenience and needs of the public, financial condition and management resources
of the BHC and its subsidiaries, and anti-competitive effects that might flow from BHC activities.
Generally healthy capitalization and sound management are preconditions for BHC expansion and
growth. The convenience and needs of the public

* In contrast, when the BHCA of 1956 was enacted, there were
only 47 registered BHC's with 7.6 percent of the nation's bank
deposits. By 2001 6,318 BHC's held 94 percent of all bank assets.
In 2003 there were 630 Financial Holding Companies (FHC's),
most of which had grown out of BHC's.

normally tends to be served by broader BHC activities with strong finances and good management. But when BHC's become too large, they may inhibit competition, or restrain trade in financial or other markets. Such anticompetitive consequences have led to constraints upon BHC expansion.

The major legislative limits on growth of BHC's applied to diversification and merger activity. But some historical background is needed to understand their development. The original Bank Holding Company Act of 1956 was designed to limit chain banking (networks with more than one bank), to restrict indirect branching activity (especially across state lines), and to prevent excessive concentration in banking through holding companies. Left open was an opportunity for "one-bank" holding companies to diversify into nearby financial activities, or perhaps other industries.

Merger limitations developed first, with the Bank Merger Act of 1960, the Supreme Court's decision in United States v. Philadelphia National Bank (S.Ct.1963), and the Bank Merger Act of 1966. (Described in the next section.) As these constraints upon bank merger expansion developed, they tended to channelize large bank growth and merger aspirations into diversification (or international banking). Major horizontal mergers among sizeable banks within the same cities became unlawful, and substantial chain banking networks between different cities were limited, too.

Meanwhile, increasing prosperity in the 1960's and a "Bull Market" for stock price appreciation made bank leaders (and stockholders) more eager for growth and diversification prospects. In 1967–69 there was a surge of bank holding company formation, involving a large proportion of the bigger banks in the country, comprising one third of the nation's commercial bank deposits. This was part of a tide of conglomerate merger activity in the economy as a whole, which peaked in the later 1960's, and resumed in the 1980's and 1990's.

Congress responded with the Bank Holding Company Amendments of 1970, which confined BHC's and their subsidiaries to activities which are "a proper incident to banking or managing or controlling banks." In applying Section 4(c)(8) of the BHCA, as amended, "the Board shall consider whether . . . performance by an affiliate of a holding company can reasonably be expected to produce benefits to the public, such as greater convenience, increased competition, or gains in efficiency, that outweigh possible adverse effects, such as undue concentration of resources, decreased or unfair competition, conflicts of interest, or unsound banking practices." 12 U.S.C.A. § 1843(c)(8). Under Regulation Y, implementing this provision, the Board allowed the following: the making and servicing of loans, such as by finance, mortgage, factoring, or industrial loan companies; fiduciary and trust account activities; closed-end investment companies; financial and investment advisory services; leasing personal and real property as a financing activity;

bookkeeping and data processing services; courier services for banks; check verification and handling services; management consulting for banks; credit card operations; foreign exchange, gold and silver trading; issuing travelers checks; underwriting some federal, state, and local securities; underwriting credit life insurance; and even real estate and business appraisals. The Board allowed securities transactions for the account of customers (and affiliations with discount securities brokers). In the later 1980's, the Federal Reserve and OCC allowed some of the largest BHC's to underwrite commercial paper, securitized mortgage-backed instruments, and even corporate bonds and stocks, so long as these activities were carried on in separate affiliates (see Section D–6. Securities Marketing, supra). Subsequently, banks have been allowed to market mutual funds, and some BHC affiliates are even developing "fleets" of funds. (See Chapter V, infra.) And some banks and BHC's were poised to widely market insurance policies and underwrite insurance, provided that their regulatory and legislative authority could be clarified. But this insurance question was strongly contested by insurance interests from the mid–1980's into the late 1990's; conflict over insurance was a major battleground in Glass–Steagall "reform" efforts.

On the other hand, the Board had excluded, for many years, land development and real estate syndication, real estate brokerage, property management services, management consulting (defined broadly for all kinds of businesses), most ordinary insurance underwriting (not credit life insurance), and travel agencies. Industries threatened by competition from bank holding companies, especially insurance, securities brokerage, mutual funds, savings and loans, etc., fought in Congress, in the courts, and with the Board to keep banks and the banking industry confined to the more traditional roles of bank finance and services,* up-dated to allow for automatic data processing and EFT technology.

Finally, in 1999, however, Congress settled many aspects of a 20 year long boundary war among financial industries. The Gramm–Leach Financial Services Modernization Act of 1999 provided that Financial Holding Companies (FHC's) could operate in banking, insurance, and securities markets. By 2003 there were 630 FHC's in the U.S., which

* It should be emphasized, however, that the Board had authority (since 1956) to grant exemptions for small bank holding companies:

(1) to avoid disrupting business relationships that have existed over a long period of years without adversely affecting the banks or communities involved, or

(2) to avoid forced sales of small locally owned banks to purchasers not similarly representative of community interests, or

(3) to allow retention of banks that are so small in relation to the holding company's total interests and so small in relation to the banking market to be served as to minimize the likelihood that the bank's power to grant or deny credit may be influenced by a desire to further the holding company's other interests. 12 U.S.C.A. § 1843(d). These provisions were used recently to allow a considerable number of BHC's to be involved with greater diversification activities, such as insurance or real estate, that had been excluded fields for larger BHC's (and not traditional for banking). But use of this loophole remained controversial.

controlled 78 percent of BHC assets (supervised by the Federal Reserve Board). Banking activities in bank holding companies are regulated and supervised mainly by the Federal Reserve Board. Insurance activities are regulated largely by the state insurance departments or Commissioners. And securities activities are largely regulated by the SEC. Important ambiguities, mutual access to data, and the coordination of over-sight will have to be worked out in the coming years. The extent to which failures, fraud, money-laundering and other problems occur will have a great impact on this evolving area of financial holding company regulation.

3. BANK MERGERS

Bank merger regulation has gone through three different stages: (1) *Between 1950–74* bank mergers were restricted to limit consolidation and preserve the traditional, largely decentralized U.S. banking market structure. Competition among depository institutions was maintained, and even enhanced by growth of savings banks, S & L'S, and credit unions. (2) *Between 1974–93* these limitations on bank growth and mergers were relaxed in a gradual, incremental pattern. But no drastic increases in concentration or reduced competition occurred, even though the numbers of U.S. banks slowly declined over these 20 years from 14,600 to 10,500, savings banks and S & L's from 5,400 to 2,200, and credit unions from 21,000 to 12,500. (3) *After 1994* there has been more drastic relaxation of bank merger and BHC restrictions, which allowed much larger consolidation mergers, big chains of mega-banks, and substantially weaker competition in many regional and local banking markets. By 2000 the number of U.S. banks fell further to 7,700 with only 1,360 savings banks and 418 S & L's, and 9,500 500 credit unions (CU's). In 2003 the top 10 U.S. banks held 41 percent of U.S. domestic bank deposits; the top 25 had 55 percent. Current banking and BHC regulation fosters even more consolidation into a limited number, say 15–20 very large bank chains and BHC networks, with most becoming new Financial Service Holding Companies (FHC's). There will be a fringe of regional and/or state banking chains, and a scattered survival of independent community banks, savings banks and S & L's. An extensive range of credit unions will still operate, although many CU's are *employer related* and not able to accept depositors from everyone in their communities.

Merger restrictions began in 1950 with the Celler–Kefauver Amendments to Section 7 of the Clayton Act (1914). Original Section 7 Clayton outlawed acquisitions of the "stock" of other companies when they "might tend to substantially lessen competition in any line of commerce in any section of the country." Unfortunately, this provision was emasculated at the outset by a blunder in draftsmanship; not covered were acquisitions of the "assets" of companies. This allowed large mergers to be carried out as "asset" acquisitions, i.e., exploiting the "asset" loophole. Considerable merger activity occurred in the 1920's, even a few bank mergers, but the original Section 7 was ineffectual as a limitation. Then the stock market Crash of 1929 and the Great Depression choked off merger activity, but mergers revived substantially in the later 1940's. Fearing a "rising tide of economic concentration," Congress enacted in 1950 the Amended Section 7 as a major strengthening of U.S. antitrust policy—to limit large mergers that could substantially lessen competition. New Section 7 governed mergers in most of the economy, although its application to bank mergers was not clear.

In 1956 Congress enacted the Bank Holding Company Act to explicitly limit chain banking and interstate banking activity (see previous sections). The BHCA regulatory standard was twofold—to prevent "substantial lessening of competition", but "convenience and needs" of the community were to be considered as well. This was supplemented by the Bank Merger Act of 1960, which used the same two factor standard—substantial lessening of competition offset by convenience and needs.

In the leading case of United States v. Philadelphia National Bank (S.Ct.1963), the Supreme Court held that Section 7 Clayton alone governed bank mergers, because "[i]mmunity from the antitrust laws is not lightly implied ... [T]here is no indication in the legislative history to the 1950 amendment of § 7 that Congress wished to confer a special dispensation upon the banking industry ... " (quoting from the Court's opinion). With respect to the merits, the Court held that this merger of the second and third largest banks in Philadelphia, comprising 36 percent of bank assets and deposits of the metropolitan area, would have substantial anticompetitive effects. This decision set a strong precedent, and indicated that "anti-competitive effects" were the primary concern in bank mergers.

But the Court clearly accepted the need for absorption mergers in failing bank situations, and even suggested that the "failing company defense" for mergers "might have somewhat larger contours as applied to bank mergers because of the greater public impact of a bank failure as compared with ordinary business failure" (U.S. v. Philadelphia National Bank).

Congress responded several years later with the Bank Merger Act of 1966. The statute employed the Section 7 Clayton Act standard, i.e., prohibiting any merger "whose effect in any section of the country may be substantially to lessen competition", unless ... the anticompetitive effects of the proposed transaction are clearly outweighed in the public interest by the probable effect of the transaction in meeting the convenience and needs of the community to be served. 12 U.S.C.A. § 1828(c)(5), (A) and (B). These guidelines largely accepted the Philadelphia National Bank decision, but allowed convenience and needs to be considered as well.

Procedurally, the BMA of 1966 established the independence of the Justice Department to challenge the legality of a bank merger on anticompetitive grounds in the courts, even if the relevant federal banking regulatory agency had approved the transaction, except where the agency "must act *immediately* to prevent the failure of one of the banks involved." This procedural scheme allows prompt evaluation of competitive effects by the antitrust authorities and banking agencies, but ensures also that banks threatened by impending failure can be quickly forced into an emergency absorption merger.

For some years the Supreme Court extended the strong policy of Philadelphia National Bank and the BMA of 1966 to smaller bank merger combinations. The ultimate development of the rule was illustrated in United States v. Phillipsburg National Bank & Trust Co. (S.Ct.1970). In this case the relevant market was Easton, Pa.-Phillipsburg, N.J., a twin city area on both sides of the Delaware River (with about 90,000 population.) The merging banks ranked 1st and 2nd of three banks in Phillipsburg alone with 76 percent of of its deposits, and 3rd and 4th of 7 banks in the twin cities area with 23.4 percent of combined deposits. The Supreme Court sustained the Justice Department's challenge under the Bank Merger Act of 1966. In the Phillipsburg decision the principle of preventing sizeable market share mergers was applied to relatively small cities.

According to strict Department of Justice Merger Guidelines issued in 1968, applicable to most industries, sizeable horizontal mergers (in the same market area) normally would be challenged under Section 7 Clayton. In substantially concentrated markets (normal in banking), the Department announced it would ordinarily challenge mergers with any sizeable market shares. (But these guidelines were relaxed greatly in 1982–84.)

Market extension mergers were regulated by branching laws in some states where significant restrictions had been placed on branch activity, e.g. unit banking or county-wide branching. But in many the holding company device represented an important loophole for indirect branching or growth by market extension merger. The BHCA of 1956 required Federal Reserve Board approval for such mergers by holding companies, thus its policies became important in shaping the latitude for market extension acquisitions. And after Philadelphia National Bank (1963) and the Bank Merger Act of 1966 the antitrust authorities had a role in challenging mergers that might have anticompetitive effects.

Thus, under either Section 7 Clayton or the BMA of 1966, a market extension merger involving one of the leading banks in a state as the acquiring firm could be an excessive weakening of the force of potential competition, when a major bank in another section of that state was acquired. On the other hand, a "toe-hold" acquisition of a smaller bank or de novo entrant bank would present little or no competitive problem, and might strengthen competition within the market area.

But in United States v. Marine Bancorporation, Inc. (S.Ct.1974), the Burger court majority relaxed this policy and allowed a major market extension merger. In this case, Marine Bancorporation, the second largest bank holding company in the state of Washington, based in Seattle, with 20 percent of all bank deposits statewide and 107 branches, acquired the third largest bank in Spokane with 19 percent of local deposits, 8 local branches and 1.5 percent of statewide deposits. Nonetheless, the courts approved the merger, reasoning that new entry by the acquiring firm was very difficult under this state's law, and consequently, there was little potential competition to be weakened, and that convenience and needs of customers in Spokane would benefit from absorption of the "target" bank into a major state banking organization.

The next major relaxation of bank merger policy was relaxation of the Department of Justice Merger Guidelines, in 1982 and 1984. The most dramatic change in the Merger Guidelines, was their redefinition of concentration thresholds in terms of the Herfindahl–Hirschman Index (HHI). The "HHI", or simply the Herfindahl index or "H" (as most industrial organization economists label it), is merely the sum of the squares of each firm's market share in the relevant market. Thus, we define

$$H = \sum_{i=1}^{n} s_i^2$$

where H is the Herfindahl index, s_i is the market share, and i is the range of 1 through n firms in the relevant market. A few illustrations will be helpful:

	"Low" Concentration	"Moderate" Concentration	"High" Concentration
Rank	(1) $15\%^2 = 225$	(1) $25\%^2 = 625$	(1) $30\%^2 = 900$
	(2) $10\%^2 = 100$	(2) $20\%^2 = 400$	(2) $25\%^2 = 625$
	(3) $10\%^2 = 100$	(3) $15\%^2 = 225$	(3) $20\%^2 = 400$
	(4) $10\%^2 = 100$	(4) $10\%^2 = 100$	(4) $15\%^2 = 225$
	(5) $10\%^2 = 100$	(5) $10\%^2 = 100$	(5) $5\%^2 = 25$
	(6) $5\%^2 = 25$	(6) $5\%^2 = 25$	(6) $5\%^2 = 25$
	others [40%] 100	others [15%] 25	others [–] —
Total	$s=100$ $s^2=750$	$s=100$ $s^2=1500$	$s=100$ $s^2=2200$

Because the squares of low market shares are small numbers (e.g., $1\%^2 = 1$, $.5\%^2 = .25$, $.3\%^2 = .09$, $.1\%^2 = .01$, and so forth), the Herfindahl index has the statistical property of diminishing low market shares to relative insignificance. Hence, use of the Herfindahl index, ''H'', puts overwhelming weight on the market shares of larger firms (e.g., $5\%^2 = 25$; $10\%^2 = 100$; $15\%^2 = 225$; $20\%^2 = 400$; $25\%^2 = 625$; $30\%^2 = 900$; $40\%^2 = 1600$; $60\%^2 = 3600$; $80\%^2 = 6400$; or $100\%^2 = 10,000$).

To compute the changes in ''H'' or $\triangle$ H resulting from mergers, simply add the percentages of each firm together, and square their new share (e.g., if firms (3) and (5) merge, in each column, then, $10\% + 10\% = 20\%^2 = 400$, $15\% + 10\% = 25\%^2 = 625$, and $20\% + 5\% = 25\%^2 = 625$). Then subtract the old shares squared (e.g. $400–100–100 = \triangle$ H=200, $625–225–100 = \triangle$ H = 300, and $625–400–25 = \triangle$ H=200) to achieve the $\triangle$ H or change in concentration produced by the merger, as measured in terms of the Herfindahl index.

The Department's new standards for evaluating horizontal mergers are framed in terms of the post-merger market concentration or H value, and the increase or change in concentration resulting from the merger or $\triangle$ H.

(a) Post-merger H below 1000

Markets in this range have relatively low to higher concentration, collaboration among firms is not easy, and the Department would not challenge mergers in this region.

(b) Post-merger H between 1000 and 1800

Markets in this range reflect relatively low to higher concentration, and depending upon the H value, the Department might challenge mergers producing $\triangle$ H of more than 100, but is unlikely to challenge mergers yielding $\triangle$ H of less than 100. Entry conditions, product differentiation, price-output visibility, past conduct, and historical performance will be taken into account in making this evaluation.

(c) Post-merger H above 1800

Markets in this range are highly concentrated, and the Department might challenge mergers producing $\triangle$ H of more than 100–200.

These new merger Guidelines of 1982–84 were a significant relaxation of horizontal merger policy. The major loosening involved less concentrated markets, and moderately concentrated markets. In markets with high concentration, sizeable mergers could still be challenged, unless failing companies are involved as the acquired firms. But relevant markets have been defined much more broadly since the Reagan era, so that high concentration occurs infrequently. Typically, commercial lending was used as the "index" for geographic markets more recently, whereas local deposits were the "index" for local market definitions in Philadelphia National Bank (1963) which governed until the early 1980's.

A substantial bank consolidation merger movement got under way by 1982–83. It featured mergers among larger banks in regional markets (when a bank was willing to sell out), and the buying up of banks in rural-suburban areas to extend BHC chains. The wave of bank, savings bank, and S & L failures of the 1980's-early 1990's also added momentum. Regional interstate banking broadened the scope for merger activity, which was extended to the entire nation by Riegle–Neal (the Interstate Banking and Branching Efficiency Act of 1994). In 1997–98 a series of mega-mergers combined some of the largest BHC chains in the U.S. (e.g. Bank America and NationsBank). Finally, Gramm–Leach in 1999 allowed Financial Holding Companies (FHC's) to combine banking, insurance, and securities (like the Citicorp–Travelers merger, already approved by banking regulators and Department of Justice in 1998).*

* Many business analysts were questioning already the "profitability" of many mega-financial mergers. Profits often decline, and many mergers failed—despite disruptive layoffs, shedding of personnel, and difficulties of combining different cultures.

How much of this greatly increased consolidation activity is necessary or desirable remains controversial. Supporters argue for wide freedom to merge. Economies of scale or integration might be involved. Fear of computerization drove many to sell out, especially when premium per share gains could shared by merger partners. Opponents, however, insist that operating efficiencies do not require mega-mergers, and that large regional institutions are big enough to be completely efficient. Consumer groups and small business interests complain that rate competition is reduced in many areas (for both deposits and lending), bank profit margins are fattening, and that service often declines in "1–800 number" banking. Getting competent, reliable attention is often more difficult. In some areas enough banking rivalry remains, including credit unions and MMMF's. But other areas suffer inadequate banking service competition. A complication is that traditional depository institutions seem to have less growth lately (see Tables II–1 and IV–1) and that large banks often place fewer "good" loans—as more big companies raise their capital internally or by issuing commercial paper at thin fees through investment bankers. If the pie of commercial banking is not growing, or even shrinking, some increased consolidation was not surprising. On the other hand, allowing too much banking consolidation hurts consumers, smaller business, and reduces the options available for financial services.

Already by the mid–1990's, for example, the top 25 securities firms had 88 percent of the capital owned by Securities Industry Association members (along with 65 percent of SIA member employees). The top 25 mutual funds had 63 percent of all assets under such management. The top 25 life-health insurers had 88 percent of their industry's revenues, and the top 25 property-casualty insurers had 94 percent of that industry's revenues. In the late 1990's the top 25 U.S. banks were increasing their market shares rapidly in this direction. (Between 1980–2003 the top 25 U.S. banks increased their share of domestic bank deposits from 29 to 55 percent, and the top 100 held 72 percent in 2003.) Now that Gramm–Leach in 1999 allowed Financial Holding Companies (FHC's) across these boundaries, more BankAmerica–Nationsbank and Citicorp–Travelers combinations can be expected. How much efficiency, good sense, and wise investment can be expected in giant financial conglomerates? Failures are harder to deal with politically for financial regulators. Oversight is more difficult. The experience of other nations suggests that government bailout and "moral hazard" dangers are substantially increased for mega-financial institutions. If giantism in finance proves burdensome, and with greater risks, losses, and weaker service, how can banking, securities, and insurance regulators turn things around? How can a mandate for more decentralized competition be implemented?

4.   EFT ACCESS AND PRICING

A vital problem for modern EFT technology and its use is the extent to which access, sharing, and pricing should be regulated by law. Modern computer engineering and electronic potentialities allow broad, integrated networks to take over, or at least facilitate, a great deal of what banks and other financial institutions have accomplished in the way of funds transfer and account management. Some of this could be integrated into service provided by the telephone systems. (In the early 1980's the U.S. phone system was substantially "disintegrated" through a voluntary fragmentation agreement, where AT & T agreed in a consent antitrust settlement to spin-off its regional phone system operating affiliates, while retaining its long lines network, its Western Electric equipment producing subsidiary, and its Bell Labs "R & D" component.) A considerable portion of the existing EFT and credit card systems involves use of telephone lines and connections, and more could be wired into that network. In one extreme configuration, the ultimate financial institution might be the phone systems, and everything involving EFT and financial transactions could be forced by law into it.

But this extreme of EFT concentration could be a monopoly outcome, requiring public enterprise or strong public utility regulation. Even though such a monopoly phone-EFT system is feasible in countries with a nationalized phone system and nationalized banking, it already has been by-passed by evolution in the U.S. Instead, we have a set of regional public utility phone monopolies, with independent competitor access and interconnect systems allowed and encouraged by antitrust law. Banks and credit card companies have already developed competitive networks for card usage and EFT linkages. Most retail establishments now use standardized card-receipt authentication routines, which accept many different cards, and check on current status by telephone. Bankcard systems are being integrated into this network, along with credit cards. In this way, maximum access to existing banks (and other financial institutions) can be facilitated. But contractual access, sharing, pricing and cost-allocation are not fully settled.

Meanwhile, considerable development of ATM (automated teller machine) "branching", POS (point of sale) linkages, CBCT (customer-bank communications terminal) interconnections, and ACH (automated clearing house) operations have already occurred. ATM branching is now regulated by many state statutes, pro-rating the opportunity for use among existing institutions, with more or less scope for expansion. Interstate (and international) bankcard usage networks are being implemented, in addition to credit card systems. CBCT connections have developed to a limited degree, but could ultimately interconnect all homes, businesses, and financial institutions with each other. ACH activities already exist, with various market developed pricing regimes for the service involved.

Most careful analysts suggest, at this transitional stage in implementing EFT technology, that we avoid drastic, freezing restrictions on these developments. Market dominance and excessive concentration is certainly to be avoided, but rigid limits on contractual experimentation can be costly, and even anticompetitive. Cooperation should be encouraged, and within limits, there should be a role for the Federal Reserve system to build up and improve its check-clearing system, without unduly inhibiting or suffocating private market developments. Under sensible regulation, the Federal Reserve clearing system can be an important component of a strong, national grid of check and EFT connections.*

Scale economies can be significant in these activities, unless general and easy access is provided by engineering, law and/or rapidly developing custom. Much of the trend toward broad use of telephones and card-receipt authentication routines with credit cards already allows lower cost access, based upon interconnection with telephone (and/or possibly cable) services. Bankcard interconnections remain to be worked out on a comparable basis. The CIRRUS and PLUS systems helped to lead the way. In time, many EFT transactions could be carried on at home, or at the office, with appropriate interconnect and authentication routines. Home and office terminals for computer linkages already are spreading significantly, and bearable costs are approaching

* Partly because of improved computer technology, Congress mandated faster check clearing deadlines in the Expedited Funds Availability Act of 1987 (Title VI of CEBA, 1987).

for multi-purpose connections that could include EFT transactions.

It should be evident, in this context, that recent branching, bank holding company, and merger law could be somewhat challenged by the possibilities implicit in EFT and its use. And yet, this new technology is so powerful that it can be made to adapt to many different institutional environments of geographic boundaries, contract access, system sharing, servicing, and cost-pricing arrangements.

Antitrust and consumer protection litigation, and to some degree, state and national legislation (and/or regulation) can be expected to influence the shape of these developments. Rivalry among various financial institutions, different kinds of banks, the 50 states, and regulatory agencies is to be expected. We can expect conflicting influences, with room for creative evolution and compromises that cannot be predicted with full certainty at this stage in EFT progress.

F. INTERNATIONAL BANKING

Multinational banking has become more important for larger U.S. banks over the last generation, and bigtime international banks spread globally in their network of deposit, loan, financing, securities transactions, and currency exchange activities. Greater affluence, thriving trade and commerce, foreign investment, and increasing use of multinational channels for tax avoidance, enhanced profits, and in some situations, flight of capital to escape regulation or even possible confiscation, have helped to create a multinational banking system comparable in size to the entire U.S. domestic banking industry. American banks still play an important role in this multinational scene, yet in 1995 only about 10 of the top 75 international banks (then with at least $75 billion in assets and $4.5 billion equity that year) were based in the U.S. About twenty-two were Japanese, eight German, five British, four Canadian, three Swiss, three Dutch, seven French, one Belgian, four Chinese, four Italian, three Spanish, three Australian, and one Brazilian.* This reflected broadened world prosperity, more involvement in external commerce, and greater concentration in many banking systems. Most major multinational banks have extended branch connections throughout much of the world, including the U.S. itself in recent years.

More recently, from 1996 into 2004, a wave of mega-mergers among U.S. and multinational banks, investment bankers, and major insurance companies has occurred among leading OECD nations (including the U.S., Europe, and Japan). As a result, the largest global commercial banks were as follows in April, 2004:**

* By the early 1990's, Japanese and European banks had moved ahead of larger U.S. banks in assets and resources. (They had higher concentration than U.S. banks, and their economies caught up with American per capita incomes.) Back in 1970 a third of the world's 500 largest banks were U.S.; in 1995 only one sixth. Among the world's largest 100 banks in 1995 only eighteen were U.S.—26 Japanese, 9 German, and 47 from other nations. More recently, in 2004 U.S. banks caught up some, with 14 of the 80 largest banks in the world from the U.S.

** Financial press estimates.

Rank	Holding Co.	"Home"	Assets*
1	Mitzuho	Japan	$1,285b.
2	Citigroup	U.S.	1,264b.
3	UBS	Switzerland	1,121b.
4	Credit Agricole	France	1,105b.
5	HSBC	U.K.	1,034b.
6	Deutsche Bk.	Germany	1,015b.
7	BNP Paribas	France	989b.
8	Mitsubishi Tokyo	Japan	975b.
9	Sumitomo Mitsuo	Japan	950b.
10	Royal Bk Scot.	U.K.	806b.
11	Barclays	U.K.	791b.
12	Credit Suisse	Switzerland	778b.
13	Morgan Chase	U.S.	771b.
14	UFJ	Japan	754b.
15	Bk. Of America	U.S.	736b.
16	ING Bk.	Netherlands	684b.
17	Soc. Général	France	681b.
18	ABN AMRO	Netherlands	668b.
19	HBOS	U.K.	651b.
20	Ind. Com. Bk.	China	637b.
21	Hypo Vereins	Germany	606b.
22	Dresdner	Germany	602b.
23	Fortis	Belgium	536b.
24	RaboBank	Netherlands	509b.
25	Commerzbk	Germany	482b.

Each giant bank is larger than many smaller countries with far flung activities around the globe; they are "powers unto themselves." Another 40–50 mega-banks have more than $100b. assets. In addition, another 30 major global investment bankers place $100b. to $600b. annually in securities or commercial paper (including 12 of the top 50 commercial banks). All of these giant banking institutions might be considered "too big to fail" from a bank regulatory standpoint. While their stockholders and principal officers would lose heavily in bank failures, these institutions would certainly receive government assistance and lending to restructure themselves.

Multinational banking extends through the next few hundred banks down to "regional banking" by international standards, say from $85 billion on down to $10–15 billion assets. Less than 15 percent of them are U.S. banks. Many regionals participate, to some degree, in multinational loan agreements, and some have branches abroad, either directly or through consortium banks. And many smaller banks are active with international banking, especially in places like London, Switzerland, Hong Kong, Singapore, Luxembourg, Lebanon, and the Persian Gulf (more recently). The most important "centers" for international banking in the 1990's were London, New York, Tokyo, Switzerland, and Frankfurt, but important banking activity also takes place in Paris, Spain, Italy, the low countries, and elsewhere, along with a broad network of tax havens, including Hong Kong, Singapore, Bahamas, Caymans, Netherlands Antilles, Panama, Luxembourg, Channel Islands, Monaco, Bahrain, Kuwait, and the United Arab Emirates.

1. U.S. BANKING ABROAD

International banking has a long history of involvement with foreign trade, shipping, and investments. Italian merchant bankers were important in such finance during the Middle Ages and Renaissance and this banking activity gradually spread north to the Netherlands and German towns. In the early modern period, Dutch, and later British, banking became increasingly prosperous and international. London took the strong lead as an international banking center during the 19th century, helping to enlarge British trade and industrial development. Britain placed a substantial volume of foreign investment in many countries, including the Americas. And London remains, in some ways, the most sophisticated international banking center today, even though much of the capital collected there is no longer British.

U.S. banking began to flow abroad earlier in the 20th century, especially during World War I and the 1920's. But the big involvement began after World War II, servicing the needs of American companies that expanded their activities into the EEC and worldwide. British banking, meanwhile, pioneered in creating Eurodollar accounts that gathered increasing amounts of liquidity to finance multinational business. (The role of the dollar as a preferred reserve currency, with less inflation than most countries between the later 1940's-late 1960's was also influential.) U.K. banking regulations and tax policy encouraged London's revitalization as an international banking center. Subsequent U.S. efforts to restrict "leakage" of capital in the 1960's, with its interest equalisation tax and other measures, actually fostered the retention of earnings abroad by American corporations, in London and elsewhere. As the momentum of Eurobanking developed, similar deposits and lending operations expanded for many clients, corporations, and even governments, drawn from around the world. When the U.S. inflation rate increased as compared to harder currencies, like the Deutschmark and Swiss Franc, in the late 1960's-early 1970's, some accounts shifted into a broader range of "Eurocurrencies" (in addition to the dollar). Then came OPEC and the "petrodollar" recycling of 1974–80. Oil-rich exporters placed a large volume of their liquid earnings into Eurocurrency deposits. As growth rates readjusted around the world, with some NIC's gaining, and especially Japan, Korea, Taiwan, Hong Kong, and Singapore, more Eurocurrency financing spilled into Asian banking centers and tax havens. The Yen became a harder currency, and Japan became a significant creditor nation with a more active role in multinational banking. In all this expansion of banking abroad, more corporations, entrepreneurs, and governments placed liquidity deposits in multinational banks for greater freedom, and to obtain maximum earnings. More borrowing needs were financed this way for international business, and even governments in recent years.

U.S. banking law put modest constraint upon this multinational banking development. (See Regulation K of the Federal Reserve Board.) The Federal Reserve Act allows national banks with $1 million capital and surplus to establish branches abroad, under regulations established by the Board. State chartered member banks must obtain Board approval, and, if there are any restrictions in state law, approval at that level, too. (State non-member bank branching abroad is supervised by the FDIC, and, to a modest degree, under state law, but only a small amount of international banking occurs in these banks.) Subsidiaries of U.S. banks abroad can be established under the same patterns of supervision as branches. Although some accountability has been imposed on U.S. international branches and subsidiaries, it is fair to say that properly managed, sound U.S. banks of sufficient size find no difficulty in setting up activities abroad. Under these arrangements, by the late 1980's, about 130 U.S. banks had created some 800 branches abroad with at least $300 billion in assets. However, the bulk of these activities were carried on by the largest 15 or so U.S. "multinational" banks.

Other alternatives are Edge Act corporations, authorized since 1919 as vehicles through which international banking can be carried on in other states. Edge Act corporations are domestic subsidiaries which confine their activities to international banking, export-import finance, foreign investments, or deposit gathering abroad for these purposes. Edge corporations may have branches and subsidiaries in other countries, and branches since 1978 in other states. Some Edge corporations emphasize banking; others are basically investment holding companies. The Banking Edges (almost 60 of them in the early 1980's) are scattered about the country, mainly in New York, Chicago, Miami, Houston, San Francisco and Los Angeles. Investment Edges are mostly subsidiaries of parent BHC's in their home cities. (Agreement corporations are similar to Edge corporations, with authority going back to 1916, but few exist.) Altogether some $14 billion in assets were held by Banking Edge Corporations in the early

1980's, with another $30 billion for Investment Edges.

In addition, bank holding companies may invest directly in foreign companies under the BHCA, also subject to Board regulations. 12 U.S.Code Section 1843(c)(13). However, limitations on transactions and lending among affiliates have somewhat constrained the use of this vehicle.

Somewhat wider latitude for U.S. banks was allowed in their international banking activities, under American law, broadly speaking, than domestic banking. Because there was no Glass–Steagall "wall" for international banking, U.S. international banks could carry on the underwriting, trading, and marketing of securities abroad, whether debt or equity. Mutual funds can be managed abroad (provided shares are not sold domestically or to U.S. residents) by U.S. international banks, along with somewhat greater latitude for insurance and business consulting activities.

Naturally, U.S. banks abroad must conform to the requirements and law of their respective host countries. Some are more hospitable than others. But the U.K. led the way, in many respects, in providing leeway for international banking in London, and various offshore tax havens in the British commonwealth. This brought leading U.S. banks into the growing London money center, along with American multinational corporations, and many others from around the world. Over time a competition developed in providing convenient, non-burdensome, and reasonably secure havens and transfer points for international banking and finance. In its present condition, the multinational banking system has achieved, in many respects, substantial independence from onerous regulation, as a network of transnational enterprises. Fear of switching assets to more hospitable bases tends to inhibit restrictions that might seriously crimp international banking activities.

The recent U.S. innovation of International Banking Facilities, since December, 1981, represented an effort to bring home some of these activities. The Federal Reserve Board acceded to considerable urging from major banks to allow IBF's in the U.S., so that some of their current offshore activity in shell branches overseas could be switched back to these new enclaves onshore. Under the regulations, IBF's can be set up by U.S. banks or other depositary institutions, Edge and Agreement Corporations, and by foreign banks through their U.S. branches and agencies. IBF's can accept deposits from abroad without being subject to domestic reserve requirements or interest rate regulations. Lending from these IBF's may be extended only to foreign residents or entities, other IBF's, or the parent institution. Minimum transactions, however, for non-bank dealings are $100,000. States can further encourage IBF's within their own borders with special regulations and/or tax subsidies.

The great majority of countries, however, try to confine the enclave of international banking activities in their countries to the sphere of foreign trade, lending, investment and exchange activities. Most nations prevent substantial poaching on the domestic deposit collection business of local banks. But this is not entirely enforceable against corporations and entrepreneurs with large international transactions, that can gather and place substantial cash flow outside local channels. In this way, international banking may lead to leakages of liquidity and capital into the world market, beyond what is publicly acknowledged, or even desirable for many nations. As governments become insecure, corrupt, or suffer depreciating currencies, these leakages may be encouraged. The modern international banking system may facilitate substantial capital flight. Exchange controls are often used to limit these flows, but are hard to maintain with complete effectiveness. No wonder the takeover of private domestic and international banks was often a first step for strongly socialist governments.

2. FOREIGN BANKS IN THE U.S.

British banking played an important role in financing the American colonies, and helped finance trade and investment after independence. But as the U.S. economy developed strength, domestic banking became preponderant. Foreign banks mainly confined their subsequent activities to financing their own exporters, trading, and selected investments, including securities in railroads and other large corporations. Some of these investments were sold off during World Wars I and II, and a major revival of foreign investment and banking in the U.S. did not get under way until the 1960's, when Europe and Japan had restored economic prosperity. Gradually, this foreign activity gained impetus, and a substantial presence of foreign banking was established during the 1970's. By 1989 some 300 foreign banks from about 60 countries were operating with offices, branches, or subsidiaries in the U.S.

Foreign banks have a range of options in the U.S. that is broader, in some respects, than alternatives U.S. banks enjoy to carry on activities abroad. Representative offices and agencies are the more limited connections, which are most widely employed. Investment companies are authorized for foreign banks in some states. Since 1978 Edge Act Corporations are allowed for foreign banks, too. But in addition, many foreign bank branches, subsidiaries, and even foreign owned U.S. banks have been established, some of which have domestic deposit collection and lending authority comparable to U.S. banks in many states. Until the International Banking Act of 1978, foreign banks also enjoyed a special freedom from the McFadden–Douglas restrictions on interstate branching. But the proliferation of foreign bank activities finally provoked Congress into eliminating most of these special interstate branching opportunities in the IBA of 1978, under the principle of "equal treatment" for foreign and domestic owned banking. Such a broad principle of parity is not generally granted abroad, especially by countries that fear influence or competition from giant multinational banks based in the U.S. or other major banking nations.

The International Banking Act of 1978 created licensing authority for the Comptroller of the Currency to license foreign bank branches or agencies in the U.S. For the most part, foreign bank branches are put under "equalized" regulatory discipline, including reserve requirements for domestic U.S. deposits and FDIC insurance. The same applies to restrictions upon U.S. domestic banking activities and diversification, but not, of course, to the foreign bank's operations outside the U.S. and its territories. Also, the Glass–Steagall Act brought complications for foreign banks in marketing securities with U.S. residents, so they needed to keep their activities segregated into a restricted U.S. domestic market category, and unrestricted operations abroad. U.S. and foreign customers adapted easily by doing business with the most appropriate division of foreign banks in the U.S. or abroad.

This legal regime allows foreign banks liberal access to many U.S. banking markets. A variety of motivations had prompted more than $750 billion worth of investments, subsidiary banks, Edge or Agreement corporations, branches or agencies in the U.S. by foreign banking interests as of the 1990's. Many wanted stronger multinational banking networks, access to U.S. clientele, and more opportunities for international investment. Access to U.S. EFT technology, banking management and practices have been useful also. When the dollar weakened relative to other currencies (in 1968–73, the later 1970's, and since 2003), the opportunity for investment and branching activity, broadly speaking, became something of a bargain. Finally, investments in U.S. banking have been a route toward greater safety in an insecure world, when risks in many countries are often alarming. For these various reasons, foreign banks have found it attractive to take part in the American banking market. The major U.S. multinational banks have not opposed this evolution, because it tends to cement stronger links for these institutions in many countries, and very likely, because international branching in the U.S. has helped to erode the McFadden–Douglas barriers to interstate banking.

3. RECENT CONTROVERSY AND PROBLEMS

In spite of the obvious benefits to multinational banks, trade and investment in many countries, this rapid growth trend has brought uneasiness and controversy about international banking developments. These concerns are fivefold: (i) Extensive tax avoidance and encouragements to capital flight from many countries; (ii) Thinner reserves, liquidity mismatching, and fragility; (iii) Excessive (or insufficient) liquidity and possible speculation strains; (iv) Undue lending to doubtful countries with political risks; and (v) Lack of limitations on loans to weaker countries, with excessive borrowing and dangers of default. Until the 1980's, these worries were not sufficiently alarming to cause any significant restriction upon the international banking system. But since the early 1980's, widespread distress, reduced export earnings in many debtor nations, and high interest rates (resulting from inflationary momentum and tighter monetary policies), caused a serious rescheduling "crisis" affecting some 60–70 nations (mostly debtors) significantly involved in the multinational banking network. This led to a reappraisal of these issues, with some additional regulatory supervision.

Extensive tax avoidance and leakages of private capital have become an awkward problem in many countries. International banking, in its present, highly developed form, with many points of access and tax havens around the world, facilitates these flows. But the incentives to avoid high taxation, onerous regulation, possible confiscation, imprisonment or worse, are reflections of "bad" national policy, demoralization or lack of social cohesion. The international banking industry disclaims responsibility for these underlying problems, and holds that each country should limit leakages with healthy self discipline. Governments suffering leakages find this explanation somewhat self-serving, and often lack the administrative capacity to prevent significant tax evasion or capital flight. Unfortunately, this may leave them with unhappy dilemmas—accepting capital flight, reduced business incentives, or drastic nationalization measures that weaken productivity. Only the healthy countries, with sound morale, broad prosperity, lower inflation, and good, honest government are likely to minimize tax evasion and possible capital flight. However, since the Mexican–Asian crises of 1994 and 1997–98, provoked by excessive capital inflows and speculation, many now favor precautionary taxes (like Chile's) on short-term capital inflows, to limit "hot money" speculation.

Reserves and net capital held by many international banking operations, even by U.S. multinationals, had become leaner than most domestic U.S. banks by the early 1980's. Competition in international activities is keen, and legal reserve and capital requirements were often less demanding. In international banking, customer confidence for deposits or lending comes from the size, reserves, capital, and reputation of their parent banks at home, and the evident determination of governments to support their financial integrity. Thus, domestic banking regulations and resources actually support international banking, its deposits, lending, and profitability. Most national governments found it necessary to back up their major international banks, or so people generally believe. Where banking systems were substantially nationalized, as in France (during the Mitterand government) and many other countries, or where central banks or governments subsidize credit (especially for exports), margins in international lending may be artificially reduced. As international banking became more crowded and competitive, and surplus liquidity built up with international trade, a situation of reduced margins with thinner reserves could be somewhat risky. (This led to the BIS G12 risk-based capital requirements of 1987, described at p. 236 below. See also, above, at pp. 129–136.)

Liquidity mismatching is inevitable for banking activities. Banks take demand, short term, or at least "mobile" liquid resources on deposit, and convert them into loan assets, securities, or other investments earning a sufficient margin to compensate for interest paid to depositors and other operating expenses. With thinner reserves and lower net capital ratios, the tolerance for error in liability-asset management is reduced. Some countries, most notably Switzerland, developed liquidity ratio regulations designed to limit the risks of mismatching maturities to some degree at least. But the more important safeguards seem to be two-fold: (i) floating rate deposit liabilities that move with loan assets using floating rates; and (ii) confidence that national governments and central banks in the major banking nations will stand behind, and support financially, their significant international banks in a crisis situation.

Deposits and lending in the multinational banking sector have grown at a faster rate since the 1970's than domestic banking for most industrial countries. This led some economists to argue that international banking, with reduced reserves and a larger multiple of high powered monetary expansion, may be contributing to (or at least reflecting) increased international inflation and/or speculation. Others said that increased flows into multinational banking merely reflect special advantages, avoidance of taxation and regulation, OPEC earnings "recycled", and the attraction of greater deposit interest rates in this sector of banking. Also, a substantial part of international banking deposits are interbank transactions, not necessarily involving real shifts from domestic into international deposits and lending. Some of those alarmed at this expansion of international bank liquidity urge the application of domestic monetary controls and disciplines to world banking. But this is easier said than done, when a large part of this liquidity prefers the freedom of international banking, and can quickly switch to other havens in the multinational basing system. Of more interest for some countries, and more amenable to control, would be the prevention of excessive flows of speculative liquidity into domestic economies. This kind of "sterilization" operation has been feasible in strong banking centers like Switzerland, when they enjoyed good productivity, fiscal and monetary restraint, and lower inflation rates. But the recent surge of OECD investments into many emerging markets, especially in 1990–98 (e.g. Mexico), showed that sterilization was more difficult in developing countries. Many economists cite these experiences, and the lack of sufficient fiscal, monetary, and/or trade-balance discipline in a large number of countries, to conclude that major problems of macro-economic coordination and instability remain unsolved. (This is why precautionary taxes on inflows are receiving favor; by contrast, taxes on outflows are more difficult, magnify confidence problems, and may not stop capital flight.)

Nonetheless, increased concern for inflation, speculation, and other disturbances lead many central banks, including the U.S. Federal Reserve, to develop more careful accounting for deposits, assets, and lending by their respective multinational banks. Detailed estimates are needed for the flows of liquidity into international banking, and the spillover effects upon domestic money markets. This implies fairly close supervision of exchange and interest rate movements, along with the balance of payments, reserves, current accounts, investment flows, and trade balances. Monetary targeting practices should take these subtleties into account, as some central banks (e.g. the Swiss National Bank) already do. It is a misconception to think that monetary developments in major industrial countries (with substantial involvement in multinational banking, investment, and trade) can be understood without appreciating the role of foreign exchange rates, capital flows, lending, investment and trade. Increased monitoring of multinational banking is unavoidable for these and other purposes.

Excessive loans to doubtful economies, with heavy government deficits and monetary stimulus, excessive wage-price inflation, and increased demands for international credit, have become a growing concern for many observers. This has provoked an extensive literature of country and political risk assessment for the international banking industry. Informally, major international banks are now setting limits on their lending commitments to specific countries, which have been strengthened as a result of central bank coordination among leading banking and creditor nations (i.e., the U.S., Japan, U.K., Switzerland, West Germany, etc.) But capital flows, lending, and trade are difficult to supervise. It has been hard to blacklist, embargo, or put ceilings on such flows, or to use formalized quotas. Instead, there has been broad support in many nations for gradually increased IMF quotas and lending support to many debtor nations. But problems of rescheduling and sustaining confidence in the international banking system remain as serious difficulties, at least until the world's prosperity is more broadly assured.

A combination of circumstances in the 1980's led to a sustained crisis of "problem country loans" with extended rescheduling, increased credits, and perhaps, lower interest rates needed to prevent a series of defaults. Some fifty nations, led by Mexico, Brazil, and Argentina, plus Poland, Yugoslavia, Turkey, Zaire, Sudan and others, got into a nasty squeeze between increased debts and interest costs, and reduced exports and foreign exchange earnings. Few anticipated elevated interest rates to last so long, or such a strong world-wide recession, or the extent to which export revenues would be reduced. International banks did not realize quickly enough how much new short term borrowing had been accumulated by some countries. By mid–1982 and early 1983 the dangers of default were evident in a number of nations. One problem was that costs of servicing past loans were approaching, or even exceeding, for some countries, the benefits of limited additional lending. In such a predicament, developing nation politicians found it painful to accept the harsh retrenchment, reduced government spending and living standards, that usually were demanded by foreign bankers and the IMF as preconditions for substantial and renewed lending. Resentment was aggravated when they felt these misfortunes had been externally imposed by anti-inflation policies among industrial nations, which had not been sympathetic to third world pleas for increased government loans at lower interest rates. Ironically, it seemed, though, the threat of defaults was forcing major banking nations to liberalize IMF borrowing quotas, and in some cases, to provide government or central bank support to debtor nations with special links to banking center countries (e.g. the U.S. and Mexico). This situation aroused plenty of controversy: (i) among creditors as to the scale of new lending, interest rates, and conditions to be imposed; and (ii) among debtors as to the consequences of default, retrenchment, and associated political strains. Awkward conflicts followed. Leading banking center and creditor nations did not find it pleasant or easy to increase credits, or subsidize international bank lending when they suffered economic distress, considerable unemployment, and budgetary strain. On the other hand, debtor nations found it no easier to "knuckle under", pay increased interest, suffer retrenchment or other adversities, and fail to deliver on widespread expectations of economic development and broader prosperity to their peoples.

Gradually, the leading banking nations (including U.S., Japan, U.K., W. Germany, Switz., France, Italy, the low countries, and Canada), worked closely with the IMF and World Bank, and fashioned a series of rescheduling agreements for most of the over-loaded debtor nations. Obligations were stretched-out over time, with reduced interest rates and fees. Some new lending flowed, especially for short-term trade finance, although net new capital flows were reduced greatly (in some countries even reversed, when capital flight was included). Loans to over-loaded LDC's (especially in Latin America) became less secure, and were discounted substantially (to the extent a secondary market developed). Large loan loss reserves were created (or provisioned) by the creditor banks, and appreciable losses were recognized from many countries gradually during the 1980's. For large U.S. multinational banks with sizeable assets used for LDC lending (and some other major creditor banks in other countries) this posed a continuing problem for regulatory supervision, Central Bank support, and IMF aided rescheduling. But by the mid–1990's, many debt-overload countries had substantially improved their situations, reduced debt service burdens, and restored economic growth. Increased capital was flowing again into many "emerging markets" in the 1990's.

Meanwhile, during the 1980's the multinational banking community were gradually improving their prudential supervision, partly in response to the softness of lending to many LDC's. Under the Basle

Concordats I (1975) and II (1983), developed by 10 major banking nations (the Group of Ten) with the Bank for International Settlements (BIS), Central Bank collaboration has been improving in other respects. Consolidated supervision was strengthened further between 1983–87. Parent country responsibilities for their own banks were stressed, and the need for ample lender-of-last resort support. Another important step was the December, 1987, 12 nation agreement (adding Italy and Sweden to the G–10) that harmonized risk-adjusted capital requirements. This was a break-through toward a more level playing field, with greater financial soundness for international banking.

Unfortunately, the Bank of Commerce and Credit International (BCCI) failure of 1991 illustrated a gap in the BIS–Concordat support system. A major bank, BCCI, that began in Pakistan and became well-established in the Persian Gulf Emirates, was not sufficiently supported by its relevant parent nations. (BCCI was designed to make supervision and accounting difficult; two linked holding companies were based in tax havens, the Cayman's and Luxembourg. In retrospect, it was only surprising that so many host countries [including the U.K., France, Switzerland, Luxembourg, S. Arabia, and others] could let such a bank develop into more than a $20 billion operation in at least 32 countries.) When BCCI failed many depositors lost substantially (although the U.S. affiliates were soundly capitalized, and made good on deposits in this country). Implicit in the Concordat regime are financial parent countries that are strong enough to stand behind their banks and guarantee international deposits.

In response to BCCI's collapse the Basle Committee on Bank Supervision (G–12) established stronger Minimum Standards: (i) All international banks should be capably supervised by a home country authority with consolidated accounting; (ii) Host countries should impose restrictive measures on unsound operations in their territories that are not well supervised. Thus, home and host countries should make effective arrangements to prevent other failures like BCCI. In this way prudential practices can be improved for banking in the global marketplace.

Also in the early 1990's, as Communism collapsed in Eastern Europe and the U.S.S.R, international concern shifted toward their problems. As these "transforming" nations applied for GATT and IMF membership, receiving considerable support from European Community and OECD nations, their large needs for additional capital, credit, and trade potential became evident. Most Western countries were inclined to be supportive, but mobilizing large resources quickly was a difficult challenge, and inhibited by uncertainties in the former Soviet Union. Meanwhile, slowdown in the U.S., Japanese, and some European economies complicated matters during 1990–92. Another round of IMF capital increases was soon needed for these purposes, but political stresses caused delay. Many banking interests also preferred that renewed capital investment for East-

ern Europe, the former USSR, and developing countries generally be flowed primarily through private
enterprise banking and multinational corporations.
Nonetheless, the IMF, World Bank, BIS and regional multilateral financial institutions have a crucial
role in maintaining global confidence, encouraging
some reasonable financial discipline, and enough
coordination among nations to avoid serious disruptions.

   In 1997–98 a wave of financial crises, with heavy
capital flight and currency devaluations hit many
countries, including Thailand, Malaysia, Indonesia,
S. Korea, and later Russia and Brazil, together with
some smaller nations (Mexico was hit earlier in
1994). Japan and China also were strained, although they continued their strong export efforts. A
series of IMF assistance packages with "reforms"
was worked out for the most troubled nations.
Political strains were aggravated, especially in Indonesia. A common theme was excessive capital
inflow into emerging markets; speculative euphoria,
panic, capital flight, and devaluation. Lessons
drawn from these experiences were that prudential
regulation of banks needed strengthening, along
with greater disclosure and transparency , and, in
many situations, precautionary taxes on short-term
capital inflows to limit "hot money."

International debate resumed on "architecture
problems" for the IMF, multilateral development
banks, international banking, exchange rates, capital and trade flows. Consensus was difficult on any
stronger measures, since few wanted to cut back on

global prosperity and trade flows. But a global euphoria toward freer trade and financing suffered a jarring setback. In this regard, the World Trade Organization (WTO) financial services agreement (FSA) of December, 1997, was more limited than many wanted in the early 1990's. An outgrowth of the Uruguay Round GATT and WTO Agreement of 1994, the FSA was limited by strong reciprocity requirements (and prudential safeguards) imposed on emerging markets by the U.S., E.U., and Japan. Thus, most emerging markets were unwilling to open up their financial sectors to heavy participation or takeover by OECD nation banks and financial institutions; in response, the U.S., E.U., and Japan would not open their financial markets much to "third world" banks and institutions. Ironically, this mutual caution proved wise, for a rapid opening to more BCCI's in the mid-late 1990's would have brought more disruptions, and hard to deal with failures and political strains. An overriding lesson seems to be that fully open capital flows should be confined to strong, prosperous, and comparable economies (like the OECD nations) that have the fiscal and regulatory resources to provide full guarantees for the activities of their banks and other related financial institutions (under Basle Concordats I and II).

Another complication since the mid–1980's is rising trade and current account deficits for the U.S. Increasingly heavy U.S. capital inflows, with surging imports and more slowly growing exports for the U.S. were problems. During 2003–2005 these

U.S. external account deficits reached $500–600 billion annually, i.e., roughly 5 percent of U.S. GNP. Most experts believed such extra-ordinary U.S. deficits were unsustainable. Already the U.S. dollar declined substantially against the E.U.'s euro, the U.K., Canadian, Australian, and New Zealand currencies—but not against most Asian currencies, which were held low to support big export surpluses into the U.S. Some feared a possible "crisis," with a bigger, broader collapse of the U.S. dollar, a major selloff in U.S. stocks and other securities, rising interest rates, and spreading global stagflation. There was widespread unease about these imbalance problems, but no consensus on the best remedies, either within the U.S. or among other significant countries. Could these global imbalances and adjustment problems disrupt international trade, finance, and banking? The coming years will resolve these issues.

CHAPTER IV

THRIFT INSTITUTIONS

The thrift institutions, mutual savings banks, savings and loan associations, and credit unions, originally were created to meet needs for saving, credit and loans of people whose resources and income were modest. Commercial banks, merchants, money lenders, and pawn shops often did not serve this demand for loans or savings as well, or with interest rates as favorable to poorer individuals and families. During the last two centuries, thrift institutions were gradually developed, therefore, by social reformers, philanthropic benefactors, religious and fraternal organizations, trade unions, employers, and thrift entrepreneurs (in most countries of the world) as a collateral type of banking or financial intermediation. With expanded prosperity and broader affluence, these thrift institutions grew more sizable, and many became more like banks in their offerings of deposit accounts and check-writing services, and sought a wider range of investment and lending alternatives for their deposit resources. This trend created a need for more flexibility in regulating thrift institutions, especially in an era of electronic funds transfer.

The regulation of thrift institutions can only be understood historically, as a response in every country to their humane origins, and partial rivalry with commercial banking. In the United States, mutual savings banks (MSB's) were the first thrift institution to prosper. Beginning in 1816, MSB's slowly became active in most Northeastern states before the Civil War. MSB's grew stronger for the next two generations, mostly in the Northeast, although their relative influence declined since World War II, with only $175 billion in assets for 1981. Savings and loan associations (or building societies) began in Pennsylvania in the 1830's, but expanded more rapidly after the Civil War, when they spread all over the nation. But the great heyday of S & L's came since World War II, with VA, FHA, and other federal encouragements for housing loans. S & L's had assets of $663 billion by 1981, (compared to $1808 billion assets in commercial banks). Credit unions came to the U.S. in 1908, significantly later than Western Europe. Credit unions began to grow more rapidly during the Great Depression, especially after the National Credit Union Administration and progressive employers sponsored them actively. Their postwar growth has been impressive, and credit unions accounted for $75 billion of assets in 1981. (See Table IV–1).

Since the S & L strains of the 1980's, however, which led to the FSLIC bailout of 1989, thrift institutions in the U.S. have grown much less rapidly than commercial banks. (See Table VIII–1.) But thrifts are still a major factor in financial markets, particularly in serving consumer households and families.

Table IV–1

Development of U.S. Thrift Institutions: Mutual Savings Banks, Savings & Loan Associations, and Credit Unions, 1816–2003

(amounts in millions of dollars)

	Mutual Savings Banks (and Savings Banks)	Assets	Savings & Loans	Assets	Credit Units	Assets
	1st Mutual Savings Banks Founded 1816		1st Savings & Loan Founded 1831			
1880	629	832				
1890	921	1,743			1st Credit Unions Founded 1909	
1900	626	2,328	5,356	571		
1910	637	3,598	5,869	932		
1920	618	5,586	8,633	2,520	191 [a]	—
1925	610	7,831	12,403	5,509	419	—
1929	598	9,873	12,342	8,695	974	—
1935	559	11,046	10,266	5,875	3,372	50
1940	542	11,925	7,521	5,733	9,023	253
1945	534	15,924	6,149	8,747	8,683	435
1950	530	22,252	5,992	16,893	10,591	1,005
1955	528	30,382	6,071	37,656	16,201	2,743
1960	516	39,598	6,320	71,476	20,047	5,653
1965	505	56,383	6,185	129,580	22,119	10,522
1970	497	76,373	5,669	176,183	23,656	15,523
1975	476	121,000	4,931	329,000	21,608	38,013
1981	448	175,000	4,347	663,300	21,119	74,700
1985	353 [b]	216,800	3,552 [c]	1,070,000	17,581	137,200
1991	451 [d]	218,000	2,216 [e]	921,000	14,549	221,000
1995	604 [f]	258,000	1,478 [f]	780,000	11,836	301,000
1999	462	270,000	1,110	947,000	10,841	407,000
2003	418	354,000	944	1,073,000	9,504	599,000

[a] 1921.

[b] FDIC insured.

[c] Stock associations 1,087, stock savings banks 306, and mutual associations 2,159; all FSLIC insured.

[d] BIF insured.

[e] Federal S&L's 628, state S&L's 770, and stock savings banks; all SAIF insured.

[f] BIF insured 604; SAIF insured 1478. But some 200 institutions were allowed to convert from SAIF (OTS supervised) to BIF (FDIC supervised).

SOURCES: *Historical Statistics of the U.S.: Colonial Times to 1970,* Bureau of Census, U.S. Dept. of Commerce, 1975; *Statistical Abstract of the U.S. 1981,* ibid.; 1986 and 1995 Savings and Loan Sourcebook U.S. League, Wash., D.C., 1986 and 1995; *Credit Union Report 1986 and 1990,* CUNA, Inc., Madison, Wisc., 1987; *1986 National Factbook of Savings Institutions,* Nat'l Council of Savings Banks, Wash., D.C.; *Federal Home Loan Bank Board News,* April 16, 1987; *Annual Reports, 1991 and 1995, Federal Financial Institutions Examination Council,* 1992 and 1995; *1995 Sourcebook,* America's Community Bankers, 1995; Federal Reserve Staff, 2000, 2004.

NOTE—Histories of specialized thrift institutions record the first Mutual Savings Bank in Switzerland 1787, the first Building Society (or Savings & Loan) in England 1781, and the first Credit Union in Germany 1850. These institutions had common origins in attempting to encourage saving by people of modest means, and often were sponsored philanthropically in their formative periods by wealthier patrons and trustees.

The Great Depression provoked a large part of modern thrift legislation in the United States, and much of the federal regulatory structure that supervises and insures most thrift institutions. (1) Savings banks (mostly MSB's) had been authorized in 17 states, and recently could also obtain federal charters. Their insurance came from the FDIC, FSLIC, or state insurance programs (e.g. Massachusetts). In 1982 almost all 448 savings banks were state chartered, and supervised by their respective states, plus the FDIC or Federal Home Loan Bank Board. But recently many stock savings banks were chartered by the Federal Home Loan Bank Board, its successor agency (the OTS), and some states. In 2003 there were 418 FDIC insured savings banks. (2) Savings and Loan Associations were chartered by every state or by the Federal Home Loan Bank Board, and since 1989 by the OTS. Insurance coverage was from the Federal Savings and Loan Insurance Corporation (FSLIC), or from a few state insurance programs; now the FDIC (SAIF) is the primary insurer. There were 3,200 S & L's at the end of 1985, though this number had shrunk to 954 (SAIF insured) institutions by 2003. (3) Credit Unions are chartered by the National Credit Union Administration (NCUA) or by the states. There were some 9,500 credit unions in the U.S. in 2003.

Since 1970 federal insurance has been available from the National Credit Union Share Insurance Fund (NCUSIF), which covers the majority, while state and private insurance programs are used by most of the remaining credit unions.

Savings institutions grew more rapidly than commercial banks between 1946–85, as S & L's and MSB's helped finance a large expansion in the housing industry. But greatly increased market interest rates and inflation brought an end to this long boom in the 1980's. This combined with Regulation Q ceilings on deposit interest rates, and a lack of flexibility on mortgage loan earnings, to put the majority of S & L's and many MSB's into an awkward financial squeeze, as their cost of funds exceeded earnings and net worth began eroding. In this crisis, tough new competition came from money market mutual funds that offered higher market interest rates to smaller depositors, and took away some $200 billion in deposit growth from these thrift institutions. Credit unions were less seriously damaged, because their interest rates on deposit accounts and member loans enjoyed more flexibility. This crisis for S & L's and MSB's between 1978–82 helped provoke major new laws, the Depositary Institutions Deregulation and Monetary Control Act of 1980 and the Depositary Institutions Act of 1982. This legislation allowed more direct competition between banks, thrifts, and money market funds for deposit accounts, and somewhat more rivalry in lending too. And more recently, since the late

1980's and into the 1990's, mutual funds again took extensive deposits from thrift institutions.

This new legal environment, together with money market accounts, NOW accounts, cash management accounts, EFT technology, and continued inflation for many years, put thrift institutions into a period of severe challenge, particularly the savings banks and saving and loan associations. When many of the S & L's suffered weakened capitalization in the early 1980's, and then received broader lending authority—especially for commercial real estate loans, hundreds of them got into big insolvency troubles with a large volume of bad loans. Those losses to thrifts badly strained FSLIC insurance reserves. A $250–350 billion FSLIC "bailout" operation was required between 1985–95. And under the Financial Institutions Reform, Recovery, and Enforcement Act of 1989 (FIRREA), most Federal Home Loan Bank Board functions were moved into the Office of Thrift Supervision (OTS) of the OCC, and FSLIC was absorbed into the FDIC. Not surprisingly, higher FDIC insurance premiums were then imposed against FSLIC insured institutions. Most former FSLIC institutions since 1989 have been insured by the SAIF portion of FDIC in contrast to the bank or BIF portion of FDIC. But higher SAIF premiums are now a competitive disability for many savings banks and most S & L's.*

* BIF insurance premiums were raised substantially between 1989–94 because of widespread commercial loan problems among larger banks, and BIF insurance reserves needed replenishment. But by 1995–96, bank capital had been largely rebuilt for BIF insured institutions, and accordingly, BIF premium charges have

A. SAVINGS BANK REGULATION

Mutual Savings banks for workmen, artisans, women, and other people of modest means were an idea that emerged in many Western countries during the later 1700's, including Britain, Germany, Switzerland, and Italy. Jeremy Bentham suggested "frugality banks" in 1797, for example, and in Britain friendly societies for savings, mutual support, and insurance developed in many communities in the early 19th century. In 1816 the first United States savings banks were chartered, the Philadelphia Savings Fund Society and the Provident Institution for Savings in Boston. In the early years, typical features were limitations on the size of deposits, wealthy or philanthropic trustees, relatively small loans, or investments in the most reliable public bonds, private securities or mortgages available. Religious and community leaders often played a key role in setting up these savings banks, and in spreading the concept to other communities.

Mutual savings banks spread through the industrial Northeast fairly rapidly in the 1820's–30's. The Panic and Depression of 1837 depleted their ranks, but MSB's became more numerous and prospered during the 1840's–50's. By 1860 deposits in about 200 MSB's were $150 million, whereas assets in the 1600 commercial banks totaled $1 billion.

been lowered to minimal levels for soundly-rated commercial banks. For years, SAIF premiums were more expensive. This differential was a cost disadvantage for SAIF insured savings banks and S & L's.

But savings banks operations were concentrated in the more industrial states, especially Massachusetts with 89 MSB's and $36 million deposits, and New York with 72 MSB's and $67 million deposits. In the agrarian midwest and south, banking remained overwhelmingly commercial and farming oriented, and MSB's were relatively rare. In many areas state commercial banks were also smaller, less pretentious, and served some of the functions of savings banks. And savings and loan associations (or building societies) largely took over the remaining role for mutual savings banks in the rest of the country.

Even so the growth of MSB's was impressive in the Northeast. By 1890 there were over 900 MSB's with $1.7 billion assets, and after closures in the 1893–97 depression, there were still more than 600 MSB's with $3.9 billion assets in 1915, as compared to 25,000 commercial banks with $21 billion assets in 1912. The majority of MSB's were in New York, Massachusetts, and Connecticut, which accounted for three-fourths of MSB deposits in 1915.

A significant reform came in Massachusetts in 1907, when MSB's were allowed to issue small life insurance policies. Louis Brandeis was a leader in this effort. New York and Connecticut later authorized comparable life insurance from MSB's in 1938 and 1941, respectively. This was helpful competition towards lower cost life insurance, though it did not lead to a big volume of life insurance business for MSB's. Nor did life insurance premiums become a large part of MSB income or resources. But this broadening of the competitive range for MSB's was suggestive, and should be considered a precurser, in expanding consumer product lines, of the NOW accounts which were offered in the 1970's and money market accounts in the 1980's.

The Great Depression was a problem for mutual savings banks, but less so than for commercial banks or savings and loan associations. While 9000 (out of 25,000) commercial banks closed between 1929–33, and 526 (out of 12,000) savings and loans failed, only eight MSB's went under this period. Although deposit growth slowed and mortgage assets declined in their value, New Deal relief measures helped ease this difficulty considerably, and greatly reduced the number of MSB failures.

Limited Depression relief came in 1932, with creation of the Federal Home Loan Bank system, a network of 12 regional Home Loan Banks supervised by the five member Federal Home Loan Bank Board. The FHLBS was patterned, in some respects, after the Federal Reserve System for commercial banks, with lending authority to support member S & L's and savings banks. Short-term loans without security and long-term mortgage loans to member institutions were authorized. Members had to purchase capital stock in their regional Home Loan Bank equal to one percent of their mortgage loans. This lender of last resort assistance was strengthened by the availability of loans from the Reconstruction Finance Corporation, although not much help came to the thrifts before the Roosevelt administration came to office.

The FHLBS was designed mainly for the nation-wide S & L and home loan mortgage industry, which suffered heavy strain as many depositors reduced thrift institution deposits in the depression, and more real estate mortgages fell into default, with substantially increased foreclosure rates. Meanwhile, property values for homes and other real estate sagged in these hard times, and some of these defaulted mortgages led to losses for thrift institutions. But most MSB's had become substantial real estate mortgage holders along with S & L's, though not usually with the same overwhelming dependence on this kind of loan portfolio. Ultimately most S & L's joined the FHLBS, whereas only about one-third of the MSB's became FHLBS members.

The new Deal brought more relief for thrift institutions. In 1933 the Home Owners Loan Corporation (HOLC) was created to target much larger government support to the distressed mortgage markets. During 1933–36 the HOLC disbursed $2.7 billion in exchange for mortgages, which included $410 million to savings banks, $770 million to S & L's, $685 million to individuals (and various trusts, estates, etc.), and the remainder to mortgage companies, insurance companies, and commercial banks. The Federal Housing Administration added substantial new mortgage money over a longer period of years, so that the revival in housing finance could be sustained. In 1934 the Federal Savings and

Loan Insurance Corporation (FSLIC) was created to offer deposit account insurance for S & L's and savings banks.

Meanwhile, MSB operations gradually revived with the economy as a whole. World War II gave a strong boost to government financed expenditure and MSB deposits increased by half during these years. Postwar expansion followed through the 1970's, though at a slower pace than S & L's. This reflected the faster growth of housing and mortgage finance outside the Northeast, together with the fact that MSB's were confined to that section, where they also faced competition from S & L's.

After World War II, however, MSB's began to put more of their assets into real estate mortgages, resuming a trend evident in the 1920's. By 1960 MSB's held two-thirds of their assets in real estate mortgages, and by 1966 three-fourths of MSB assets had become real estate mortgages. Eventually, MSB's became more like S & L's, except that MSB's tended to be bigger institutions, with more deposits than S & L's, and MSB's were concentrated mainly in the Northeast.

But a broader latitude for investment activity, along with savings bank life insurance in key states like Massachusetts, New York, and Connecticut, proved significant in encouraging a bolder attitude toward innovation and expansion outside real estate finance. The most important development by the savings bank industry came from Massachusetts, where these thrift institutions developed the Negotiable Order of Withdrawal (NOW) account.

NOW accounts were developed in the early 1970's in Massachusetts, where the MSB tradition was strongest, and many institutions were as large as sizeable commercial banks. The NOW account was a modified savings account, which paid interest, but on which checks could be written. It was more convenient than an ordinary passbook or time deposit account, and closer to a commercial bank checking account. Congress enacted authority for NOW accounts in 1976 for all federally regulated institutions, including commercial banks, in the six New England states. This was later extended to New York and New Jersey. Some variations developed in practice, with respect to required minimum balances, charges for checks, and the allowed number of checks. But the competitive advantages from NOW accounts were somewhat helpful in gathering new depositors for thrift institutions, which enjoyed the ¼ percent higher interest rates allowed by Regulation Q (the differential applicable after 1973 and until 1982).

NOW accounts were not desired by all thrifts (especially smaller ones) in most parts of the country, but once introduced in an area by large MSB's or S & L's, they were normally offered by the other institutions. Competitive pressures were building up when the Depositary Institutions and Monetary Control Act of 1980 authorized nationwide use of NOW accounts effective January 1, 1981. But as part of a trade off package, Congress imposed uniform reserve requirements for all transactional accounts (checking and NOW accounts) to be phased in during five years, and an end to Regulation Q ceilings and differentials on deposit interest rates within six years. Thus, thrift institutions and commercial banks would be treated more alike, and would be more directly competitive to this extent. In addition, under the DIDMCA federally chartered S & L's could invest up to 20 percent of their assets in consumer loans, commercial paper, and corporate debt, and federally chartered MSB's could make business loans up to 5 percent of their assets. But these enhanced powers were less important for MSB's, which enjoyed most of this latitude already, and some thrifts felt the DIDMCA was a net loss for them in phasing out the Regulation Q interest rate advantage over commercial banks, despite the nationwide extension of NOW account authority. It should be borne in mind also that NOW accounts did not bring in much new money to thrift institutions as a whole; only $2.3 billion were in NOW accounts by the end of 1981 or 1.5 percent of MSB deposits.

Meanwhile, the most serious disintermediation crisis for thrift institutions (MSB's and S & L's) was building up in the late 1970's, and hit with full force on their earnings in the early 1980's. Increased inflation and higher interest rates came in three major stages, the late 1960's, 1973–74 and 1978–82. But the strongest surge of inflation, elevated interest rates, and disintermediation occurred in 1978–82. Regulation Q deposit rate ceilings were kept firm, but market interest rates went 5–10 percentage points higher. Money market mutual funds offered more competitive deposit rates, and $200 billion of new deposits were taken away from other institutions. MSB's and S & L's lost substantial deposits, and began suffering an earnings squeeze when their rising cost of funds (especially from larger denomination CD's, with higher interest rates) exceeded their mortgage interest revenues (weighted down with a substantial inventory of lower yield, older mortgages). The majority of MSB's and S & L's fell into a period of negative earnings in the early 1980's. This prompted efforts at self-help, such as variable interest rate mortgages, widespread conversion from mutual to stock forms of ownership, switching from state to federal charters, merger activity among thrifts, some acquisitions by banks, closer relations with mortgage bankers, and government relief, including broadened thrift powers, new liability instruments and accounts, and emergency financial assistance. But these problems and remedies cannot really be understood for MSB's without encompassing S & L's, because they were involved together as part of the overall problems of mortgage and housing finance, survival of thrift institutions as a whole, and the restructuring of competitive relations among banks, thrifts, money market funds, the securities industry and financial institutions generally.

B. SAVINGS AND LOAN ASSOCIATION REGULATION

Savings and loan associations (or building societies) were another kind of cooperative thrift organization that focused lending upon the desire for home ownership and construction by families of modest income. Building societies like this had been developed in Britain around 1781, and had become widely established. The first S & L in the U.S., The Oxford Provident Building Association, formed in 1831 at Frankford, Pennsylvania, a small town on the outskirts of Philadelphia, was patterned on the British model. Its founders were two local manufacturers, a physician, and a schoolteacher-surveyor, together with 33 other local resident members. Members were required to contribute $5 initial deposits and $3 monthly dues. Accumulated savings would be offered as loans among the members, though restricted to nearby residents within five miles. Withdrawal was permitted after a month's notice, but with a 5 percent penalty charge on accumulated contributions. Small fines were imposed for a failure to make monthly contributions.

A modest spread of building societies (S & L's) occurred before the civil war in eight states, but a more permanent type of organization was needed. The original prototype in Frankford, Pa., only operated for ten years, when it wound up, distributed the accumulated resources, and a new association of similar name succeeded for another decade, and so on. This early type of "terminating" association had inherent limits on growth potential, and was supplanted by two varieties, the "serial plan" and the "permanent plan." The serial plan issued successive blocks of shares to provide more continuity, and allowed continuous operation with no disruption or need to terminate. Most serial plans strongly encouraged regular contributions or dues, both to accumulate enough savings for home loans, and to enforce thriftiness. But the serial plan was less suitable for larger organizations, and was inconvenient for irregular savings or withdrawals.

The "permanent plan" proved to be readily expansible and more successful in most parts of the country. The most widely known prototype developed in Dayton, Ohio, about 1880, although a few precursers can be found even earlier, including one in Charleston, South Carolina. In the permanent plan shares are issued (or accounts opened) at any time, net earnings or dividends are paid regularly. The modern "S & L" is an outgrowth of the permanent plan, with larger resources, often with branches, a variety of deposit accounts, and lending potential extended into multi-family housing, or even other kinds of credit in recent years.

Savings and loan associations spread through the entire country between the civil war and 1890, and by 1900 there were 5,356 S & L's with $571 million in assets. (See Table IV–1) By contrast, only 626 MSB's (or savings banks) were concentrated in the Northeast, with much larger assets of $2,328 million in 1900. At the turn of the century, an average sized S & L held a bit less than $100,000 deposits, whereas the average MSB or savings bank had nearly $4.5 million deposits. S & L's were more informal, and often had only part time offices without regular employees. Also, S & L's assets consisted almost entirely of smaller home mortgages, while MSB's held more corporate securities (mainly bonds) than real estate mortgages at that stage.

Regulation of S & L's was largely non-existent in this early period, but these associations became increasingly popular because they served a useful purpose. Local attorneys, realtors and builders, over the years, also became common organizers, because an S & L might serve their business interests, too. Once the problems of continuity and permanence had been solved, this kind of building society had broad appeal.

Unfortunately, this appeal led to some exploitation by irresponsible promoters, and in particular, the rise and fall of the so-called "nationals." The first of these was the National Building, Loan, and Protective Union, which began in Minnesota around 1887. This outfit sold shares of "$100 par value", with monthly dues of 85 cents, from which 10 cents went to "expenses", 15 cents to "insurance", and 60 cents to the "loan fund." In addition, there was a $2 membership fee which paid sales commission agents. There was no withdrawal or surrender value, so a member lost everything contributed with a lapse in payment of dues. Liberal commissions and expenses, however, encouraged growth in the early years, with traveling sales crews signing up a local attorney and respected citizens in each community (often compensated) to enable substantial recruitment. The success of such promoters led to 11 other "nationals" in Minnesota within a year, and more were set up around the country. By 1893, 240 "national" associations existed in the U.S., as compared to 5,598 local building and loan associations. Between 1887–95 the nationals collected an estimated $250 million, and loaned $150 million (a lower percentage than the locals).

The local building and loan organizations naturally felt outraged at the high promoter expenses and unsound finance in these "national" fly-by-night operations. The United States League of Local Building and Loan Associations in 1893 (later U.S. League of S & L's) was prompted in large part by need to organize this opposition. State legislation on S & L's was mainly inspired by this controversy. Some states required $100,000 cash deposits (or in mortgage assets) as a condition for the nationals to do business in their jurisdiction. In other states bonds were required for the sales agents to secure against fraud. Some states made formal investigations, which tended to be unfavorable to the "nationals", their selling practices, and financial soundness. But what ultimately destroyed the "nationals" was a series of failures, beginning in 1896 with the largest, Southern Building and Loan Association of Knoxville, Tennessee. Within several years none of the significant "nationals" remained. And yet, most S & L experts believe this episode was, in the end, constructive, for it led to some sensible regulation,

helped teach the importance of sound accounting
and actuarial techniques, and emphasized the posi-
tive benefits of community knowledge, reputation
and cooperation that caused the spread of local S &
L's in the first place.

Serious supervision of S & L's began in New York
in 1875 (along with MSB regulation) with a requirement of annual reports. This was enlarged to visitation authority in 1887, and annual inspections in
1892. During the late 1880's-early 1890's such regulation spread to many other states, and this supervision had become near universal by the 1920's. The
main objectives were to minimize fraud and embezzlement, and to enforce reasonable prudence and
care on the part of trustees and directors, many of
whom served merely part-time, and were not necessarily experienced business people. Results were
uneven, but local interest normally served to sustain reasonable honesty and competence.

Savings and loan institutions prospered in the
period 1900–1929. The number of S & L's grew
from 5,356 to 12,342, and their assets mushroomed
from $932 million to $8.7 billion. This compares
with a slight decline in the number of MSB's, i.e.,
from 626 to 598, and a slower growth of $2.3 billion
to $9.9 billion in MSB assets. Meanwhile, commer-
cial banks trebled in number from 10,800 to 30,000
between 1900–21, although shrinking to 25,000 in
1929. Commercial bank assets grew from $9 billion
in 1900 to $62 billion in 1929. As a whole, thrifts
roughly maintained their share of financial institution assets as compared to commercial banks, but S

& L's grew more rapidly than MSB's, and approached the MSB's in total assets—even though the average S & L's $700,000 assets was still much smaller than the average MSB's $15 million assets.

The Great Depression brought widespread distress to the S & L industry, more severe than that suffered by MSB's, though not so drastic as the fate of 9000 failing banks. Some 536 S & L's failed in the years 1929–33, but the Federal Home Loan Bank board, the Federal Savings and Loan Insurance Corporation (FSLIC) insurance system, and the Home Owners Loan Corporation (HOLC) were created in time to save the industry from epidemic closures. (See pp. 250–252 in the preceding section.)

The initial problem for S & L's brought by the Great Depression was liquidity. Cash and liquid reserves had never been very large for S & L's. But as the economic crisis deepened, with business failures and growing unemployment, withdrawals increased, and some associations suffered the loss of their bank deposits when the latter failed. A considerable number of S & L's became "frozen", i.e., withdrawals were no longer allowed, except as limited amounts of new deposits flowed back in. This would not necessarily require closure of the institution, particularly when accounts could be segregated in some manner, with staggered rights of withdrawal over time. Gradually, liquidity could resume flowing through the S & L, as its situation began to unfreeze, and more new deposits were added to the association.

More serious solvency problems developed later for S & L's in communities plagued by heavier unemployment, losses of job income, and heavy foreclosure rates on home loans. Less attractive or poorly constructed homes tended to depreciate more rapidly, and this often applied to multi-unit and lower-grade income properties. The fraction of S & L assets consisting of "real estate owned" gradually arose from less than 3 percent in 1930, to 20 percent in 1936 and 1937, and did not fall back below 5 percent until World War II. Foreclosed assets in these conditions moved slowly, and market prices for real estate had declined substantially during the depression, not recovering fully until the latter part of World War II.

What proved essential for the survival of many S & L's in the depression was generous and sustained support from government. First, there was emergency refinancing support through the Reconstruction Finance Corp., Federal Home Loan Bank Board, and, especially, the Home Ownership Loan Corp. (HOLC). RFC emergency loans to S & L's totaled $118 million in 1932, with another $275 million of capital loans to S & L's between 1933–42. HOLC support to S & L's absorbed $770 million of mortgages between 1933–36, which refinanced 13 percent of the outstanding mortgage holdings of S & L's (commercial banks took $525 million from the HOLC to refinance 26 percent of their mortgage portfolios). The FHLB loans in the 1933–42 period are not so well documented, but added another source of short and long term lending to member S

& L's. It is no great surprise, in these circumstances, that more than 90 per cent of the nation's S & L's weathered the depression, and did not have to terminate operations.

Second, there was regulatory support through the Federal Home Loan Bank Board, and strong collaboration with the savings and loan industry (and the U.S. League of Savings and Loan Associations). One of the few areas of vigor in President Hoover's policy was support for S & L's and regional discount land banks (patterned after the Federal Reserve for commercial banks), which even antedated the Depression. Although commercial banks, insurance companies, and private mortgage bankers opposed these plans, Hoover, the S & L's, and enough supporters in Congress combined to get the Federal Home Loan Bank Act into law in the summer of 1932. As explained before, this legislation created the Board and its structure of 12 regional banks. An initial capital subscription of $125 million came from the U.S. treasury, with another $600 million of FHLB debenture authority. Unsecured short-term loans were authorized and also secured long-term loans, which could be made to member S & L's (or MSB's). Members merely subscribed with payments for stock in their regional banks worth 1 percent of their home mortgage loans outstanding. Each regional bank had 11 member boards of directors, nine representing member institutions and two public representatives.

By the end of 1933, 2,086 savings associations or 19 percent of the S & L's (with 34 percent of S & L assets) were FHLB members (and a few MSB's). Gradually, membership increased as more S & L's regained the liquidity to subscribe, and as membership advantages became more evident. Ultimately, by the end of 1981, there were 4,034 S & L members in the FHLB system (1,912 federally chartered, and 1,872 state chartered), or about 93 percent of the nation's S & L's. In addition, 144 MSB's had become FHLB system members, or 32 percent of the MSB's in the country.

The third major development was account insurance from the Federal Savings and Loan Insurance Corporation (FSLIC). This was offered in 1934 (paralleling FDIC insurance for commercial banks and MSB's). Initially accounts up to $2,500 were insured, now the limit is $100,000 per account. By the end of 1981, most S & L's (representing more than 98 percent of the assets) had FSLIC insurance. The remainder, mostly smaller institutions, were under state S & L insurance plans in Massachusetts, Maryland, North Carolina and Ohio. A few savings banks are also FSLIC insured. This insurance protection has been emphasized increasingly by S & L's in marketing their deposit accounts against the strong new competition from money market funds.

A fourth development was federal chartering of S & L's. Up to the Great Depression, the chartering of S & L's (along with MSB's) had developed exclusively as a state activity. There was considerable diversity, especially in the earlier period of S & L growth. But gradually S & L charters tended toward similarity, as this institution became more popular and widely accepted throughout the country. Federal chartering increased this standardization process. Chartering standards became a significant part of S & L regulation by the Federal Home Loan Bank Board, influenced also by the U.S. League and state regulatory experience. Gradually, the proportion of S & L's with federal charters increased. By 1940 about 1400 S & L's or 19 percent of the industry were federally chartered. At the end of 1981, 1,907 S & L's or 44 percent of the industry had federal charters (and 2,440 state charters).

Additional support for the housing industry came from the Federal Housing Authority (FHA) between 1934–42, which subsidized a substantial minority of the mortgages issued in these years. The U.S. Housing Authority also began a program of public housing in 1937, building 10 percent of the new homes constructed between 1939–42. These programs enlarged the supply of housing activity, and the HOLC and FHA led the way in lengthening mortgage maturities to 15 and 20 years, breaking older, more conservative traditions of 10–12 year limits on mortgage finance. Interest rates also declined in these years, partly as a result of government policy, and because of the continuing depression, slack and high unemployment.

These government programs began to revive the housing industry in the later 1930's. But the financial strains of the depression caused a very substantial consolidation or merger movement among S & L's. The number of S & L's declined from 12,342 in

1929 to 6,093 in 1946. Most of those associations disappeared by consolidation or merger with existing associations. Less than 600 failed in the depression, though many more troubled institutions were consolidated under strong encouragement from the Federal Home Loan Bank Board. Significant S & L consolidations and mergers continued after in the postwar prosperity, offset largely by a considerable flow of new S & L entrants from the late 1940's thru 1980's. Policies varied among the states, and some states experienced more consolidation and branching activity by larger S & L's.

World War II brought a temporary consolidation of housing programs (including the FHLBB, FHA, and U.S. Housing Authority) into the National Housing Agency. War-time controls limited new construction, restricted credit, and included some rent ceilings. But as the war ended, plans were developed to support housing more strongly, including veterans housing loans. After a brief adjustment period, the post-war housing boom took off.

Federal housing policy encouraged and helped sustain this boom in home construction and ownership. FHA loans were supplemented by VA loans (Veterans Administration) both subsidized by the Treasury, Federal National Mortgage Administration (FNMA), Government National Mortgage Administration (GNMA), and the Federal Home Loan Mortgage Corporation (FHLMC). VA loans provided a powerful boost of subsidized lower interest, longer maturity, and low down payment lending to veterans. Since so many young men (and some women) had served in the war, this gave support to family home construction and liberalized conventional mortgage terms substantially. FNMA ("Fannie Mae") was created in 1938, but became more significant after the war in providing a secondary market in which VA, FHA, and conventional mortgages could be auctioned off for their yield value on a reliable basis, thus assuring liquidity to financial institutions that emphasize mortgage asset portfolios. When FNMA became a completely private corporation in 1968, part of its role was taken over by GNMA ("Ginnie Mae"), a government owned corporation operating within the Department of Housing and Urban Development (HUD). GNMA markets mortgages acquired from other agencies, and supports mortgage programs that subsidize low-and middle-income housing and other targeted activities. In 1970 FHLMC ("Freddie Mac") was organized under the Emergency Home Finance Act of that year as a corporation making a secondary market for government-supported and conventional mortgages, with its capital owned by the 12 regional federal home loan banks. This accumulated network of federal support, securities issues, and financing was coordinated, more or less, over the years with FHLBS, FHA, VA and HUD regulations. This effort promoted and encouraged home ownership, construction, and financing beyond the level of private market activity, and these policies broadened prosperity and participation in the private enterprise system.

This support of housing markets became an important dimension of national financial and banking policy. Money and credit markets were significantly affected, and it became customary for fiscal, monetary and banking policies to be worked out consciously in the light of housing finance and the various institutions involved. The U.S. House and Senate Banking committees included these matters as part of their detailed work and jurisdiction, and regular lobbying shaped legislative and regulatory policies, budgets and credit support in their favor.

Tax policy was used also to encourage and complement housing policy (along with other sectors of the economy). Until 1951 most thrift institutions had been exempt from federal income taxes, because they were mutual savings institutions. Although Congress removed this special treatment in the Revenue Act of 1951, thrifts continued largely exempt, for practical purposes, under very liberal bad debt accounting provisions until 1962. Thereafter, income tax treatment for commercial banks, S & L's and MSB's became more comparable. (Some even complained that commercial banks received somewhat better treatment.)

More importantly, tax law encouraged substantial investments in real estate financed by mortgages, with the expensing of interest payments, and through liberal depreciation treatment. But interest charges are expensed generally for business borrowing, and depreciation is often quite liberal for capital equipment and other investment outlays. Thus, the encouragement of housing finance through tax policy is hardly unique, and its consistent Congressional support is not really surprising.

In this postwar housing era, typical mortgage maturities lengthened to as much as 25 or 30 years (when credit markets were not being restrained, as in the Korean War 1950–52), loan-value ratios were increased, and low down payments became customary, and FHLBB supervision of standard mortgage contracts became generally accepted. Some mortgage supervision proved unfortunate in later years, however, when housing market and thrift institutions adapted too slowly to increased inflation rates, and the growing severity of disintermediation strains in the late 1960's, 1973–74, and the most serious crisis recently, 1978–82. Nonetheless, a large part of this housing support and financing system has been worthwhile, beneficial to the economy, and helped broaden the distribution of wealth.

C. INFLATION, DISINTERMEDIATION AND CRISIS

When the economy approached full employment in 1965–66, and the Vietnam War brought an additional surge of government spending and a deficit, the Federal Reserve significantly tightened monetary policy. Growth of the monetary aggregates was halted in the second half of 1966, and interest rates rose sharply. Significant disintermediation began to occur from savings accounts, which shifted towards T-bills and other investments paying higher interest. In this context the Interest Rate Control Act of

1966 extended rate ceiling controls to the thrift institutions, under coordination of the Federal Reserve Board through Regulation Q (and involving the FHLBB and FDIC). As a stop-gap measure, it was hoped that "temporary" upward pressures on interest rates could be contained, the cost of funds for thrifts and housing credit kept down, without much need to choke off the 1961–66 economic prosperity. In this way, Regulation Q was transformed from a loose rein on excessively generous bank interest rates that might endanger bank solvency into a general, seriously restrictive, and protectionist effort to keep savings account and mortgage interest rates below market levels, at least briefly.

As the economy slowed the Federal Reserve eased restraint late in 1966, but the broadened Regulation Q limitations were retained, with some slight easing for large CD's over $100,000. This policy allowed banks and thrifts to get some additional "price sensitive" funds by paying more for them, and yet hold the larger portion of existing deposits at somewhat below market rates. At this stage, the Vietnam War surtax closed the budget gap, which eased the fiscal pressures toward inflation. But, unfortunately, in the meantime, wage-price discipline broke down, the administration's guidelines were increasingly disregarded, and the inflationary spiral gradually increased momentum.

In 1969 monetary policy was tightened significantly, stock market prices fell off appreciably, and some slack developed in the economy. Yet inflationary momentum eased only slowly, and interest rates did not fall much. But Regulation Q ceilings were raised slightly, and disintermediation was less serious. In the summer of 1971 a run on the dollar developed in foreign exchange markets (reflecting a buildup of Eurodollars abroad and weakening confidence in the U.S. economy). Nixon was forced into the first U.S. devaluation since 1933–34. The administration reversed course, imposed Phase I–II wage-price controls, and switched to more stimulative monetary and fiscal policy. The economy improved with reduced inflation and falling unemployment. But after successful re-election, the administration abandoned most controls, and inflationary momentum rebounded in 1973–74, aggravated greatly by world market food scarcities and the OPEC oil price increases. Inflation rates quickly reached double digit levels, the worst since the end of World War II.

In 1973–74 short-term interest rates rose very sharply above Regulation Q ceilings, and another serious disintermediation period developed (a flow from savings and thrift accounts into higher interest alternatives). This time the Regulation Q ceilings on large deposits over $100,000 were raised more significantly. Once again, however, this was designed to allow banks and thrifts some additional high cost CD funds for liquidity and new lending purposes, while trying to keep the bulk of their lower interest deposits intact. This assumed that inflation and higher interest rates were brief, transitory phenomena, and any disintermediation would be limited and bearable. If inflation rates had been brought quickly under control, and reduced to low levels in the mid-late 1970's, these two disintermediation episodes might have been passed off as limited disturbances, with no significant, lasting impact on thrift institutions.

But inflation and higher interest rates developed stronger, renewed momentum in the later 1970's-early 1980's, and only began to abate after severely restrictive monetary policy (between 1979–82), record high interest rates, and the worst recession of the postwar era. This third higher round of inflation and elevated interest rates built upon an increased underlying inflation rate, that lasted much longer, leaving residual inflation after 1982 of 3–4 percent annually, that would have been considered unacceptably high in the late 1960's-early 1970's. Interest rates began declining in 1982, yet remained unusually high into 1986, sustained by increased federal budget deficits (reaching 5 percent of GNP for 1983–86, with fears of a possible renewal of higher inflation). This situation led to a severe world-wide recession, and a sustained period of strain for international banking, as many debtor nations found it hard to pay increased debt loads at high rates of interest.

This third round of disintermediation also produced the worst crisis for thrift institutions (S & L's and MSB's) since the Great Depression, with far reaching consequences. In 1978 major withdrawals began from thrift institutions, aggravated by a new factor, the rapid rise of money market mutual funds (MMMF's). By 1982 more than $200 billion in deposits had been accumulated by MMMF's, much of which would have gone to savings accounts, especially in thrift institutions. For MSB's there was a net outflow of $25 billion in 1978–82, and for S & L's a net outflow of about $50 billion between 1979–82. This loss of deposits, by itself, might have been manageable, but the cost of funds for thrifts (with increased rates on CD's and other high rate deposits, which increased as a proportion of liabilities) began to exceed asset earnings (weighted down with older, low yield mortgages, and not sufficiently increased with a smaller volume of new, high rate mortgages) during 1980–82. For the majority of S & L's (at one point nearly 85 percent of them) earnings became negative for awhile, and their net capital or reserves declined appreciably. Many were forced into consolidation mergers as a result. For MSB's this distress was not so widespread, because their reserves were normally larger, but, unfortunately, severe financial distress was concentrated upon some of the largest MSB's.

There was belated recognition that mortgage interest rates for S & L's and MSB's should have floated upwards with their increasing costs of funds. But although the FHLBB eventually began liberalizing mortgage terms, and even encouraged variable interest mortgages in one form or another, this came late. The large majority of older mortgages in thrift portfolios had been fixed rate conventional mortgages. These low interest mortgages could not be floated, and, in fact, turned over (were paid off) less frequently as new mortgage rates went higher.

In retrospect, this failure to develop floating rate mortgages earlier was a blunder. But government officials in charge during the late 1960's, 1973–74, and even the mid-late 1970's, did not expect such strong inflation and elevated interest rates, and were reluctant to mandate a substantial increase in mortgage costs for consumers (with immediate inflationary impact).

In the end, the U.S. effort to hold down mortgage interest costs and savings account rates was a failure for thrift institutions. Market forces, with increased inflationary pressure, proved too strong. Thrift institutions were saddled with asset portfolios that could not move up sufficiently with market rates, and while ordinary passbook rates were kept artificially low throughout, net disintermediation greatly reduced the volume of these low cost accounts as a source of funds. Instead, thrift institutions had to get more and more of their funds through higher interest CD's, retail "repos", and ultimately, after the Depositary Institutions Act of 1982, money market accounts. In other words, thrift institutions had to pay market rates of interest in the end, but got stuck with too many low yielding mortgages that squeezed their earnings, and brought widespread distress, forced mergers and consolidations.

In contrast, the British and Canadian experiences were more successful. Floating rate (or rollover) mortgages were developed much earlier, and regulatory authorities placed no limitation comparable to Regulation Q on their deposit account rates and access to funds. Consequently, in these countries the thrift institutions (building societies and savings associations) saw their earnings and deposits move up with market interest rates, there was no significant disintermediation, and thrift institutions have remained healthy and vigorous, with an adequate, continuing supply of mortgage financing.

D. REGULATING THRIFTS IN TRANSITION

Thrift institutions during the early 1980's experienced a painful transition period, with increased rivalry for deposits from money market funds and commercial banks, and for many of them, serious strains on net capital resulting from low earning mortgage portfolios. The Depository Institutions Act of 1982 provided some access to net capital assistance and long-term government borrowing authority. It was hoped that this assistance, plus substantially reduced interest rates, lower inflation, and a more traditional yield curve (with higher interest rates again on long term mortgages than short term deposits) would help their prospects greatly. For the majority of S & L's and older MSB's, prospects and performance did improve in 1983 and beyond.

But a large minority—including many that transformed themselves into new, stock-type ownership, with more aggressive, high interest and rapid growth strategies (attracting higher yield deposits for more speculative lending)—got into serious trouble with loans. Such asset quality problems became especially widespread in Texas and other energy "boom" areas after oil prices collapsed in 1986, along with parts of the Sunbelt where excessive real estate speculation occurred. By late 1988 and early 1989, hundreds of these thrifts had become seriously insolvent, with hundreds more in trouble. This led to an emergency FSLIC "bailout" in 1989 under FIRREA, and a transfer of S & L supervision and insurance responsibilities to the banking regulators (the OCC and FDIC respectively).* Massive FSLIC liabilities had developed which required a huge clean up operation. By early 1992 at least $160 billion in outlays had accumulated between 1985–92 to close or merge insolvent thrifts (and to dispose of "assets" taken in receiverships). Another $200–300 billion in ultimate interest costs were projected by some experts.

How did this situation get out of hand? First, many S & L's had suffered weakened capitalization by 1982 as a result of interest rate "squeeze"— losses caused by limited earnings from lower rate mortgages, and a rising cost of deposits in the 1978–81 inflation surge. The FHLBB tried to help weakened S & L's by allowing lower capitalization,

---

* The Financial Institutions Reform, Recovery, and Enforcement Act of 1989 (FIRREA) folded the FSLIC into FDIC, and the FHLBB into a new Office of Thrift Supervision (OTS) within the Office of the Comptroller of the Currency (OCC). The New OTS Chief became another member of the FDIC (joining the FDIC Chairman, Comptroller, and two independent FDIC members). FIRREA also created the Reconstruction Trust Corporation (RTC) to manage and sell off the assets of failed institutions. RTC took over the Federal Asset Disposal Association (FADA), which had similar responsibilities between 1985–89.

and more relaxed accounting (especially for "good will" taken from seriously troubled thrifts that were normally merged into somewhat stronger thrifts). Before 1980 the minimum net worth for FSLIC insured thrift institutions had been 5 percent of liabilities (reasonably close to the 6–7 percent capital/total assets that was customary for most commercial banks). The DIDMCA of 1980 relaxed S & L minimum net worth to a range of 3–6%, with the FHLBB setting the specific ratio. Then the Bank Board reduced these minimum net worth requirements to 4 percent in 1980, and later to 3 percent in 1982. Meanwhile the Net Worth Assistance program authorized by the Garn–St. Germain Act of 1982, i.e., the Depository Institutions Act (DIA), allowed all thrifts (or banks) to borrow medium-term from the FSLIC (or FDIC) to replenish net worth, if their mortgage portfolios equaled 20 percent or more of outstanding loans.*

In addition, the Bank Board relaxed accounting rules by allowing deferral of loan loss recognition

---

* Access to net worth assistance borrowing was restricted to "viable" institutions, i.e., those with a net worth of at least $\frac{1}{2}$ percent of assets *after* receiving net worth assistance. The assistance formula worked as follows:

Net Worth	Level of Assistance
3 percent or less	50 percent of period loss
2 percent or less	60 percent of period loss
1 percent or less	70 percent of period loss

In this way, more needy institutions could get greater support. [With hindsight's wisdom, unfortunately, the DIA capital assistance program assumed that FSLIC could monitor bad loans and capital levels closely and accurately. These assumptions proved unrealistic, when FSLIC was overwhelmed with too many troubled and increasingly insolvent thrifts between 1986–89.]

and allowing many insolvent thrifts to be absorbed into acquiring institutions with unrealistic "good will" valuations. Both accounting devices were extensively employed to somewhat overstate the asset or capital values in troubled thrift institutions, and to delay full recognition of their actual or impending insolvency. By 1984, the combination of these liberal accounting devices allowed some 600 institutions, with over one-third of the industry's assets, to avoid reporting insolvency. [These deviations from Generally Accepted Accounting Principles (GAAP) became known as Regulatory Accounting Principles (RAP). Even under GAAP, it should be emphasized, the deterioration in soft "A,D,C" mortgage assets was not recognized as quickly as mark-to-market procedures might require. On the other hand, it's not that easy to up-date market evaluations, when business and real estate projects face real world uncertainties.]

Second, the widespread encouragement of new thrift entrepreneurs in the early-mid 1980's, with additional capital (converting mutuals into stock institutions or chartering new stock savings banks) brought many aggressive, high growth oriented managements into commercial real estate lending. Conversion of thrifts from the older, traditional mutual forms into stock S & L's or stock savings banks had become a priority in the early 1980's. The advantages of conversion were three-fold: (i) to attract additional equity capital, with potential for leveraging effects and greater earnings for stockholders; (ii) extra profits and stock-option benefits for managers becoming equity shareholder; and (iii) mergers more easily arranged with stock associations or savings banks. In a context of weakened net capital for thrifts, with many mergers and consolidations inevitable, the advantages of conversion seemed important. A great many conversions occurred quickly, such that there were 1,285 stock S & L's by the end of 1988 (1,644 remained as mutuals). More stock thrifts followed in later years, some by conversion, and others by new entry, with others by acquisition over the years as well.*

Third, broader commercial real estate lending powers up to 40% of assets and 10% of assets for other commercial lending (including "junk bonds"), and unrestricted interest rates on deposits had been granted as relief to S & L's under Garn–St. Germain, the Depository Institutions Act (DIA) of 1982. This was designed to help troubled thrifts make more money, and attract more deposits. A few key states, Texas, Florida, and California, went even further with much broader lending authority for state chartered S & L's and/or savings banks. These

* There was concern about unfair or deceptive conversion plans that did not give proper distribution of the existing reserves or net worth to depositor-members of mutual S & L's and savings banks. But regulations were developed by the FHLBB and some states to reduce these risks. Regulatory approval was required for conversion plans and good will distribution, with public notification procedures to depositor-members. Only limited discounts on purchase should be allowed to existing depositor-members, and no larger discounts should be offered to directors, officers or other association employees. There are restrictions on take-overs by other companies or affiliates (from other industries) within three years of conversion. Initial pro-forma stock values in the conversion are based upon recent earnings and expected income from the increased capital base.

states offered great potential for speculative real estate investments, and many of the worst case institutions developed in these states. Unfortunately, giving troubled thrifts a much longer leash allowed many of them, with high risk-rapid growth strategies, to get into much bigger trouble.*

Fourth, regulatory supervision relaxed somewhat in 1982–85 under a deregulation oriented administration, and with budget constraints on staffing and excessive turnover among examiners. When oil prices slumped heavily in early 1986, many more substandard, doubtful loans (especially for "A,D,C" purposes—acquisition, development, and construction of real estate—office buildings, shopping centers, apartments, condos, and even tracts of new homes) quickly accumulated in many S & L and new savings bank portfolios in the Southwest–Sunbelt States.* Meanwhile, a potential landslide of

* Broadened powers for thrift institutions, especially for the S & L's which had been more limited than MSB's, were a major development. Earlier steps included authority to make mobile home and home equipment loans for federal S & L's in 1968; federal authority for NOW accounts in 1973 for Massachusetts and New Hampshire, all of New England 1976, New York 1978, and New Jersey 1979; and under the DIDMCA of 1980, nationwide NOW account authority; and expanded investment latitude of up to 20 percent of assets in consumer loans, corporate debt securities and commercial paper. The Depository Institutions Act of 1982 added authority to accept demand deposits from commercial, corporate, and agricultural customers who had established loan accounts; commercial, corporate, and agricultural lending authority up to 10 percent of assets; expanded non-residential real estate lending authority up to 40 percent of assets; and enlarged authority for investment in government securities (including obligations of state and local authorities).

* An unfortunate "cost-saving" measure by the FHLBB in 1983–84 also disrupted regional supervision, without any con-

risky commercial real estate loans had been building up in 1983–86. And more of the "bad" loans were concentrated in a few hundred institutions, often with the most aggressive growth strategies, sucking in deposits with premium interest rates through deposit brokers. The biggest concentration of this questionable loan expansion was in Texas, and to a lesser extent Louisiana and Oklahoma.

Thus, with hardly any criticism or doubt expressed by financial experts in the early to mid–1980's, the foundations were being laid for a very costly disaster. The FSLIC fiasco of 1987–92 flowed from four factors operating together: (i) extensive under-capitalization tolerated by the regulatory agencies; (ii) greatly increased latitude for commercial real estate lending, with significant potential for speculation; (iii) encouraging new managements and entrants (partly to improve capitalization levels), many of which became over-aggressive and risky in growth and investment strategies; and (iv) substantially relaxed supervisory discipline, when weakened or undercapitalized thrifts could get into much bigger trouble.

During 1985–87 the Bank Board and FSLIC gradually realized that more insolvencies and troubled institutions were developing. The Bank Board attempted to limit riskier thrifts by restricting deposit brokers in 1984, but the courts promptly held this

scious intent to do so. The FHLBB moved its Little Rock, Ark., District Office (which supervised Texas, Louisiana, New Mexico, Arkansas, and Mississippi) to Dallas. Many senior staff wouldn't move. This weakened supervision at a critical stage, when it was more urgent than ever in oil "boom" states.

regulation illegal and unenforceable. In 1985 the Bank Board began to restrict deposit growth slightly for under-capitalized thrifts, and raised prospective net worth targets in 1986, and somewhat further in 1987. Supervision staffs were significantly rebuilt after 1985, too. But a mushrooming number of thrift insolvencies quickly overwhelmed the supervision staff and the FSLIC's net deposit insurance reserves.*

Constrained by limited FSLIC reserves, the Bank Board developed the Management Consignment Program in early 1985—a provisional holding status for insolvent thrifts under new caretaker managers that tried to contain further financial losses, so that mergers or other less expensive resolutions could be worked out later. More than 100 insolvent thrifts were put into this MCP "limbo" between 1985–88; 26 still remained for disposal at the end of 1988. But additional FSLIC resources were needed to properly close or assist disposal for the expanding roster of insolvent thrifts.

In early 1986 the Bank Board had proposed a $15 billion borrowing program for FSLIC (based on future deposit insurance premiums, and $3 billion

* By the end of 1984 FSLIC reserves were only $5.6 billion, and 71 institutions with $15 billion assets were already insolvent under RAP. Under traditional GAAP accounting 374 thrifts with $95 billion assets were insolvent at end 1984. Meanwhile, FSLIC and FDIC insurance premium rates had been modest; only $\frac{1}{12}$ of one percent for deposits. Previous failures had been few and involved relatively small losses before the early 1980's. Although the Bank Board levied special assessments that increased FSLIC premiums 150 percent in 1985, this yielded only $1 billion in additional reserves.

current net worth in the Federal Home Loan Banks). But Administration and Congressional leaders were slow to appreciate the seriousness of thrift insolvencies, and 15 months passed without significant action. Then the General Accounting Office reported FSLIC itself insolvent, since its contingent liabilities for unresolved thrifts exceeded reserve assets. Meanwhile the thrift industry resisted extensive closures, preferring more forbearance. This led to more caretaking for "Zombie" thrifts. Finally, in July Congress enacted the Competitive Equality Banking Act (CEBA) with $10.8 billion additional borrowing authority for FSLIC.

With this funding, the Bank Board and FSLIC tried to dispose of more thrifts quickly. By the end of 1987 there were 351 RAP insolvent thrifts with $99 billion assets (and net worth of $–21 billion). Texas thrifts alone accounted for roughly half these losses. Accordingly, the "Southwest Plan" received top priority. Of 205 thrifts "disposed of" in 1988 (with $100 billion assets), 81 were Texas thrifts.* Sixty percent of the $30 billion disposal costs that year went for Texas thrifts. These disposals were controversial, however, because of substantial losses incurred by FSLIC, and relatively generous terms conceded to thrift purchasers—often with guarantees against loss by FSLIC.

Neither Congressional nor Administration leaders chose to highlight FSLIC problems during the 1988 election year. But by year end, despite many dispos-

* Most of these involved assisted mergers, or 179 acquisitions with $27 billion FSLIC costs.

als, 243 thrifts with $74 billion assets were still RAP insolvent; about 500 thrifts with $300 billion assets were insolvent on a tangible net worth basis, and a third of the industry was still unprofitable. Once elected, President Bush felt obliged to clean up the FSLIC mess promptly, and get it all over with quickly. Congress went along, because the FSLIC crisis was obvious now.**

A big FSLIC "bailout" through massive borrowing was authorized by the Financial Institutions Reform, Recovery, and Enforcement Act of 1989 (FIRREA). President Bush proposed in early February to borrow (mostly off-budget) what was needed to clean up and dispose of the remaining insolvent thrifts. Congress responded promptly, and by August FIRREA was enacted (largely as proposed). The Bank Board and FSLIC were abolished, and transferred into the OCC and FDIC, respectively.* A new Office of Thrift Supervision (OTS) in the OCC took over supervision, while the FDIC's deposit insurance funding was divided into separate parts—the Bank Insurance Fund (BIF) and Savings Association Insurance Fund (SAIF). Deposit insurance premiums were raised substantially, though more rapidly at first for thrifts. [Ironically, within

** Political observers noted that "blame" for neglect of thrift insolvencies couldn't be assigned on a partisan basis. Leaders in both parties—the President, Treasury Secretaries, Federal Reserve Chairmen, House and Senate leaders, Congressional Committee leaders, regulators and most industry lobbyists had all played roles in not facing up to thrift problems earlier.

* Only a modest "rump" of the FHLBB survived, a new Federal Housing Finance Board (FHFB), to provide oversight for the Federal Home Loan Banks (owned by the thrift industry through its District Banks).

several years FDIC bank deposit insurance premiums were as high as thrift premiums, because of increasingly expensive commercial bank failures in 1989–92. Many larger banks got into trouble with bad real estate loans and highly leveraged corporate lending.]

Heavy FSLIC bailout borrowing began in 1989 ($20 billion *on budget* from the Treasury, and $30 billion *off budget*). By early 1992 $160 billion in FSLIC liabilities had accumulated, with some experts projecting another $200–300 billion of borrowing costs. (The majority of costs will be borne by taxpayers—a lesson in the social costs of excessive forbearance with insolvent institutions.) Meanwhile, the Resolution Trust Corporation (RTC) became the new "garbage can" for collecting bad loans and foreclosed assets from failed thrifts. RTC took over the role of the Federal Asset Disposal Association (FADA), a FSLIC affiliate between 1985–89. By the mid–1990's, it was hoped, most of the RTC's assets, largely real estate mortgages or assets, would have been sold off or liquidated.

FIRREA had important effects in other areas: (1) Mergers and acquisitions by banks of S & L's and savings banks were generally allowed under FIRREA. Under the DIA of 1982 only failing institutions had been allowed to merge across these traditional boundaries, with clear preferences for mergers among institutions of the same type and, so far as possible, within the same state. (2) Higher net worth or capital standards were to be phased-in over several years under FIRREA, so that S & L's, savings banks, and banks would operate together under the same "leverage" (3 percent) and "risk-based capital" requirements (8 percent) as established for banks in 1987–89. Note—Under the risk-based capital requirements, *residential* real estate, (*conservatively appraised*) carries only a 50 percent risk rating. Thus, effective capital needed for *residential* real estate lending is only 4 percent under G–12 international standards. *Commercial* real estate, however, would carry the full 8 percent capital requirement for *these* loan assets. (3) Enforcement powers, civil penalties, fines and criminal sentences were strengthened under FIRREA, with enlarged authority to remove officers and directors, and explicit FDIC power to suspend or terminate deposit insurance for thrifts or banks. (4) The "Qualified Thrift Lender" (QTL) test was strengthened in FIRREA, so that S & L'S and savings banks enjoying some tax, credit, and accounting advantages must hold at least 70 percent of their assets in housing related assets. The earlier CEBA of 1987 had initiated the QTL test with a 60 percent requirement. This QTL test was designed to encourage and reward more conservative, traditional thrifts that did not get into overly risky, dangerous, and speculative diversification. (Some questioned these QTL restrictions, however, wondering whether diversification had been the main problem—as opposed to under-capitalization and weakened supervision. But many felt that an excessive, sudden surge of commercial lending by inexperienced thrift managements was a major part of the FSLIC fiasco.) (5) Because a limited number of thrifts got into very serious trouble with heavy investments in "junk bonds," thrifts were generally prohibited under FIRREA from investing in corporate debt securities below "investment grade." Transition rules were provided to phase out most of such low grade investment by mid–1994. (6) Many of the worst managed, most costly thrifts were state chartered (in Texas, Florida, or California), where much wider investment latitude had been allowed. Therefore, FIRREA generally prohibited state chartered thrifts from any investment activity not allowed to federally chartered institutions, unless the FDIC determines there is no risk to its reserve fund, and the thrift is fully complying with capitalization standards.

Clearly, a major consequence of the FSLIC fiasco, and the heavy costs of cleaning up nearly 1,000 insolvent or seriously troubled thrift institutions, was an increased consciousness of the need for supervision, prudential regulation, and adequate capital for financial institutions generally. Attitudes in Congress, the press, and the public clearly shifted somewhat away from a deregulation enthusiasm of the early-mid 1980's. The FDIC Improvement Act of 1991 reflected the new mood (described at length in Chapter 3, at pp. 132, 149 and 155).

More recently, however, much of the thrift industry recovered their financial health. Generally the "problem" institutions had either failed or recovered by the mid–1990's. But the consolidation movement that hit the U.S. banking industry since the mid–1980's continued throughout the full range of depository institutions. Commercial banks declined in numbers from 14,285 to 7,700 between 1985–2003 while bank assets grew from $2,350 billion to $6,680 billion in these 18 years. Savings banks and S & L's declined from 3,905 to 1,362 between 1985–2003, but thrift assets (S & L's, savings banks, and credit unions) grew modestly from $1,414 billion in 1985 to $2,026 billion in 2003.* Substantial numbers of thrift institutions, and their assets, had been acquired by commercial banks in these years. Also significant was a disparity in FDIC insurance premium assessments for BIF (bank insurance fund) institutions—as compared to SAIF (savings association insurance fund) insured S & L's and savings banks. (While BIF insurance premiums did increase greatly in 1989–93 when many commercial banks failed, BIF insurance premiums dropped down by 1995–96, as most commercial banks improved their capitalization.) Meanwhile, other cost pressures, computerization, and increased competition from mutual funds (especially money market mutual funds) adversely impacted some S & L's and savings banks. This squeezed their profit margins, which encouraged some mergers and consolidation among thrifts and by banks.

E. CREDIT UNION REGULATION

Credit unions were the last major thrift institu-

---

* Credit unions declined substantially in numbers, i.e., from 17,581 in 1985 to 9,500 in 2003.

tions developed in the United States. They began as another type of small scale, cooperative borrowing and savings institution in Germany during the 1850's. The leaders were Herman Schultze–Delitzsch for people's banks (volksbanks), and Friedrich Wilhelm Raiffeisen for more rural credit coops. These credit cooperatives spread to other countries including Scandinavia, Switzerland, France, and Italy, but became especially strong in Germany, where before World War I there were 1002 volksbanks and 16,927 Raiffeisen credit societies. The credit union concept spread to the U.S. through a few key leaders, including the philanthropist department store owner, Edward Filene of Boston, Alphonse Desjardins, founder of "caisses populaires" in Quebec, and Pierre Jay, Commissioner of Banks in Massachusetts. The first U.S. credit unions were founded in 1909, including the Industrial Credit Union of Boston, Caisse Populaire of Saint Jean Baptist Parish Church, Lynn, Mass., and St. Mary's Coop. Credit Association, Manchester, New Hampshire. The first general statute was the Massachusetts Credit Union Act of 1909, and that state quickly became the pacesetter in credit union development.

What distinguished credit unions from MSB's and S & L's was their emphasis on a common bond of workers, church members, or people in a local area, wanting to borrow relatively small amounts at reasonable interest rates from each other, and help each other save to meet these short-term needs. Their goal was to provide a low interest rate alternative (6–9 percent and preferably the lower) to loan sharks or pawnbrokers. In the U.S. credit unions developed mainly among urban or smaller town workers, and did not do so well among farmers as in Northern Europe. Credit unions became the smallest and most informal of thrift institutions. And the credit union objective of making installment loans at modest rates with their deposits was quite different from MSB's or S & L's, whose asset portfolios stressed security and good returns to savers. Many early credit unions emphasized borrower needs more than saving, although some diversity among credit unions developed in the growth of this movement.

During the next decade credit unions spread unevenly on a modest scale. Philanthropic backers were important in some early credit union societies, although democratic self rule and elected officers were an organizing theme, along with virtues of thrift, regular work, and mutual assistance. By 1920 there were 64 credit unions in Massachusetts, 68 in New York, 33 in North Carolina (all rural), and relatively few elsewhere. The next year the nation had 190 credit unions altogether, with only 72,000 members (an average of 375 each). At this stage a lawyer, Roy Bergengren, from Lynn, Massachusetts, was hired by Filene as the director of an organizing campaign for credit unions. They established a Credit Union Extension Bureau (CUNEB), financed largely by Filene's foundation, the Twentieth Century Fund. This began a productive partnership, which eventually created a strong national association, Credit Union National Association (CUNA).

By 1929 there were about 1,000 credit unions with 265,000 members, spreading into more states (with credit union chartering laws in a dozen states). Members were mostly employees with some local or occupational common bond. Massachusetts was still leading with 296 credit unions and 98,000 members, but an important endorsement had been achieved in 1928 from the national Catholic Welfare Conference, which assisted further organizing efforts. Yet the aggregate resources of credit unions remained modest, only $54 million in outstanding loans to individuals (or an average of $50,000 per credit union). The Great Depression reduced the deposits available to credit unions, and their total loans dropped to $16 million in 1932. But the number of credit union societies had grown to 1700 by that year, and the broader cooperative movement began to strengthen interest in credit unions.

When Roosevelt's New Deal came to Washington in 1933, Filene and Bergengren made their push for a federal credit union law, and they also sought discount privileges for credit unions at Federal Reserve banks. Although the Treasury and Federal Reserve opposed the discounting idea, there was little opposition to federal chartering for credit unions. Accordingly, Congress passed the Federal Credit Union Act of 1934, which provided federal chartering authority, and a small staff to facilitate organizing efforts. The Credit Union Section of the Farm Credit Administration was established in the

Agriculture Department. Shortly thereafter Credit Union National Association (CUNA) was founded. One of its first priorities, apart from organizing efforts, was an insurance affiliate, CUNA Mutual Insurance Society set up in 1935. This offered credit life insurance for CUNA loans, and helped to strengthen the reliability of installment credit assets. A few years later an independent CUNA Life Insurance Co. was established to offer smaller life insurance policies to members.

There were controversies in the credit union movement as it grew. There was conflict over the proper interest rate charges on loans to members, i.e., borrower-oriented 6 percent versus a saver-oriented 7–10 percent. How was expansion to be financed? Through CUNA dues, income on CUNA affiliate insurance, or federal FCA staff budgets? CUNA dues for credit unions became the main resource for expansion. In this period Bergengren moved the CUNA headquarters to Madison, Wisconsin, a more central locale with a strong cooperative movement. In 1937 Filene died, after 18 years of support and financial assistance, and the FCA ruled it could no longer take the initiative in forming new societies. But CUNA's momentum was now self-sustaining, and by 1941 there were 9,891 credit unions, with 3.3 million members and $320 million assets. Credit unions held 3.3 percent of consumer installment loans in 1941.

In World War II credit unions were restricted by Regulation W, which limited installment credit loans (along with other policies to control war-time inflation.) This cut credit union lending roughly in half. But improved wages and earnings expanded credit union deposits and assets by 50 percent, even though membership and the number of credit unions declined slightly. Another complication proved awkward, when the Credit Union Section of FCA was transferred to the FDIC. CUNA soon began to complain of FDIC restrictions, delays in chartering, and a prohibition of CUNA credit life insurance. Therefore, CUNA sought to move the credit union section, and its chartering responsibilities to a more friendly agency, the Federal Security Agency (social security). The transfer was achieved in 1948, and the section became the Bureau of Federal Credit Unions, which facilitated chartering activity again.

CUNA added automobile insurance to its offerings for credit unions in 1949, through private insurance company contracts it sponsored. Yet CUNA opposed any federal credit union guarantees on accounts (like FDIC or FSLIC insurance), preferring to maintain CUNA affiliate bonding insurance for credit union officers responsible for funds. This, the majority argued, was a sufficient safeguard against the risk of theft, embezzlement and fraudulent credit union managers, which would be cheaper, and allow lower cost borrowing by credit union members.

By 1960 there were 20,047 credit unions, with 12 million members and $5.6 billion assets. These societies were becoming more mature, many had full-time staffs and offices, and some were sizeable institutions. The common bond for most credit unions was still the employment relationship, but credit unions were becoming commonplace among employers, especially those with larger work forces. Some kinds of employees were especially prone to credit unions, including government workers, the military, teachers, aerospace, universities, hospitals, IBM, and some public utilities. In the late 1960's, some new credit unions were organized with OEO (the poverty program), but by this time credit unions were no longer oriented mainly to poorer workers, and this new drive did not become a major part of the credit union network. In 1969 23,731 credit unions were in operation, with 21 million members and $16 billion assets. Their average size was nearly 10,000 members and $675,000 assets, a far cry from modest beginnings. At this stage regulatory maturity was established, with basic new legislation.

In 1970 the National Credit Union Administration (NCUA) was created, which took over the chartering, supervision and examining function for federal credit unions. State authorities continue to supervise state chartered credit unions. In 1970 Congress also established the National Credit Union Share Insurance Fund (NCUSIF), administered through NCUA, to insure credit union accounts. By 1981 12,000 federally chartered credit unions, and the majority of nearly 9,000 state chartered credit unions, were insured by NCUSIF, with limits on insurance raised to $100,000 per account. By 1995 97 percent of credit union savings were NCUSIF insured, with most of the remainder insured under state plans or privately. Like the Federal Reserve and the FHLBB, NCUA is self-financing, with income from chartering, examination, supervision, and insurance fees. NCUA is now administered by a three member board, appointed for six year terms, under a chairman designated by the President.

In 1978 Congress added another feature to NCUA, a National Credit Union Central Liquidity Facility. This provides discounting and loan support to credit unions, and supplements previously established mutual support arrangements and borrowing. Among the latter institutions is the private U.S. Central Credit Union, with $22 billion assets, which provides support and financial services to the "corporate" credit unions (most of the stronger credit unions became members of the "corporate" credit union network).

The distribution of common bonds in the credit unions active in 2003 was 70 percent occupational (or employer related), 15 percent associational, and 15 percent residential. Within the employer related group, 10 percent of all credit unions were in manufacturing, 11 percent governmental, 10 percent educational and health, and the remainder scattered through other sectors. In 1998 the U.S. Supreme Court in a 5–4 decision tried to narrow the scope for broadening credit-union membership by blocking small-business employees or lower-income residents from joining occupationally bonded institutions. NCUA v. First National Bank and Trust Company (S.Ct.1998). But Congress promptly and overwhelmingly passed corrective legislation (H.R. 1151), the Credit Union Membership Access Act of

1998, that restored credit union leeway to liberalize their common bonds and broaden membership.

In 2003 there were 9,504 credit unions (according to CUNA, Inc.), with 85 million members and $599 billion assets. This represented a large minority of the entire U.S. population, and accounted for $400 billion in loans to members. Aggregate assets of U.S. commercial banks at $6,600 billion still dwarfed the credit unions, and the $1,426 billion for S & L's and savings banks were greater, too. But credit unions have become significant financial institutions, with more substantial growth in the last decade than S & L's and savings banks. (But note that money market mutual funds held more than $2,224 billion by 2003 with much faster overall growth than banks, thrifts or credit unions.)

Fortunately, credit union failures were relatively infrequent, and involved only small institutions. For the most part, credit unions stuck to their knitting and didn't get into serious trouble. They continued consumer-family loans, e.g., cars, furniture, home renovations, house mortgages, etc., and avoided risky new areas—like commercial real estate, which became the downfall of so many S & L's and savings banks. Average capital to assets was 10.4 percent in 2003, appreciably stronger than for commercial banks, savings banks, and S & L's. (The only significant exception to this pattern was a group of credit union failures in Rhode Island, with a state funded deposit insurance scheme that became overwhelmed in the 1980's like a little FSLIC. Their problems stemmed largely from bolder lending activities, including real estate, which got some credit unions into deeper waters where some of them foundered.)

Credit unions (like banks, MSB's and S & L's) differ greatly in size. The largest, Virginia Navy Federal Credit Union of Merrifield, Va. held $8.4 billion assets in 1996, and in 2003 around 250 credit unions had more than $500 million assets, and another 400 credit unions at least $200 million assets. But the average credit union in 2003 held only $60 million assets; the great majority, 63 percent of credit unions, were still small operations, with $50 million or less assets.

This varied size, with different mixtures of educational background, income, and outlook among members, leads to somewhat divergent policies, expectations of service, and management capacities. The large, more affluent credit unions normally offer a wider spread of financial services, and may emphasize saver perspectives more than borrowers. Small credit unions, on the other hand, confine themselves to one or a few basic accounts, and more limited loans for automobiles, furniture, and other personal or family needs. However, most credit unions include a range of members, some older, others younger, with more or less income, so that a portion will be substantial savers, while another will be borrowers. Most credit unions are net savers overall, with surplus invested in various assets, whereas others may be net borrowers for their members. Their asset and liability structures reflect such emphasis, with more or less investment outside the credit union, some liquid reserves, and perhaps, limited borrowing to meet service needs. This helps explain why the mutual support, borrowing, and lending operations among credit unions, through the U.S. Central Credit Union and the National Credit Union Central Liquidity Facility, and other external borrowing and investment activities, have become so useful to the credit union network.

Supervision, examination and correction of credit union malpractices by the NCUA and state regulatory authorities is comparable to the supervision of other thrift institutions. Thus, NCUA employs rule-making authority, along with powers to suspend charters, remove officers and directors, and impose involuntary liquidation for insolvency or violations of charters, by laws or regulatory requirement. In this way, misconduct by irresponsible officers and directors, and misappropriation of funds can be minimized. Bonding requirements for officers and directors, and NCUSIF insurance provide further safeguards.

Charters for credit unions are either federal or state, with similar requirements. But compared to banks and other thrift institutions, the process of chartering credit unions is simple, relatively inexpensive, and does not require legal counsel. Perhaps most important, chartering does not encourage protestants to resist increased competition. Rivalry among credit unions is limited normally by the fact that each common group is served by only one society. Provided that an employer company, institution, locality, or government agency is agreeable to a credit union, minimum requirements for members, initial contributions, and bylaws provide no real barrier to entry for sizable groups of employees. Usually employers find the credit union helpful as a fringe benefit of employment, and it tends to improve employee morale. The main requirements for a charter are a showing of (i) a common bond (occupational, associational or locational) that provides an adequate foundation, (ii) sufficient economic prospects, and (iii) an initial group of responsible leaders and sample subscribers. Federal and state chartering agencies are helpful in explaining new charter procedures. And CUNA, Inc., has a network of fieldworkers in every state to provide instruction and charterings kits, along with expert advice. In contrast to other financial institutions, entry into the marketplace is facilitated for new credit unions.

There has been extensive consolidation activity among credit unions, as when mergers occur among companies, or for other reasons of convenience, and liquidations occur (usually voluntary) for credit unions that don't catch on or retain adequate membership. The peak in numbers of credit unions was reached in 1970 with about 23,700, and the figure for 2003 had declined to 10,841 (according to CUNA data). But the overall membership in credit unions, and assets held by them, have increased steadily over these years, from 22.7 million to 85 million members, with assets growing from $18 to $599 billion in the same period 1970–2003.

A modest employer "subsidy" was typical for credit unions, at least in their early stages. Office space, equipment, and supplies are frequently furnished. Officer and directors, elected from employee ranks (often personnel administrators, accountants or engineers) are not discouraged from these responsibilities, for the benefit of the company or institution involved. As assets and earnings build up most credit unions hire part or full-time employees for filing, bookkeeping, and member services. Eventually, full-time salaried managers take over as earnings justify overhead expenses. Among the important advantages of a credit union is being part of the personnel system of a responsible employer. This involves access to personnel records, and the employment relation greatly facilitates reliable debt collection.

Interest rates paid by credit unions reflected more flexibility than passbook savings accounts in commercial banks, S & L's or savings banks. On the other hand, credit unions normally charge somewhat lower interest rates to borrowers than consumer finance companies or other institutions for small loans. This thinner margin is justified by low default rates, reduced credit risks, and lower cost operations in credit unions. Good employers with quality, reliable employees, in particular, afford an inherent economy of integration to credit union activities.

Although the growth of new deposits for credit unions slowed somewhat in 1978–82, there was no disintermediation or outflow from credit unions comparable to that suffered by other thrift institutions (S & L's and MSB's). Nor did credit unions suffer as serious a squeeze on earnings. Three factors explain the better fortunes of credit unions: (i) greater loyalty of credit union members to their institutions; (ii) somewhat higher interest rates and more flexibility for credit unions; and (iii) much less involvement for credit unions in real estate mortgages, generally speaking. However, the broadened use of money market accounts since the fall of 1982 (and the DIA) by commercial banks, S & L's, savings banks, and mutual funds gave more competition to credit unions in their gathering of member savings deposits.

Yet it remains to be seen how intensely this competition for credit unions may develop. Credit unions traditionally have been more differentiated from commercial banks, savings banks, savings and loan associations, mutual funds, and insurance companies. Credit unions were set up mainly to take smaller, passive deposit accounts, and to make relatively small consumer loans to members. Bigger, higher yield deposit and investment accounts would go elsewhere, if the other financial institutions bid for them effectively. Meanwhile, more of the home mortgage finance, consumer durables, and other consumer lending probably will continue with other financial intermediaries. But credit unions have become a respectable, extensive, and useful form of competitive discipline for the financial institutions industries. More of the older mutual tradition survives among credit unions, in fact, than in most savings banks or savings and loan associations. This can be helpful to credit unions in retaining a substantial role within the thrift sector in a period of challenge for financial institutions generally.

Banking lobbies, however, have been challenging the tax exempt status of credit unions as mutual, non-profit savings associations. Banks reason that credit unions should lose their tax preference (exemption from federal and state income taxes), because some credit unions are becoming larger, offering more services, and acting more like banks. This critique focuses upon the NCUA's recent "liberalization" of common bond requirements, particularly the allowance of locational bonds that permit some credit unions to emphasize geographic area "bonds" more like banking market areas. But CUNA replies that banks and "stock" thrifts (investor owned) vastly exceed credit unions in size and strength. Altogether "stock" banks and thrifts had roughly $7,500 billion assets in 2003, whereas credit unions had only $600 billion assets that year.* Furthermore, in an era when large-scale bank and stock-thrift consolidation and merger activity is reducing competition among depository institutions, the survival of credit unions as a marketplace discipline against commercial banks is becoming more important than ever. Most credit unions are sound; capital at nearly 9,504 federally insured credit unions in 2003 averaged 10.4 percent (a higher capitalization rate than banking). Nonetheless, bank criticism of credit unions can be expected to persist, with regu-

* At the end of 1994, there were 1,000 "stock" S & L's and savings banks with $900 billion assets, and 1,000 "mutuals" with $208 billion assets.

lar proposals for stronger supervision and reductions in the tax preference for credit unions.

Finally, one other development deserves mention in the thrift institution sector. For more than 30 years there have been proposals for additional cooperative banks, community development banks, or low-income designated credit unions to supplement existing financial institutions with a "mission" of outreach to provide more credit and business advisory services to "poor" communities. Various efforts were made over the years to charter banks, thrift institutions, or credit unions that target poor or minority communities. The Clinton administration efforts at expanded CRA enforcement—see Chapter III, Section 13 on *Discrimination*, also were designed to provide more credit to poor areas.

CHAPTER V

SECURITIES MARKET REGULATION

A. ROLE OF SECURITIES MARKETS

Securities markets and financial intermediaries help to mobilize the savings, loanable funds, and resources available for investment in society. These resources are gathered by appropriate incentives, interest payable, and profits shared (or some kind of taxation), through financial intermediaries, securities markets, and government operations. Although some saving and investment occurs internally within households, business enterprises, other institutions, and government, the larger portion of savings in a complex industrial society flows through financial intermediaries and the securities markets. (See Chart V–1.) In this way, specialized information, talent, and risk pooling makes safer, more productive allocations for many investments than would otherwise be feasible within households (or other direct resource holding organizations). The allocations within each alternative channel for intermediation and investment should be optimized by free market price competition. The constantly adjusting network of markets, supplies, demands, and prices tends to equilibrate real rates of return, adjusted for risks and uncertainties. Thus, every decision-making unit in society (whether a household, business, institution, or element of government) tries to make the most efficient and productive use of resources, and this allocates the optimum flow of resources through each channel for savings and outlays—internal investments, financial intermediaries, securities markets, and government. (See Chart V–1)

Chart V-1

Financial Intermediation and Securities Markets

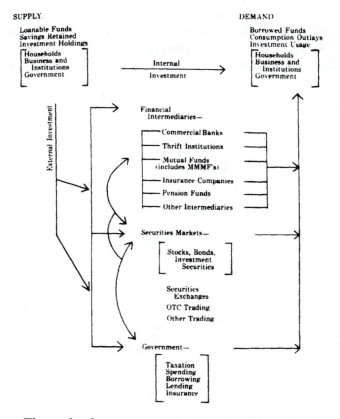

The task of government is to set healthy rules for this network of economic activity. Savings and investment should be encouraged to foster greater productivity, increase output, and enlarge real living standards and social well-being. The role of financial intermediaries and securities markets is to facilitate this process. Government may also provide some services, regulation, and to a limited degree, perhaps, financial intermediation, insurance, or support through tax and spending policies. The test or guideline normally employed by economists for government intervention is that net social benefit should result, i.e., government should only get involved when it can improve upon the private marketplace, financial intermediaries and securities distribution. Hopefully, regulation of the securities-financial system should reflect a political consensus in each country on what seems to work best.*

Securities markets are an outgrowth of mercantile prosperity. Whenever trading flourishes there is opportunity for joint venture deals and investments. Joint stock companies and modern business corporations evolved over the last few centuries as a further refinement in this process. Trading in stock, bonds, and other investment securities developed naturally in the larger mercantile centers. Stock exchanges merely formalize this trading more efficiently. They provide buyers and sellers of securities a convenient focal point, where trading takes place quickly, with better information, more reliable brokers, and competitive prices. Britain created the

* [NOTE—The big difference between the more "socialistic" and "free enterprise" oriented countries is the desired scope of government. Socialist societies find more shortcomings in the private marketplace, and a larger role for government activity. Free enterprise nations see more healthy performance in the marketplace, and less need or competence for the government.]

first modern stock exchange at London in 1773, and similar stock exchanges spread through the more prosperous countries of Europe and America in the 19th century. The London Stock Exchange set a pattern for the New York Stock Exchange (NYSE), the American Stock Exchange (AMEX), and regional exchanges. Limited membership for professional traders, specialists inside the exchanges for many securities, self-regulation for the convenience and protection of members, efforts to restrict outside dealings, and policies enforcing integrity of traders for the public's benefit were characteristic features. In most nations, these standards were developed privately by the exchanges, but government regulation has tended to reinforce and supplement them, especially since the Great Depression.

Table V–1

U.S. Securities Facts

Securities Firms (2003)

6,679 Broker–Dealers	$3,050b.	Assets (2002)
(with 37,300 branch offices)	$222b.	Revenues(2002)
172,404 Registered Representatives	$15b.	Pre-tax income (2002)
553,000 Securities Employees	$142b.	Equity Capital (2002)
	101.2m	Customer Accounts

Exchanges (2003)
NYSE, AMEX, Chicago, Pacific, Philadelphia, Boston

Stock Trading (2003)
All exchanges $14.1 trillion

Mutual Funds (2003) [incl. MMMF's]	88m.	shareholders
8,126 Mutual Funds		
(Total)	$7,414b.	Assets
[MMMF's—973	$2,016b.	Assets]
[Equity Funds—4,601	$4,122b.	Assets]
[Income and Bond Funds—2,043	$1,241b.	Assets]

Total Shareholders (2003)   (Direct
                                                                   and
                                                              Indirect)

50 percent of families   84m. investors

Total Share Value Outstanding $12,158b. (NYSE—End 2003)
Total Bonds Value Outstanding $1,355b. (NYSE—End 2003)

SEC Registrations (cash sales each year)

Registrations		Common	Preferred	Bonds, Notes
1940	306	$210m	$ 110m	$1,112m
1960	1426	$ 7,260m	$ 253m	$4,224m
1980	3263	$31,631m	$ 2,841m	$40,907m
1989	n.a.	$26,000m	$ 6,200m	$320,000m
1997	n.a.	$82,400m	$29,800m	$811,000m
2003	n.a.	[combined $120,300m]	[combined $120,300m]	$1,574,000m

Sources: *SEC Annual Report 1986, 1990, 1998, and 2003.* Securities and Exchange Commission, Washington, D.C.; *Securities Yearbook 1999–2003,* Securities Industry Association, 1996, 2003; *Statistical Abstract of the U.S., 1999, 2004–2005* Washington, D.C., 1999, 2005.

B. UNITED STATES SECURITIES REGULATION SYSTEM

Securities market regulation in the U.S. developed mainly since the Great Depression. Earlier securities trading had developed informally, regulated by contract and corporation law (mostly at the state level), and through evolution of the NYSE, AMEX, and regional exchanges. The Stock Market Crash of 1929, and the depression which followed, were traumatic events that led to the present system of regulation. (See Chart V–2 Summary.) Its main elements comprise: (i) statutory registration and disclosure disciplines to enforce more complete, accurate information for market participants; (ii) Securities and Exchange Commission (SEC) supervision and regulation of the disclosure process, the stock exchanges, over-the-counter market, and National Association of Securities Dealers (NASD); (iii) enforcement of disclosure and anti-deceptive practice disciplines by the SEC and private litigation encouraged under the law; and (iv) Securities Investor Protection Corporation (SIPC) insurance for accounts held for customers by brokerage firms, though not securities owned directly by the public.

In contrast to the banking and thrift regulatory systems, where federal (and state) regulatory authorities impose trusteelike accountability over such institutions and their managers, with strong efforts to preserve and regulate growth of the "money supply", the SEC's supervision of securities markets is much more limited. So long as adequate disclosure is assured, deceptive practices and market manipulation minimized, the securities regulation system assumes investors should take their own risks. Thus, investments, for the most part, are considered to be more risky, hopefully more profitable, and not deserving of government safeguards to the same degree as demand or other liquid deposits in financial institutions (like banks, MSB's, S & L's or credit unions). Thus, the major theme of securities regulation is registration and disclosure enforced by SEC and private remedies. The firms participating in the securities business, exchanges, underwriters, dealers, brokers, investment companies, mutual funds, and their sales forces are subject to much lighter, though not inconsiderable, regulation than financial institutions.

Money markets, liquidity and their regulation (See Chapters II, III and IV), clearly impact securities markets, especially through interest rates. But monetary policies do not attempt, with very limited exceptions, to regulate securities directly. And, for many years (1933–99) the Glass–Steagall Act provisions largely separated commercial banking from securities distribution and marketing. Hence, securities regulation is substantially different from banking and insurance regulation.

Chart V–2

Securities Regulation System

Scope

Stocks, bonds debentures, investments certificates, variable annuities, and profit sharing interests.

Exemptions for deposits, accounts, and CD's in financial institutions; ordinary life insurance and annuity policies; and many pension funds, along with most IRA's and Keogh's in Exempt categories.

Registration and Disclosure Disciplines

[Securities Act of 1933; Securities Exchange Act of 1934, Public Utility Holding Company Act of 1935, Trust Indenture Act of 1939, Investment Company Act of 1940]

Underwriting and Distribution—
Fed'l registration requirements

State Blue Sky laws

Administrative enforcement
Private remedies

Publicly Held Companies—
Periodic disclosure and reports
Proxy solicitations
Takeover bids and tender offers
Insider trading and "short swing" profits

Trading—
Securities exchanges—
Self regulated under SEC supervision
Members and specialists

Industry Regulation

Investment Bankers and Underwriters—
Disclosure discipline
Separation from commercial banking (eroding)

Domestic underwriting
Int'l underwriting

Broker-Dealer   Network (NASD)—
Responsibilities
Net capital rules
Segregation of customer funds and securities

SEC supervision

Securities Investor Protection Corporation (SIPC)—
Account insurance
Assessments and borrowing authority
Protective supervision and remedies

Investment Companies—(including Mutual Funds)
Regulated operations
Registration and reporting
Assets and capital
Management restrictions
Selling and price restrictions
Money market mutual funds

Investment Advisors—
Registration requirements
Advisory contracts and compensation restrictions

Antifraud, Deceptive Practice and Manipulation Remedies

Administrative enforcement
Private remedies (including class actions)
Margin regulation
Arbitration remedies
Commissions

OTC Market—
NASD trading outside exchanges
National Market System (computer linkages)

Other Trading—
Institutional trading
Other private transactions

1.   SCOPE OF SECURITIES REGULATION

Registration and disclosure requirements administered by the SEC apply to "securities." Securities are defined under the Securities Act of 1933 as shares of stock, bonds, debentures, evidence of indebtedness, certificates of interest or participation in profit-sharing agreements, investment contracts, variable annuity contracts (reflecting profits), mutual fund shares, money market fund shares, fractional undivided interests in oil, gas or other mineral rights, or rights and warrants to obtain or purchase any of the foregoing. Similar definitions of securities apply to the Securities Exchange Act, Investment Company Act, and most state securities laws. But most accounts in banks or financial institutions, trust accounts, share accounts in thrifts, or certificates of deposit in such institutions are exempted from the securities laws.* Likewise ordinary insurance policy contracts (not involving variable annuities or profit sharing) are not considered securities.

A limited category of securities is exempted from registration requirements under the securities acts, including federal, state, and local government obligations. The 1933 Act (but not the 1934 Act) also exempts securities issued by banks, savings and loan associations, and religious and charitable or-

* On the other hand, banks received more authority in recent years to sell securities or mutual funds to their customers. But these securities "products" must be registered with disclosures like other securities under the law.

ganizations. Short-term notes (with less than 9 month maturity), known as commercial paper, are exempted securities under both acts. [To deal with the gap for government obligations, Congress created the Municipal Securities Rulemaking Board in 1975, and after June 30, 1983, there was a registration process for new municipal (state and local) securities. Considerable information had already been disclosed, however, and forms the basis for privately published ratings on these securities. Some reporting also is required under the Internal Revenue Code to obtain tax-free status. Subsequently in the mid 1990's, the SEC began some anti-fraud enforcement in the municipal bond area. The Orange County municipal bankruptcy also added to public concerns, with a highly publicized insolvency proceeding.]

Finally, federal registration requirements for securities do not apply to private placements, intrastate offerings (though these may be regulated by State Blue Sky Law requirements), and certain small offerings. Thus, investments among relatively small groups of investors, often involving limited partnerships, are routinely made without the cost, disclosure, or safeguards of formal registration.

2. REGISTRATION AND DISCLOSURE PROCESS

Under the Securities Act of 1933, no "security" (as defined previously) may be offered or sold to the public unless it is registered with the SEC. This requires a "registration statement" meeting SEC requirements, and acceptable disclosure has become a precondition for general marketing of such securities to the public. The registration statement comprises a prospectus, a copy of which must be furnished to every purchaser, and other information filed and available for inspection with the SEC. The method of offering, description of security, business of issuer, management and control, and appropriate financial statements must be included, according to SEC regulations, guidelines and staff approval. This means, in practice, that statements required by SEC staff as to "risk factors" might be needed. This disclosure discipline is applied to the initial distribution or flotation of the securities by the issuing company, the underwriters and dealers, or in secondary offerings by those persons who control the issuer.

These disclosure requirements impose legal responsibility for material misstatements of fact or omissions. The most important enforcement discipline is civil liability to purchasers, either individually or as a class, for any resulting damage or losses. Those responsible may include the issuer, its principal executive, financial and accounting officers, the directors involved, along with each accountant, appraiser, engineer, or other expert named as having prepared or certified the registration statement, and every underwriter. But the issuer is generally liable for damages, and the others for breach of their duty of due diligence in discharging particular responsibilities. In addition to these liabilities, dealers and sales people may be liable for their written or oral misrepresentations or omissions of material fact, but only for the consideration paid by customers.

These civil liabilities for failure of disclosure are supplemented by SEC authority to make investigations, conduct hearings, bring injunctive actions, obtain cease and desist orders, and achieve ancillary relief (including recision, return of profits, and even receivership for corporations suffering pervasive mismanagement). Wilful violations may lead to criminal sanctions, fine or imprisonment, in cases recommended by the SEC to the Justice Department.

3. PUBLIC COMPANIES AND TRADING LIMITATIONS

Once securities have been distributed additional responsibilities for disclosure and the avoidance of misrepresentation apply to publicly-held companies. Most of these requirements come from the Securities Exchange Act of 1934 as amended. Annual reports, quarterly reports, and solicitation of proxies for shareholder voting are the major requirements. These disclosure duties have been extended to any company with assets over $10 million and at least 500 shareholders of one class of equity securities. Enforcement by the SEC through administrative proceedings applies to material misstatements or omissions of material facts, along with private rights of action for damages or other appropriate relief. However, dissident shareholders are limited in their rights to injunctions, and normally would have to show injury to the company or shareholders as a whole in order to change corporate policies (unless minority interests are being unfairly prejudiced).

Special disclosures and restrictions apply to corporate "insiders", defined as officers, directors and owners of 10 percent or more of a class of equity securities. Under Section 16 of the SEA of 1934 such insiders must report their purchases and sales of equity securities. In order to inhibit unfair insider trading in these securities at the expense of other shareholders, the "short swing" profits (resulting from sale or purchase within less than six months) can be recovered by the corporation involved, or through derivative suits brought by any shareholder on behalf of the corporation. However, this provision is not enforceable by the SEC itself.

More recently, the Williams Act of 1968 added disclosure requirements for possible takeover and tender-offer situations. Under amendments to the SEA any person or group becoming owner of 5 percent or more of any class of registered securities must file a statement with the issuer and the SEC within 10 days. This statement must set forth the background of the person, corporation or group making the acquisition, along with their purpose, source of funding, number of shares owned, and any relevant contracts or understandings. Private rights of action enforce these disclosure obligations, including those brought by the issuer (or target company) and its management.

Manipulation of markets in securities by underwriters, the issuer, and others with the purpose of artificially encouraging purchases or sale of securities is regulated under Sections 9 and 10 of the Securities Exchange Act of 1934. However, some efforts which are limited to stabilizing the offer price as part of the initial distribution for the securities are specifically permitted. See SEC Rules 10(b)–6, 7, and 8. In general, however, these prohibitions on manipulation may be interpreted as attempts to limit unfair, deceptive, and distortive interventions (upwards or downwards) in the market for a security by powerful economic interests. Such manipulations are subject to SEC administrative remedies and private rights of action. But such misconduct is not easy to document or prove in practice, and there has been only limited enforcement effort.

Most of the litigated malpractices involving securities trading have concerned deception and fraud. Deceptive and manipulative practices in the purchase or sale of securities are outlawed generally under Section 10(b) of the SEA, as implemented with SEC Rule 10b–5. Since 1946 the courts have enforced 10b–5 civil liability in private lawsuits involving securities fraud or misrepresentation, in addition to SEC enforcement proceedings. More recently, however, some court decisions have given a narrower, more conservative reading to this rule. Furthermore, the Private Securities Litigation Act of 1995 placed some further restrictions on access to relief by private litigants. Nonetheless, it is still accurate to say that the principal goal of securities regulation in the U.S. has been to maintain a regime of "truth-in-securities", so that investors can allocate funds intelligently and minimize waste on undeserving investment projects.

4.   MARGIN TRADING RESTRICTIONS

Margin credit requirements for securities trading are regulated by the Federal Reserve Board. Under legislation enacted in 1934, the Federal Reserve was empowered to prevent excessive speculation through margin account trading on securities. Excessive credit on securities trading with low margins had been significant in aggravating the stock market boom of the late 1920's, and this vulnerability aggravated the Crash of 1929, and the ensuing depression. This regulatory authority is established now as part of the "Fed's" influence over money and credit markets.

More specifically, the Margin Requirements Act (15 U.S. Code Sections 78g), allows the "Fed" to set margin credit limits within a broad range. Currently, the extension of margin credit by broker-dealers is governed through Regulation T, the extension of margin credit by banks through Regulation U, by other persons through Regulation G, and with respect to some additional creditors and borrowers through Regulation X. (Regulation W on consumer credit had been in effect during World War II and Korea, but the enabling legislation for it was repealed in 1952.)

The importance of margin credit regulation by the "Fed" is that a speculative stock market boom, or even a surge in stock trading through margin credit, can be curtailed by an increase in margin credit requirements (e.g. from 50 to 75 percent, thus reducing this kind of speculation). In contrast, margin requirements can be relaxed in a serious slump as a prod to recovery in stock market trading and prices. The Federal Reserve Board (not the SEC) was given this authority, because it relates to monetary policy, restraint over money supply, credit conditions, and interest rates, and the SEC might find it harder to clamp down on speculative momentum.

Recently, however, there were proposals to terminate Federal Reserve supervision of margin credit in securities trading. Not surprisingly, the primary thrust for this "de-regulation" came from the securities industry (including the Securities Industry Association). Liberalization of margins would allow more speculative potential, and some eventual risks. The SIA proposed a securities industry committee to police itself in this regard. Others questioned whether such a change was necessary or desirable. The SEC, CFTC, and other government agencies considered these matters. But after the October, 1987, stock market "crash" (or correction), the dangers of speculation, panic, and disruption in securities markets seemed more believable again.

Following the October, 1987, slide in stock prices, a Presidential Commission studied these events and made recommendations. Some experts felt that computerized "program" trading (especially involving futures and options) exaggerated the severity of this slump. But many also believed that speculative optimism had driven stock prices somewhat too high in many countries, and that a substantial, downside correction was unavoidable. Some suggested that limits be set on daily stock price variations, although this idea lacked universal support. The whole episode, while alarming to the public, did bring constructive benefits. Greater attention was drawn to the dangers of speculation, over-leveraging, and a need for improved U.S. fiscal responsibility. Many suggested that (i) Better coordination was needed among securities and financial market regulators; (ii) Improved clearing arrangements and data dissemination would be helpful; (iii) Somewhat higher margin requirements (then only 8–12 percent) for options and futures transactions might be desirable; (iv) Considerable interest was focused upon "circuit breakers" and possible limits on daily swings in trading; and (v) Specialists on the exchanges seemed overwhelmed in the October 1987 meltdown, although substitute arrangements were controversial. While some urged a new "super-agency" to regulate national (even international) securities markets, neither the SEC nor Federal Reserve wanted drastic overhaul; only more limited measures seemed likely within the established framework of financial regulation.*

* The Market Reform Act of 1990 authorized the SEC to collect extensive data on automated and program trading, facilitate coordinated clearing, and regulate activities that contribute to extraordinary volatility (including emergency powers to sus-

5. SPECULATIVE DANGERS

More recently, as a strong "bull market" resumed in the U.S. between 1993–2000, concerns resumed in the late 1990's about the dangers of U.S. speculative excess. Greater global market integration and capital inflows could bring fragilities along with some resiliency. "Excessive" capital inflows reinforced a U.S. recovery. But few commentators (not even Greenspan's Federal Reserve) were eager to halt the boom with tighter credit and sharply rising interest rates. Perhaps computerization, "globalization," and a new round of innovation did justify faster growth in the U.S. and Asia. But speculative excess was recognized properly in Mexico's boom-bubble-devaluation of 1994–95. Soon afterwards boom-devaluation crises hit Asia in 1997–98 (Thailand, Malaysia, Indonesia, Philippines, and S. Korea), and later in Latin America (Brazil, Ecuador, and Argentina). Ironically, their distress only accentuated capital flight into the U.S. and its stock market boom (1993–2000). This super-charged the American stock market boom-bubble, which peaked at record high prices in 2000. The Dow Jones trebled and the NASDAQ ballooned six-fold between 1993–2000.

In the big U.S. stock market correction that followed in 2001–2003, bad corporate scandals exploded. Enron, Andersen, World Com, Adelphia, Global

pend trading activity). Limited "circuit breaker" remedies were developed to suspend trading in extremely wide swings of the daily market averages.

Crossing, Health South, and Tyco were among the worst examples. These corporate scandals involved over-stated profits, fraudulent accounting, aggravated misuse, and default on pension fund obligations. Such corporate abuse threatened global confidence in U.S. capital markets. Public and Congressional outrage demanded stronger legislation. Renewed corporate accountability, government prosecutions, and private damage actions were needed to restore the reputation of Wall Street. This led to passage of new legislation the Sarbanes–Oxley Act of 2002.

The Sarbanes–Oxley Act is the most important U.S. securities legislation since 1933–34. The new law: (i) strengthens criminal penalties for fraudulent corporate executives, auditors, and lawyers; (ii) creates a new Public Company Accounting Oversight Board (PCOAB) to supervise auditing standards, quality control, and ethics; (iii) imposes periodic review by the SEC of public company financial reporting; (iv) requires CEO and CFO certification of public company financial reports; (v) mandates independent audit committees for publicly listed companies; (vi) requires prompt disclosure of material changes in financial condition and operations; (vii) obligates lawyers representing fraudulent companies to withdraw and disclose breaches of fiduciary duty by company leaders and auditors; (viii) prohibits most loans by companies to their executive officers and directors; and (ix) protects corporate whistleblowers. Most of the scandalous abuses by corporate leaders in 2001–2003 were targeted by Sarbanes–Oxley. In many respects, the new legislation tries to mandate what had been understood as "best practice" by responsible and enlightened leadership for U.S. public companies. (Not provided were limits on "excessive and greedy" executive compensation for top level CEO's. Some critics insisted that this goal should have been included. But Sarbannes–Oxley focused upon corporate responsibility, enhanced CEO and CFO liabilities, and responsibility for auditing and financial reporting.)

From a comparative law standpoint, Sarbanes–Oxley strives to restore the integrity of U.S. corporate securities markets. While some foreign company issuers of U.S. securities chafe at higher U.S. requirements, they gain the respectability of U.S. shares and bonds. Better capital access was why many foreign companies wanted to be listed in the U.S. capital markets. The SEC, however, is making substantial effort to be reasonable and not unduly burdensome.

Meanwhile, the International Organization of Securities Commissions (IOSCO) was evolving as an increasingly important multinational agency (representing 181 countries by 2004). IOSCO began as a Western Hemisphere cooperative association of securities regulators in 1983, which moved toward near universal membership between 1986–98. IOSCO goals are to promote high standards of securities; responsible securities regulation; fair, efficient and transparent markets; and effective surveillance of international securities transactions. While consensus is lacking on international accounting standards, the thrust of this harmonization effort does strengthen sound investor protection and disclosure in global markets. This could gradually improve market transparency and knowledgeability by a process of competition for international investments.

C.   SECURITIES EXCHANGES AND TRADING

Stock exchanges have been convenient and efficient places to trade securities, once issued through a network of underwriters, brokers and dealers. Although securities exchanges developed as private membership organizations of merchants and bankers active in trading securities, their economic importance led to government regulation (e.g. Securities Exchange Act of 1934). In the U.S. the NYSE and AMEX were the dominant exchanges, with leading issues listed on the New York Stock Exchange. Regional exchanges (including Boston, Philadelphia, Chicago, and Pacific) listed some other issues. Many additional securities were traded in the OTC (now NASDAQ) market, which comprises hundreds of dealers throughout the country (the largest have seats on the major stock exchanges). This dealer network is linked together by telecomputers and other communications in the NASDAQ (NASD Automated Quotation System), through which current information on securities and trading activity is widely available. Comparable links exist among leading world banks and brokerage firms to other important financial and money market centers around the globe. In addition, large blocks of securities held by institutions (banks, mutual funds, insurance companies, pension funds, and others) are often bought or sold off the exchanges and OTC–NASDAQ market through negotiated transactions for greater confidentiality, and because big trades may disrupt the market against the interest of large block holders. But current exchange and NASDAQ prices are usually the benchmark for other transactions, so that regulation of exchanges and OTC activity affects all securities trading generally.

Self-regulation of the exchanges under SEC supervision has been a major theme of U.S. regulation. Continuous auction trading for listed securities is carried on through specialist-members who handle the more important securities, and by floor brokers acting on behalf of member firms and their customers. Exchange rules are largely conveniences to this trading process with elements of protection for members and their firms. The SEC exercises supervisory authority under the law, with oversight responsibility over exchange rules and commission rates (in light of industry needs and the public interest). While the SEC exercises primary jurisdiction under its statutory mandate for these purposes, the Supreme Court has held that antitrust principles should be taken into account in reviewing the SEC's supervision of securities markets.

A major development of 1970–75 was the gradual elimination of fixed commissions on trading at the exchanges. Under pressure of increasing competition on large trades from third market transactions, Congress and the SEC forced negotiated, competitive pricing practices upon member firms in the exchanges. A collateral reform was SEC elimination of the rule which prohibited exchange members from making off-market transactions for customers. This strengthened competitive disciplines for securities trading. But considerable trading still occurs outside exchanges, especially when confidentiality and exceptional volumes are involved.

Memberships or seats on the exchanges had become strictly limited and increasingly valuable as scarce "property" rights. Except for some regional exchanges, institutional investors have not been allowed to obtain memberships. This added some pressure for off-market transactions, but negotiated prices for large block trades have eased this difficulty.

The role of specialists on the exchanges provoked controversy for years. Specialists are supposed to reduce erratic swings in security prices by making markets on a regular basis for the securities they handle. But competition among specialists on securities within each exchange was generally not feasible, so that their profit margins were questioned. And yet without specialists there might be wider price fluctuations in trading, with more opportunities for manipulation. In any event, long established practices on the exchanges, including the role of specialists, have been substantially retained under SEC supervision.

Some believe that securities exchanges should evolve into a national (conceivably international) grid of computerized trading that might obviate the need for existing exchanges and specialists. Congress proclaimed the goal of a National Market System in 1975 as a partial expression of this idea, but authority was delegated to the SEC for its implementation. Some steps have been taken in that direction. They include a nationwide transactions tape, a composite quotations system, and electronic links between exchanges and World markets (used by most significant broker dealers). The current trend toward enforcing more of an "open book" in computerized data processing helps encourage more efficient trading and marketplace competition. Clearly, the SEC should regulate the exchanges and the NASDAQ in light of these evolving market practices (taking into account all domestic and international developments).

Congress also mandated in 1975 a national clearing system for securities to improve "back office" efficiency and the securities certificate transfer process. More might be done in this direction, conceivably yielding simplified card-like security certificates, easier to handle in the mails and thru automated processing (like the check clearing system).

D. REGULATION OF SECURITIES FIRMS

The securities industry comprises a variety of firms, largely members of the NASD. Included are nationwide underwriter-dealer-brokerage firms like Merrill–Lynch, major underwriters without retail distribution networks, exchange specialists, floor traders and brokers, regional broker-dealers, and many small brokers with varied emphasis or specialization. Many investment advisers are also NASD members, as are the selling arms of mutual funds and investment companies. Since the Maloney Act of 1938 and formation of the NASD in 1939, the SEC has had supervisory authority over this self-regulatory organization, its rules and practices.

1.   UNDERWRITERS AND INVESTMENT BANKING

Underwriters support the initial distribution of new securities. They provide risk capital or "investment" banking resources for this purpose. Brand new companies or projects involving substantial uncertainty or risk must accept a significant discount, spread, or fee to compensate their underwriters, say 8–15 percent off the gross offering price. Some new issuers even take a "best efforts" arrangement from the underwriters to sell whatever volume of securities investors will absorb, with a substantial commission to the underwriter. On the other hand, highly successful corporations with strong reputations obtain underwriting commitments for much smaller fees or commissions. Blue chip issuers negotiate or let bids for the lowest possible commission or issuing cost to market their securities. Thus, underwriting or investment banking involves a wide mixture of risk possibilities that may go considerably beyond normal commercial banking for collateralized loan accounts. And yet, some international bank lending, especially to problem countries with default vulnerability, really involves investment banking risk exposure. For these reasons a considerable part of international bank lending has been allocated among syndications like domestic underwriters and investment bankers put together for securities issues.

The major underwriters in the domestic U.S. securities market comprise leading dealer-broker organizations like Merrill–Lynch, which have excellent opportunities to float large blocks of securities to the public, along with a few important investment bankers that concentrate more directly on institutions. Regional underwriters and dealer-brokers may participate actively in selected issues, especially in their marketing areas. Large domestic commercial banks recently participated in this underwriting process, although restricted by Glass–Steagall Act limitations on securities distribution. (However, in 1987–90 the bank regulatory agencies allowed some of the largest U.S. banks to underwrite commercial paper, securitized instruments, and even domestic bonds and stocks, provided that such underwriting was handled in separate affiliates, and in moderate amounts compared to other activities.* See Chapter III—D–6. Securities Marketing.) In international banking, however, there

* With the Gramm–Leach Financial Modernization Act of 1999, Financial Service Companies (FSC holding companies) could integrate banking, securities, and insurance affiliates under appropriate supervision of their respective regulatory agencies.

were no Glass–Steagall restrictions, and there was extensive overlap and commingling of activities between investment and commercial banking (for U.S. and foreign banks).

Apart from the securities disclosure, registration, and anti-manipulation disciplines described previously for underwriters, dealers and brokers, there is little specific regulation of investment banking under U.S. law. NASD membership and its supervision applies, generally speaking, but this adds little further regulation to underwriting or investment banking. Thus, there are no comparable entry or chartering requirements, only modest capital or solvency regulation, and no merger, holding company, or branching restrictions for domestic investment banks, in contrast to the extensive supervision of commercial banking. (See Chapters II and III.) One basic reason is that investment banking or underwriting outlays are a specialized type of risk-taking entrepreneurship. Although often highly profitable, the underwriting of securities is not considered generally a normal, prudent investment for public deposits of liquidity. Commercial bankers are not allowed to take such underwriting risks in domestic banking operations with depositor monies, and investment bankers must use their own equity capital to play the underwriting game. Accordingly, investment bankers do not need to be constrained for the sake of depositor protection or insurance requirements.

The main social problem with underwriters or investment bankers has been marketing questionable securities to the public. Hence, the primary thrust of underwriter-investment banking regulation has been to enforce the disclosure-antifraud disciplines of the securities laws, and to protect potential purchasers of the securities against incomplete disclosures or misrepresented investment opportunities. There has been no shortage of capital or underwriters willing to play this profitable game, since most entrepreneurs are welcome.

Some suggestions have been made to expand restrictions against conflicts of interest involving underwriters. While a duty of sufficient disclosure seems well-established in the present legal system, should this duty be strengthened to a fiduciary or trustee-like responsibility? And, if so, to whom should obligations flow? The original issuer? Current management? Early stockholders? Later stockholders? Potential stockholders? Can underwriters serve competing enterprises? Can an underwriter support a client in takeover battles with previous or current clients? What remedies, if any, should enforce fiduciary obligations? Investment bankers like to suggest as a marketing strategy that their services go beyond access to credit, lending, and transitory securities distribution. Good underwriting service is partly entrepreneurial, in the sense of a joint venture, for a short period at least. But is it realistic for clients or the law to expect more?

In commercial banking such questions are not so serious, because borrowing liquidity on a loan basis is a more neutral, objective process. Some advice may flow in a good bank-client relationship, with mutual education and business gains. But the nature of investment banking is more entrepreneurial, like a quasi-partnership (at least for the period in which securities are being issued). Part of the legal difference in U.S. law flows from the securities-disclosure tradition built up by the SEC and 10b–5 responsibilities over the last generation, in contrast to more detached, arms-length creditor relationships in traditional commercial banking. For commercial banking the law creates a primary responsibility to depositors for safety and prudence in maintaining liquid funds on deposit, with equity profits going to bank managers who provide this service efficiently. In contrast, investment "bankers" or underwriters are really capital-raising deal makers, who place their capital at stake as seed money in promoting investment projects. Thus, underwriting and marketing securities is really a substantially different business from commercial banking, which was separated by custom and under U.S. law by the Glass–Steagall Act.*

2. DEALER–BROKER NETWORK AND THE NASD

Broker-dealers (along with underwriters) comprise the main marketing effort for new securities, and most of the public conduct their trading activi-

* But does this differentiation of underwriting from deposit-taking and commercial lending justify a prohibition against Financial Service Companies (FSC's) that combine banks, securities firms, and/or insurance companies? (See Chapter III and Chapter VIII.) In any event, Congress decided in 1999 to abolish the Glass–Steagall "wall."

ties through dealer-brokerage firms. Therefore, the disciplines for disclosure and avoiding misrepresentation are logically extended from issuers and underwriters to the dealer-broker network, in order to support trustworthy securities, improve responsible securities market behavior, and encourage wiser investment activity.

But dealer-brokers are subject to extensive additional regulation for the protection of customers. Most importantly, "dealers" and "brokers" must be registered with the SEC if they handle registered securities or engage in interstate commerce (which requires, in practice, universal registration). Many brokerage firms, in addition, register as investment advisors. Such registrations may be revoked, suspended, or censure imposed, for violations of the securities laws. Along with liability for engaging in misrepresentation, manipulative, or deceptive practices, more specific rules have developed with respect to possible conflicts of interest, suitability, markups, segregation of customer funds, financial responsibility and net capital requirements. Also, since 1970 the Stockholder Investor Protection Corporation has been set up to provide further assurance that valid customer claims will be paid in the event of broker-dealer insolvency.

Under many cases securities broker-dealers are held to be under an obligation not to over-reach their customers, or to exploit them. NASD Rules of Fair Practice provide that broker-dealers should not recommend a security unless they have reason to believe it is suitable to the customer's financial situation and needs. The NASD's fair spread or profit rule has been interpreted generally to allow markups of no more than 5 percent (although in some limited circumstances up to 10 percent may be reasonable). A large number of disciplinary proceedings have been brought against excessive markups. Other disciplinary proceedings have been brought against "churning", the systematic encouragement of excessive transactions. The SEC has attacked "scalping", i.e., the systematic recommendation of securities purchased by an investment advisor (without disclosing this to a customer), so that extra profits could be made when the price rises after recommendations. "Boiler room" operations have been challenged where high pressure telephone or other campaigns have been mounted to tout securities with exaggerated claims.

Some potential for conflict of interest and abuse of customers remains unavoidable, and is built into the combination of independent dealing activities for the account of the broker-dealer, and brokerage activities for the account of customers. It would be difficult, politically and practically, to sever this connection between dealers and brokers. Hence, the law, SEC and NASD have tried to reduce this conflict with rules and specific proceedings against over-reaching, excessive markups, churning, scalping, and other misconduct involving serious deception, fraud or manipulation.

Misuse of customer funds can occur in many ways: churning of accounts where brokers have authority to manage them, misappropriation of securities owned by customers to the advantage of brokers or their sales people, or conversion of cash held on account for customers. Such abuses have been dealt with by specific SEC disciplinary proceedings and private litigations, and by general SEC rules. Under SEC rules now in force brokers must maintain records, and properly segregate the accounts and securities fully paid by customers. Brokers, however, may hold margin account securities as pledges for loan obligations, and brokers may commingle the cash left on deposit with brokers and earn interest on it (along with the broker's own cash funds).

Financial responsibility standards have been strengthened since 1969–71, when many brokerage firms were over-extended and suffered losses in a slump of stock market prices. During that period of strain on brokerage firms the SEC informally encouraged many mergers among broker-dealers (with industry support), so that customer losses were minimized. Under SEC net capital rules, SEA Rule 15c3–1, most broker-dealers must maintain "net capital" (or net worth) of at least $250,000, and they may not let their aggregate indebtedness exceed 1500 percent of their net capital. (A complicated list of adjustments for different circumstances are made under this regulation, based on the broker-dealer activities of each firm.) Alternatively, a broker-dealer can qualify under Rule 15c3–1(a)1)ii), a simpler formula, which merely requires net capital equal to the greater of $250,000 or 2 percent of the aggregate debit balances attributable to transactions with customers. These requirements are comparable to, though less demanding, than the net worth and reserve requirements of commercial banks.* Securities underwriters have only brief capital risk exposure (days or weeks) during the sale of each issue, while brokerage activities merely require sufficient net assets or liquidity to meet customer obligations (and limit sizeable losses for the Securities Investor Protection Corporation).

3.   SECURITIES INVESTOR PROTECTION CORPORATION

While the New York Stock Exchange established a trust fund in 1963 to pay customer claims when a member firm failed, this fund was inadequate to deal with the widespread securities brokerage crisis of 1969–71. The SEC responded by encouraging a great many consolidation mergers among brokerage firms, using its registration authority with widespread industry support. Congress also enacted at that stage the Securities Investor Protection Act of 1970 (SIPA). SIPA created the Securities Investor Protection Corporation (SIPC), which required al-

* Capital "adequacy" for investment banking (wholesale) activities are not closely comparable to commercial banks. Investment banks use their own capital (and long-term borrowing) to finance deal-making; they do not hold large deposits from the public like commercial banks. And retail brokerage operations for securities customers provide transactional services and "street name" accounts for customers (who assume their own investment risks). Some risk of insolvency does operate, but this seems most likely to occur in stock market meltdowns or currency devaluation crises; major fraud and embezzlement is less likely (but would be covered by SIPC guarantees).

most all registered broker-dealers to become members. SIPC is administered by a seven member board, including one representative of the Treasury, another from the Federal Reserve Board, and five presidential appointees.

SIPC's function is to satisfy claims of customers against broker-dealer firms when the latter's assets are insufficient. To meet these responsibilities SIPC maintains a reserve fund, which is supported by modest assessments against member firms, based on their gross revenues. In the event this fund were inadequate, SIPC may borrow from the Treasury. The SEC may levy additional charges of not more than $\frac{1}{50}$ of 1 percent of all transactions value in the stock exchanges and OTC markets to assure repayment of Treasury loans. (At the end of 1994 there were 7,614 member firms paying assessments, of which 4,537 were NASD members). Thus far, relatively few firms have failed, so that premium charges have been quite low.

Current protection levels to customers reach a maximum of $500,000 per customer, but no more than $100,000 with respect to claims for cash. Note that FDIC, and NCUSIF directly insure depositor accounts, whereas SIPC is more limited and merely provides a guarantee-backstop of funds to assure satisfaction of claims. Delays of 6 months or more may be involved.

In recent years, most large brokerage firms have developed and offered supplementary private insurance to cover the risk of firm insolvency. Thus, up to $10–60 million more of additional customer account protection is covered in many plans. However, this coverage must be understood realistically. It does not cover the risk of reduced value in an investor's stock or bond portfolio; that risk remains with the investing customer. The risk covered is simply that the securities firm becomes insolvent and cannot meet customer obligations. Moderate charges are imposed for this supplementary insurance, and brokerage firms increasingly use this coverage as a sales tool to encourage customers to leave larger amounts of stock, bonds, and other securities in the "street name" accounts held with the brokerage firm. Interesting questions are the insurance coverage for misuse of funds or breach of fiduciary duty by a representative of the brokerage firm.

But the SIPC does have some emergency authority. When the SEC or NASD determines that a broker or dealer is approaching financial difficulty, the SIPC must be notified. If the SIPC finds the firm has failed or is in danger of failing to meet its obligations to customers, it may apply for a court order, trustee and receivership. The trustee's responsibilities are to return customer property, complete the firm's contract commitments, and liquidate the business. SIPC will meet the firm's deficiencies, up to the limits specified previously. Obviously, the SIPC parallels, in a more limited way, the bank examination regime, and the FDIC, FSLIC, and NCUSIF disciplines. But SEC and SIPC supervision is weaker, and less comprehensive in data gathering authority.

Some interesting case law has developed in recent years illustrating the importance of broker-dealer obligations, where pension, retirement, or health insurance funds are being handled as customer accounts. Obviously, SIPC coverage limits don't go very far if the individual pensioners or employees cannot recover from the SIPC when the brokerage firm fails. And yet, many smaller pension plans use brokerage firms or mutual funds as their securities fund custodians. A sizeable gap in effective risk guarantee and fiduciary responsibility has developed this way. Oversight for securities firms and their financial condition could be improved.

E.   INVESTMENT COMPANIES AND MUTUAL FUNDS

Investment companies are designed mainly as vehicles for smaller investors to select and diversify investments in securities. The most popular kind of investment company, the open-end (mutual fund) company, most of which used to invest largely in equity stocks, grew rapidly in the years after World War II, especially since the 1950's. A variant of the mutual fund which invests in money market instruments, the money market mutual fund (MMMF), subsequently became even more important in the late 1970's and early 1980's. Inflation, high interest rates, money market mutual funds, and most recently, since late 1982, money market accounts for banks and thrift institutions, have increased competition significantly between banking, thrifts, and securities firms.

Investment company shares are securities, and accordingly, their distribution has been regulated under the Securities Act of 1933 and the Securities Exchange Act of 1934. Marketing efforts by registered broker-dealers are further regulated under that legislation by the SEC and NASD. So the scope of securities disclosure, antifraud, non-manipulation policies extends to investment company activities, and the marketing of shares in such companies.

In addition, investment companies and mutual funds are regulated by more specialized legislation, primarily the Investment Company Act of 1940, and the Investment Advisers Act of 1940. These laws require separate registration with the SEC of investment companies and investment advisors (even if affiliated with broker-dealer firms). Investment companies must make registration statements disclosing their investment policies, annual reports, and maintain specified accounts and records. The company's investment advisor must be disclosed, with details of its advisory contract, including compensation arrangements. Investment advisers must report their activities, affiliations and background, and relevant financial information prescribed by SEC regulations.

Investment companies are divided into three categories: (1) face amount certificate companies, which offer fixed income bond and debenture securities; (2) unit investment trusts (similar to REITS), offering interests in a fixed block or portfolio of securities; and (3) management companies, which includes all others. The most important investment companies are the latter, especially "open-end" companies or mutual funds. Open-end companies offer shares continuously, with prices reflecting the current net asset value of its portfolio per share, and allow redemption at any time. Closed-end companies have a fixed number of shares outstanding at any time (like most corporations), and their value fluctuates accordingly. In terms of customer investments and popularity, "open-end" companies are much more important than the other varieties, although unit investment trusts (often corporate and municipal bonds) have had considerable play as well. (The Real Estate Investment Trust Act of 1960 created an analogous fixed block real estate investment security [REIT's].)

Investment company assets must be held by a responsible custodian, a stock exchange member, bank, or under other strict safeguards. Officers and employees with access to the securities or cash owned by the company must be bonded.

Capital structures of investment companies are regulated to protect customer interests. For open-end investment companies (mutual funds) no senior securities (debt or preferred stock) may be issued, although bank indebtedness, expenses, and adviser fees are proper charges on the fund's earnings. Closed-end companies may issue one class of debt securities, provided the asset coverage is at least 200 percent, and one class of preferred stock, with asset coverage of at least 300 percent. For all investment companies, there must be an initial net worth of $100,000 before a public offering can be made of its securities.

At least 90 percent of the investment company's net earnings must be distributed to the shareholder's fund each year in order to avoid double taxation, and this ensures that shareholders benefit directly. Internal Revenue Code Section 852(a)(1). Dividends must come, for the most part, from the fund's current or last year's earnings, so that the company is confined, largely, to being a conduit from the fund's security earnings (including accumulated capital gains) to its shareholders. Of course, with an equity portfolio, the larger part of accumulated gains for a mutual fund is likely to be stock value appreciation, rather than direct dividends. On the other hand, a money market mutual fund normally earns interest income only, and remits this directly (with minimum expenses) to shareholders as their dividends.

It must be emphasized, in this connection, that investment company and mutual fund investments (or customer accounts) are not insured. Thus, the risk of loss is real, and falls solely upon the customer-investor. There is no counterpart to FDIC, FSLIC, or NCUSIF insurance for these investments, and SIPC guarantees do not apply to mutual fund or investment company accounts. SIPC guarantees only apply to funds held for customers by brokerage firms or broker-dealers.

Every investment company selects its own investment strategy at the outset, and any significant changes (or dissolution) must be ratified by the majority of shareholders at that time. There are only limited restrictions on managerial discretion within these constraints, however, and there is no obligation to produce any particular level of return (or even to avoid losses). The only enforceable, general obligation is conformity with the advertised investment strategy. But investment companies may not invest more than small percentages in any other single investment company. Investment companies should not make margin purchases of securities, sell securities short, or make commitments to underwrite securities with more than 25 percent of their assets. Beyond these limits, competition among informed investors is the primary discipline to encourage and reward investment company (or mutual fund) managers. The penalties for weaker performance are slow sales of shareholder interests and reduction in growth (for open-end companies or mutual funds) of the resources available for investment, advisory fees, and managerial compensation.

Management has broad latitude within the advertised investment strategy. Most investment companies contract with an investment adviser for management services. Typical fees for this service are ½ to 1 percent annually of the net assets in the investment company's funds. The investment advisor may be a large brokerage firm or its affiliate, or a smaller corporation or partnership. Investment advisers commonly serve a number of funds, and most large brokerage firms now sponsor or use a family of funds or investment companies. A typical range might include separate funds for money market liquidity, corporate bonds, tax-free municipals, international bonds, large corporate stocks, small firm growth stocks, and so forth. Easy and low cost transfer of customer shares may be encouraged within each family of funds to provide more flexibility.

The law requires that at least 40 percent of the board of directors for an investment company be independent (for open-end companies). This means they should not be involved as officers or partners in the company, its investment adviser, a broker-dealer affiliate, as legal counsel, or employed in any other material or business relationship. (For closed-end companies only one independent director is required.) This safeguard is designed to encourage some independence and integrity of management for the fund.

More significant, perhaps, are restrictions on transactions with affiliates. There is potential for abuse in investment companies affiliated with dealer-broker organizations, in that funds might be used for "scalping" or "dumping" less desirable securities, because they are a captive customer. Section 17 of the Investment Company Act attempts to limit such abuses, and tries to assure fair and equal participation for the fund in a broker-dealer's trading activities. On the other hand, SEA Section 27(e) allows investment companies some latitude in the commissions paid to broker-dealers, if these charges are believed to be reasonable for brokerage and research services. The most important discipline, overall, tends to be competition among different funds for customer investment based on their relative performance.

Selling prices are restricted for fund shares to some extent under ICA Section 22. Subsection 22(d) provides that fund shares must be sold at the prospectus price, i.e., resale price maintenance is required by the law. This has been criticized as an encouragement to higher service charges and load fees, and as an overly generous concession to broker-dealer organizations and their sales representatives. But the industry defends this practice as needed for orderly marketing and to provide distribution incentives.

Price levels for the investment company's services to their customer investors are not closely regulated, although an upper limit of 8½ percent on the "reasonable" load charge for investor participation has been established under ICA Section 22(d) through NASD standards. Such load charges are commonly assessed at the "front-end" or entrance into the fund, although funds might impose the charge upon redemption, and there are some "no-load" funds, usually mail-order operations.* Most broker-dealer sales representatives promote mutual funds with front end load charges, because they receive a substantial commission on sales. No load funds are sold largely through advertisement in the financial and general press.

* In addition, the SEC's Rule 12b–1 regulates annual fees charged by investment companies with further implementation by the NASD. Typical fees range between .5 to 1 percent of total assets each year.

It should be emphasized, however, that most money market mutual funds were established with much smaller fees and no load charges, so that prevailing interest rates on money market instruments are passed along to investor customers. This lighter load of charges and fees was based upon the minimal expenses, risk, and management effort required to purchase and maintain such a portfolio. An important reason for the great success of money market mutual funds, which grew faster and to greater aggregate size than equity mutual funds in the late 1970's—early 1980's was their low cost. They became an excellent, reliable investment for customers who could not obtain rising money market interest rates, to the same extent, from commercial banks and thrifts, which were restricted by Regulation Q until the Depositary Institutions Act of October 15, 1982 (which finally allowed money market accounts with comparable interest rates).

A typical portfolio for money market mutual funds would comprise CD's from U.S. and foreign banks, high-grade commercial paper (short-term) from corporations, and/or short-term government securities. Average maturity of this portfolio for MMMF's would be 30–40 days. Such a portfolio is reasonably secure, reliable, and dividend yields float with portfolio yields (minus expenses). There is little danger of such a fund's liquidity or solvency failure—unless there were a major crisis in the domestic or world economy. Normal expenses for such funds average less than 1 percent on assets.

This is a thin margin for operating expenses among financial institutions.

Increasingly important contributors to mutual fund activities are IRA (individual retirement account) and Keogh plan (self-employed income) tax-sheltered investments. (See Chapter VII.) Recent trends in tax law liberalized these opportunities, and a large number of people found it appropriate to make such investments. Mutual funds have taken the lead in recent years in recruiting such investments from the public. But commercial banks and thrift institutions are seeking IRA and Keogh account deposits as well. Insurance companies have been active in this area, too, with annuity and other policies designed for tax-sheltered retirement savings and investment. (See Table VII–1.)

Some wondered about the prospects for money market mutual funds now that banks and thrift institutions compete more effectively with money market deposit accounts, since the DIA of 1982. Much depends on the sustained willingness of brokerage firms (and their MMMF's), independent mutual funds, commercial banks, S & L's, MSB's, and credit unions to offer thinner margin, higher money market yields to their investment customers. If enough of these institutions continue to do so, the remainder have the choice of doing the same and offering competitive yields (and expenses), or losing a significant chunk of liquidity investments or deposits (and the access to clientele that may be associated with such deposits or investments).

A trend of lower interest rates would reduce the net yield to customers (investors or depositors), and beyond a certain point it might seem difficult to narrow the margin for intermediation any further. In the long run, free market competition should keep the expenses for this type of passive, stable liquidity account at lean, moderate levels appropriate to the real rate of interest (plus risk and service costs for intermediation).

For equity-oriented mutual funds or investment companies, prospects are related to the industrial and business economy and its growth. This will depend upon overall macro-economy policy in the leading nations, and revival in the world economy. But investment companies and mutual funds will prosper in that environment so long as they offer a reasonably attractive share in such prosperity for their customer investors.

CHAPTER VI

INSURANCE REGULATION

Insurance companies are important financial intermediaries gathering large funds from the public and business enterprise. Insurance premiums paid on private life, health, property, marine, liability and surety coverage accounted, in the U.S., for roughly 10 percent of national income in 2003. The $4,850 billion assets held by these insurers represented major blocks of institutional investment for the securities industry, real estate and agricultural finance. Their reserve assets provide, along with premium income revenues, the resources from which insurance claims are paid, and the profits or dividends taken by insurance companies for their stockholders and policyholders. In providing these services, insurance companies act as specialized financial intermediaries between those who contract for such risk protection and investment activity, and the business enterprises, farmers, individuals, and real estate projects that use insurance company investment (in the form of bonds, stock, mortgages, and other interests).

The regulation of insurance companies bears a strong resemblance, in part, to the regulation of banks, savings institutions, and securities markets. Insurers must be chartered, meet capital and solvency requirements, and conform to restrictions on their investment portfolios. Their financial adequacy is supervised by Commissions or Departments of Insurance (at the state level of government), so that the public can place greater reliance on their contractual and investment commitments. These regulatory authorities try to limit irresponsible failure of insurers. Fairness in dealing with the public is encouraged, along with limits on misrepresentation or unreasonable discrimination. Standard form contracts are supervised by these agencies to provide more reliable insurance protection, and to minimize over-reaching and fraud.

And yet, unique features distinguish insurance regulation. The wide variety of risks to be insured or protected against requires a much more complicated range of product and contract variations. Rate-making procedures have developed which sometimes inhibit pricing rivalry, although competitive forces do have impact on long run insurance rate levels. Most strikingly, perhaps, insurance regulation is a responsibility of state governments. This represents a dramatic contrast to the federal-state "dual" regulation of banking and thrift institutions, and the largely federal regulation of securities markets. But the state insurance regulation system enjoys substantial momentum, the insurance industry finds major advantages in this tradition, and it will not easily be displaced or changed radically in the near future.*

* But the increase of insurance premiums (of all kinds) in the GNP, *i.e.*, from 6 to nearly 10 percent between 1984–2003, is causing concern. Is all of this increase legitimate or desirable?

Nonetheless, recent competitive trends and inflationary distortions have affected insurance companies, along with other financial institutions. For these reasons, insurance company product offerings, their attractiveness to the public, and the regulation of insurance is better understood in conjunction with banking, thrifts, securities markets, and government policies affecting capital and financial markets generally.

A. DEVELOPMENT OF INSURANCE AND REGULATION

The oldest uses of insurance protection were associated with joint ventures and risk pooling investments for caravans and shipping. Contracts for these purposes can be traced back to ancient Mesopotamia and the Code of Hammurabi. Modern insurance underwriting began with marine risk coverage by medieval Italian merchants, which gradually spread through Europe. As British seaborne commerce expanded in the late 17th century, Lloyd's coffeehouse in London became a convenient focal point for such underwriter contracts with shipowners. Each underwriter at Lloyd's took a portion of the risk in a projected voyage, pledging his unlimited personal liability in support. If the vessel or cargo were lost, each underwriter would be liable up to his portion. This type of insurance coverage was investor-underwriting, and well suited to a merchant city like London with many investors willing to take these risks for a sufficiently profitable premium. The rates or premiums charged reflected current risk exposure, including storm damage, war losses or piracy. The South Sea Bubble of 1718–20, a rapid boom and collapse in joint-stock company prices, had a significant impact in strengthening the role of Lloyd's underwriters, because Parliament promptly outlawed joint-stock companies for underwriting marine insurance risks (except for two companies). In 1774 Lloyd's moved to the Royal Exchange (no longer selling coffee), and their investor-underwriting became more routine with general form policies. Lloyd's received a parliamentary charter in 1871, which recognized and protected their dominant role in British marine insurance, mandated data collection activities (including Lloyd's register of shipping), and allowed their society internal regulatory authority. Bear in mind that Lloyd's underwriters have been willing for a long time to insure a considerable variety of risks, beyond marine insurance, including the most exotic insurable interests, at relatively high premium rates.

Meanwhile, other British and European insurers developed early fire insurance and rudimentary life insurance contracts in the 18th century. Most fire insurance developed on a joint stock company or friendly society basis, among the more prosperous merchants of cities, and it did not much attract the higher profit seeking underwriters of Lloyd's. Early fire insurance insurers also helped sponsor some fire prevention measures and building codes, and local governments occasionally sponsored these insurance companies or mutual organizations. Life insurance evolved even more slowly, partly because mortality experience and survival likelihoods were not well understood. Some tontine contracts and related gambling risks were underwritten, but life insurance, generally speaking, was not really a serious business until the 19th century.

When the United States became an independent nation, insurance companies were among the first chartered corporations, especially in Pennsylvania, New York, and Massachusetts. As in Europe marine and fire insurance developed initially, followed more slowly by limited experiments with life insurance. But because America lacked a major city with extensive merchant wealth, early efforts to transplant Lloyd's-type exchanges of underwriters were not very successful. Joint stock companies proved essential for early U.S. insurance to mobilize enough capital. It was somewhat more difficult also to collect premiums and enforce claims in a federal republic spreading over a large territory, and this gradually encouraged the development of new insurers as other cities grew and prospered.

Table VI–1

U.S. Insurance Facts

Growth of Life Insurance, 1787–2003

	Number of Companies	Insurance In Force	Premiums Received *	Policy Reserves
1759	1			
1787	3			
1820	6	$92.0 thousand		
1835	15	2.8 million		
1850	48	4.7 million		
1870	129	2.0 billion		
1895	67	10.5 billion		$1.0b.
1915	295	21.0 billion	$.8b.	4.4b.
1930	438	106.0 billion	3.5b.	16.0b.
1935	373	98.0 billion	3.7b.	20.0b.
1955	1,107	372.0 billion	12.5b.	75.0b.
1981	1,992	4,063.0 billion	108.0b.	428.0b.
1989	2,350	8,694.0 billion	244.4b.	1,083.7b.
1998	1,563	14,471.4 billion	355.3b.	2,377.4b.
2003	1,123	17,792.4 billion	503.9b.	2,831.6b.
				($3,806b.
				total assets–
				2003)

Other Types of Insurance

Health Care Costs—$17,000b. (2004)—15 percent of GDP

2004   (35% private plans, 5% other private, 17% Medicare, 16% Medicaid and child assistance, 12% gov't programs, and 14% out of pocket)

Property–Liability Insurance

2003   3,330 companies $1,045b. assets $406b. premium receipts $360b. policy holder's surplus

Principal Lines	Premiums Written		
	1981	1990	2003
Automobile Liability (169m. vehicles)	$41.1b.	$95.4b.	$176.8b.
Medical Malpractice	1.3b.	4.0b.	8.8b.
General Liability	6.0b.	18.1b.	n.a.
Fire, Home, Farm and Commercial	23.1b.	44.0b.	91.7b.
Workmen's Compensation	14.6b.	31.0b.	32.9b.
Marine	3.6b.	5.7b.	10.6b.
Surety and Fidelity	1.4b.	2.8b.	4.6b.
Total Property—Liability	$99.3b	$217.8b	$407.6b.

Federal Flood Insurance 2003 $673b. (in force) $1.8b. flood premiums.

SOURCES: J. Owen Stalson, *Marketing Life Insurance: Its History in America,* McMahon Foundation–Irwin, 1969; *1990 and 2004 Life Insurance Factbooks,* American Council of Life Insurance; *Property/Casualty Factbooks, 1991 and 2005,* Insurance Information Institute; *Statistical Abstract of the U.S., 2004– 2005,* Census Bureau (2005).

Early insurance regulation began with Pennsylvania, New York, and Massachusetts, and slowly spread to some other states. It started with restrictions upon out-of-state insurers, and was designed to protect local companies and citizens (Pennsylvania 1810 and New York 1814). New York added a premium tax on out-of-state insurers in 1824, and other states followed with some retaliation. Further requirements included filing of information on out-state companies, powers of attorney for local agents, and minimum capitalization or deposits. Some disclosure and safeguards already existed for in-state companies through the state chartering process, and the community standing of their local leaders. The Married Women's Act of 1840 in N.Y. gave an important boost to life insurance marketing, because it allowed policy proceeds to be paid directly to widows and orphans (free of the deceased husband's creditors). In the 1840's local companies began to be regulated also, and N.Y. passed the first general law on insurance companies in 1849. It provided for filing of information and capital requirements for local insurers, equivalent capital or bonding for out of state insurers, and the separation of life insurance from fire or marine insurance. Access to insurance company books, fines for wrongdoing, and procedures for dissolution followed several years later. Some restrictions were placed on investments to promote more reliable reserve funds. In 1859 N.Y. set up a Department of Insurance under a bonded Commissioner, supported by filing fees to meet expenses.

Massachusetts evolved in a similar direction, with its Married Women's Act in 1844, a Board of Insurance Commissioners in 1855, state valuation of policies in 1856, visitation powers in 1858, and between 1859–67, the leadership of Elizur Wright as Insurance Commissioner. Wright was an important pioneer of American insurance development. He was the son of a minister, trained himself for the ministry, although becoming a mathematics teacher, and later an actuary. Wright's advocacy significantly influenced insurance law, standard policies, and strongly encouraged mutual companies. Other specific reforms traceable to Wright were the first nonforfeiture law for accumulated life insurance premiums in 1861, injunctive authority to correct insurer abuses in 1862, power to halt sales of unsound companies in 1863, along with a dramatic demonstration of vigorous supervision and lobbying. His work helped make insurance policies more reliable, less expensive, and expanded sales of responsible companies over the long run.

Other states followed this trend, including Connecticut and Pennsylvania, and became centers for responsible insurance company development. By 1873 twenty states had set up insurance commissions, departments, or supervision of some sort. Gradually, other states did the same so that by World War I the state insurance regulation system had become virtually nationwide. The quality of supervision varied greatly from state to state, to be sure, but the best regulated states were insurance industry leaders, for the most part, and their policies were cheaper and more reliable in nationwide competition. State capital, bonding and information requirements for out-state insurers were easier for the larger, more successful companies to satisfy, so that leading companies (and, especially, mutual life insurers) which offered a better deal to policyholders were rewarded with faster growth.

Meanwhile, an important legal milestone had been passed in 1868 with the U.S. Supreme Court decision of Paul v. Virginia (S.Ct.1868). In this litigation an insurance agent challenged the constitutionality of a Virginia statute requiring the deposit of $30–50,000 in bonds for out-state fire insurers that he represented. The Court held that neither the privileges or immunities of citizens, nor the commerce power of the federal government, would preclude regulation of insurers from other states in this manner. This landmark decision clearly allowed the states to proceed with regulation of insurance in their best judgment, even though some protection of local interests might be involved.

Insurance marketing expanded greatly since the 1840's, when mutual companies took the lead with somewhat reduced premiums (especially for life insurance), and rapidly expanded agent sales forces. Commissions for agents varied considerably in this era, with some life insurance companies offering as much as 30–50 percent of the initial premium and nothing on renewals, while others offered 10–15 percent of the initial premium and 5 percent on renewals. The latter practice tended to encourage more responsible, financially sound insurance companies, with stronger reserves, and it gave local agents an incentive to keep customers happy over the long run (because the agent's income was tied to renewals). Elizur Wright and the more responsible insurance industry leaders fought hard against high initial commissions and premiums, and they also opposed premium rebates that might weaken an insurer's proper accumulation of reserves.

The number of new insurance companies increased sharply in the 1840's and 1860's, with more frequent failures of weaker companies following. Entry and growth slowed in the 1870's–1880's, but picked up more strongly until the Great Depression. The pricing of life insurance was based on mortality tables, and increased longevity and expanding policy sales made them profitable. Fire, property, and casualty insurance grew substantially also, though in these fields rate-making bureaus became important later in limiting price competition, protecting reserves, and facilitating insurance company profits.

Insurance companies as a whole did not experience any drastic reversal of fortunes in the Great Depression, mainly suffering more policy cancellations and a reduction of premium income. Although a considerable number of mergers occurred, with some discontinuance and failure of smaller companies, the reserves of sound insurance companies were not badly affected. A reduction in policy obligations might even leave sound companies in a stronger financial position, although current expenses had to be reduced in line with lower premium revenues. Loans on life insurance policies increased somewhat, but this did not weaken investment income appreciably. For these reasons, the insurance industry and its regulation were not that seriously affected by the depression period, and nothing comparable to the changes in banking or securities regulation occurred.

Rather, the insurance industry and its state regulatory institutions continued their evolution. World War II and the postwar prosperity brought greatly expanded sales for life insurance, though an increasing proportion of this came to be annuities and group life policies at lower rates. Health and disability insurance became increasingly important, and was marketed often as an adjunct to group life policies. Meanwhile, the gradual expansion of tort and legal liabilities was encouraging an enlargement of property and casualty insurance coverage, with additional lines and types of insurance being written. The varieties of life insurance, endowment, and annuity contracts also proliferated, as "product innovation" became more important for insurance and its marketing.

Over the post-World War II era, there was a substantial flow of new entrants into the insurance business. Life insurance company assets multiplied forty-fold, and property-casualty insurer assets increased even faster in the last twenty years. Profitability remained strong with expanding sales and economic growth, although inflation during the last decades made life insurance less attractive for investment (though useful for protection against risk of death). Leading insurers have grown substantially larger, albeit the ranks of medium-sized and smaller companies have increased. Many new entrants have been smaller companies, however, with limited marketing territories and impact.

The major challenge to this pattern of development came from antitrust enforcement, and United States v. South–Eastern Underwriters Association (S.Ct.1944). The Antitrust Division of the Justice Department had indicted a rate making cartel of 200 insurers for fire and allied lines under the Sherman Act, charging concerted boycotts and restraints of trade to enforce price fixing through state "supervised" rate bureaus. The insurers defended by asserting insurance was not interstate commerce (citing earlier precedents, including Paul v. Virginia), and the District Court granted dismissal. The Supreme Court reversed, holding that the modern insurance business is interstate commerce, and, therefore, that a price fixing cartel, boycotts and restraint of trade would be challenged properly under the antitrust laws. Congress responded promptly with the McCarran–Ferguson Act, 15 U.S.C.A. §§ 1011–1015, which granted antitrust exemption for insurance activities to the extent that they were regulated by state law. In subsequent cases, courts have held coercive boycotts by insurance companies to be antitrust violations and not protected by McCarran–Ferguson. See, for example, United States v. New Orleans Insurance Exchange (E.D.La.1957). On the other hand, where there is comprehensive state insurance regulation, the courts will not inquire into its effectiveness, or excessive rate levels supervised by the states. Ohio AFL–CIO v. Insurance Rating Board (6th Cir.1971) (Douglas dissenting). Thus far, Congress and the courts have allowed the partly industry-oriented regulation of insurance companies to continue as an area of substantial exemption from antitrust law.

For the most part, sources of healthy growth and profitability for the insurance industry have remained operative throughout the postwar era. Life insurance risks have favored insurers with improved longevity, while increased expenses of disability, medical and hospital coverage have been handled with cost plus contracts. Inflation recently limited the attractiveness of life insurance investment policies, although variable annuity and tax-deferral policies were developed, in part, as a response. Property-casualty coverage has grown with costs and inflation, thanks, in some degree, to ample rate increases allowed by many states. Somewhat greater price competition has come to portions of the insurance industry, however, from "direct writer" insurers, which narrowed more traditional sales margins. On the whole, however, premium income for insurers has been growing substantially and allowed considerable profit in the insurance business.

Chart VI–1

Insurance Regulation System

Scope

Insurance Companies—
Life, Annuity, Disability Pensions and Health
Property, Marine, Liability, Surety and Fidelity

State Regulation

Key States and Industry Associations
National Association of Insurance Comm'rs (NAIC)
Trade Groups
Main Themes—
Standard Form Contracts
Capital and Reserves
Investment Regulation
Authorization and Marketing
Rate Filing System
Socialized Risks

Entry, Underwriting and Marketing

Life and Health
Life and Annuity
Groups and Pensions
Health Care
Disability
Property, Marine, Liability, Surety, and Fidelity
Multiple Lines and merger activity

Competition With Other Financial Intermediaries

Banks and Trust Departments
Investment Companies and Mutual Funds
Securities Broker-Dealers
Pension Funds
Government

Industry Regulation

Chartering and Authorization
Chartering requirements
Out-of-state insurers
Agent activities

Potential Regulatory Expansion

State Regulation Problems
Industry Influence on Regulatory Process
Reduced Antitrust Exemption
Financial Service Holding Companies
Insurance Guaranty Funds Solvency Safeguards
Capital, Reserves and Solvency—
Minimum capital
Reserves requirements
Liquidation procedures
Examination and valuation
Rate Making and Filing—
Property-Liability
Prior Approval
Open Competition
Direct Writers
Life and Group
Health and Disability
Standard Contracts—
Standardization
Limits on Harshness or Cancellation
Socialized Risks—
Extreme Costs
Limited Incomes
Unaffordability
Taxation—
Premium taxes
Assessments
Contributions

Federal Regulation

McCarran Act
Antitrust exemption
Socialization of Risk
Social Security
Health Care
Flood Insurance
Crime Insurance
Export Financing

Portfolio and investment management are more sophisticated for insurers in recent years. As insurance companies became large institutional investors, many have become more professional, skillfully diversified, sometimes aggressive, and their portfolio performance is watched carefully. Many insurers did well with higher interest rates and investment earnings. For many insurers, investment profitability became more significant as a means to improved earnings. For some insurers, however, earnings weakened, and a limited number suffered loan losses, with occasional up-surges of insolvencies.

Another aspect of insurance development is the growth and increased sophistication of risk management services. More business enterprises, particularly larger corporations, comprise a sufficient spread of activities to self-insure in some degree. Developing insurance for these organizations requires skillful judgment and collaboration with management, and may require tailor-made pricing and negotiated rates, often with discounts. Even smaller business enterprises become insurance "savvy", particularly in regard to estate-planning and tax avoidance by leaders and executives. More of the market for insurance today is in these areas, which requires better trained, tax-sophisticated, and entrepreneurially minded sales efforts.

B. MAIN FEATURES OF INSURANCE REGULATION

The established system of U.S. insurance regulation is comprehensive, highly developed, with much technical detail. There is a trend toward greater uniformity in statutory provisions, reflecting the influence of key states (including New York, Mass., Penn., Conn., and more recently Wisc., and Calif.), and most importantly, the National Association of Insurance Commissioners (NAIC). The NAIC serves a progressive, consensus building role, and develops a great deal of model statutory language and uniform laws in the insurance area. Some insist that more public interest advocacy is needed within the NAIC, but its impact, in many respects, has been constructive, and consistent with the main themes of American insurance regulation.

1. CHARTERING, ENTRY AND LICENSING

The state insurance departments charter new insurance companies under standards set by local law. These requirements involve minimum capital, financial reporting, disclosures of initial organizers and principals, and acceptance of regulatory obligations. Groups meeting these standards are normally free to enter, without any showing of public convenience or necessity. Most insurers charter themselves in only one state as a primary legal domicile.

For out-of-state insurers seeking to market insurance policies through agents within a state, licensing requirements usually must be satisfied. Agents for service of process and litigation must be designated, capital or bonding requirements met, and any appropriate fees or premium taxes paid. Mail-order-insurance may avoid these requirements, but non-compliance with other state laws could bring sanctions. In most states local agents or brokers could, on occasion, also place "surplus line" business with non-admitted insurers, but only under special restrictions: (i) unavailability of such insurance in the state; (ii) acceptance of legal process, financial data filings, bonding or trust fund requirements, and (iii) premium taxes (often higher than for admitted insurers).

Agents, brokers, and adjusters selling insurance in each state are separately licensed. Written examinations are common, and the trend has been toward some tightening of these requirements.

The effect of licensing requirements is to enforce supervision upon all insurers and sellers of insurance policies within each state. Failure to comply with state insurance laws may justify various penalties, suspension, or revocation of a charter or license. Thus, companies participating in the insurance business are subject to the laws and discipline of every state in which they do business.

2. CAPITAL, RESERVES AND SOLVENCY

Adequate reserves are needed to support insurance company obligations under their contracts. A major theme of state insurance law and regulation is to enforce reasonable reserve requirements. For life insurance companies these reserve requirements are based upon mortality tables and interest accumulation projections, so that normal premium revenues would provide a comfortable flow of resources adequate for these purposes (after expenses are deducted). For property and liability insurers loss reserves and unearned premium reserves must be maintained. The loss reserve is an estimated liability for claims and settlement expenses. Standard formulas or loss ratios are employed. The unearned premium reserve equals the unearned portion of the gross premiums of all outstanding policies at the time of valuation. These requirements are designed to provide adequate resources for expenses and to prevent any insurer insolvency, though care should be taken to limit over-reserve buildup, for this can result in excessive rates. Competition among insurers, if vigorous and healthy, is supposed to limit excessive rates and premiums, while reasonable reserve requirements, if enforced, ensure the availability of funds to meet claims.

Examination of assets and valuation of policies is needed to enforce these reserve requirements, and to make sure that insurance company managers do not dissipate, waste, or encumber assets needed to support policy obligations and solvency. There are obvious dangers of fraud, embezzlement, or bad investment that could put an insurer into insolvency. For these reasons, insurance companies, like banks and other financial institutions, need the discipline of regular and competent examination, and financial accountability. Modern computer technology allows this to be done more effectively, although insurance company examination and valuation routines have not been developed to the same level as bank examination procedures. While insurance companies are not subject to a risk of "runs" or mass withdrawal by depositors, insolvencies do occur among smaller insurers. Most states, therefore, have guaranty funds and insolvency associations to settle claims against insolvent insurers, which assess the costs of failure among surviving companies.

Capital stock and policyholders' surplus represents the equity or ownership interest in an insurance company. The states require paid-in surplus for stock companies, and comparable surplus funds for mutual insurers. These surplus or capital requirements are another financial constraint upon the dissipation of assets, and a limit upon excessive growth of policy obligations (especially for property-liability insurance) relative to surplus and capital accounts. Rules of thumb used for property-liability insurance are that net written premiums should not exceed several times the policyowners' surplus (ratios of 2 to 1, 3 to 1, and perhaps even 4 to 1 are employed). A major purpose of this cushion of surplus or capital is to help offset any unexpected operating losses, above and beyond the other reserves required. In life insurance there is less risk of a wide variance in loss experience, or a bunching of policy claims in any given year, so that less regulation applies to surplus as a constraint upon life insurer growth "capacity" in the short run.

Dividends payable to policyholders have been regulated in some states, along with accumulated surplus. Reserve requirements, in one form or another, can prevent overly generous dividends, but some states have found it desirable to limit surplus accumulations, and thereby encourage reasonable distribution of dividends to policyholders (or, perhaps, stockholders).

Investment regulation is another route toward protecting solvency and maintaining reserves or assets for insurance companies. Overly bold investment strategies could impair financial soundness, and state laws try to limit unwarranted risk and impose some requirements. Although state laws vary considerably, they tend to set limits for investment in different categories. For life insurance companies, earnings and growth performance are more important, so that they are allowed more equity stock investment, along with mortgages. Property-liability insurers need more liquidity, and are given less latitude for equity securities, and usually hold more bonds and government securities. Diversification rules may be employed, along with constraints upon self-dealing and insider lending. However, asset quality supervision is generally not so strict as for commercial banks, or even thrift institutions.

In situations involving fraud, embezzlement, or dissipation of assets or reserves through irresponsible management, most state insurance authorities could take action to suspend or revoke charters or licenses, and, if necessary, impose liquidation and receivership. However, insurance examination is not as systematic, well-developed, or regular as with bank-style examination. Some states have enacted the Uniform Insurers Liquidation Act, which provides more fairness in allocating claims among the creditors of different states. But the NAIC was relatively late in seeking to strengthen accountability procedures.*

New and tougher Risk–Based Capital requirements (RBC's) were developed in the early-mid 1990's as Model Acts by the NAIC that brought significant progress, and enhanced capitalization for life, property and casualty, and later, health insurance companies. In addition, the NAIC developed an Insurance Regulatory Information System (IRIS), which includes Financial Analysis Solvency Tools (FAST), to flag attention on troubled companies. Increasingly used, these measures facilitate financial review and earlier corrective action (analogous to CAMEL ratings and tighter capital standards for banks and thrifts). A reduced rate of insurance company insolvencies has been achieved. In the years 1989–94 insurance company insolvencies totaled 389 (an average of 57 annually—with 170 life and 212 "P & C"); in 1995–96 there were only 13 insolvencies each year (4 life and 9 "P & C").

Furthermore, the NAIC has pressed state insurance commissioners to improve their oversight and staffing through an accreditation program. Most

* Insurance company failures increased in the late 1980's-early 1990's, but were still less frequent than banks or thrifts. All 50 states now have Insurance Guaranty and Insolvency Funds financed by assessments (with more or less taxpayer backup), but not all lines of insurance are fully guaranteed. NAIC accreditation standards were being tightened up in the 1990's, partly under the pressures of proposals to federalize solvency protection. Capital adequacy greatly improved, too.

State insurance departments are now "accredited," with improved capabilities.* It will be interesting to see how these developments work out, their transparency, and collaboration with bank and securities regulators, and regulators in other countries.

3.   RATE MAKING AND FILINGS

The general guideline for insurance regulators with respect to rates has been adequate, not excessive, and not unreasonably discriminatory. Rate levels for property and liability insurance are regulated in most states under rating laws. These laws normally require "adequate" rates in light of past and prospective loss experience, reasonable margins for underwriting, and overall financial conditions for insurers. Yet rates should not be "excessive" and provide too much premium income. Hopefully, competition among insurers limits insurance prices, if this is allowed to operate. For mutual insurers, where policyholders get the benefits of unneeded surplus and dividends, there is a further corrective for overly generous rates. This helps explain a tendency for most state insurance departments to emphasize adequacy, which has been criticized by consumer advocates as leading to more expensive coverage (at least for ordinary policyholders). Insurers, however, stress the dangers of cutthroat competition, rate wars, and the possibility of inadequate reserves or insolvency.

* Increasingly, state insurance commissioners have corrective order authority, together with powers for conservatorship, rehabilitation, or when appropriate, liquidation.

Sensible classification according to risk experience is an established insurance practice, and regulatory standards take this into account. Thus, insurance regulation merely tries to prevent "unreasonable discrimination." Obviously, the creation of preferred risk categories can be a means to reducing rates and premium income, so that regulators try to supervise (at least loosely) such developments. On the other hand, certain risk classifications have become controversial with consumers, such as younger automobile drivers and high rates. In these matters regulators tend to follow industry trends, and they rarely interfere with risk classification used by insurers.

Rate bureaus are employed widely for property and liability insurance. The most commonly used model rate filing law is a compromise between "prior approval" and "file and use", which allows filed rates to be used after a limited interval, unless specifically disapproved by the state authorities. Unusually low rate filings have been challenged and litigated by bureau insurers in some states. This framework has permitted reductions in rates by some insurers, when they believe this to be in their interest for expanding sales. Other states require mandatory membership in rate bureaus or insist upon regulatory approval, which involves more cartelistic pricing. On the other hand, many states employ permissive rate filing laws (on some lines of insurance at least), under which insurers are free either to follow or not follow bureau rate levels.

Even in these states, though, bureau rates tend to be influential.

Direct writers have become more important in some lines of insurance. While mail order insurance (sometimes TV advertised) is one form of direct writing, that dispenses with commission agents and expenses, this is not a very substantial fraction of the insurance sold. Much more significant as direct writers are large insurance companies such as State Farm Mutual, Allstate, Liberty Mutual and Nationwide Mutual, which use exclusive agent networks, with bigger sales volume, direct billing procedures, and lower commissions. Direct writers are active with automobile insurance, and are spreading into residential, home, and some commercial property insurance.

With respect to life insurance, rate practices have been different. Generally speaking, life insurers are free to set their own policy rates and prices, except, in some states, for group rates. This reflects great variability of risk, including age, sex, and occupation, together with different sizes of policies, and other relevant circumstances. Another factor has been a strong role for mutual insurance companies in the earlier, formative years of life insurance development. Indirectly, of course, life insurance rates are regulated through reserve requirements and solvency supervision. Unduly low rates and premium revenue undermine solvency for a life insurer. But normally it is only large, strong insurance companies (often mutuals) that reduce prevailing rate levels somewhat for individual life policies.

On the other hand, group life insurance is much cheaper, with lower marketing costs than ordinary individual policies. By 2003 about 42 percent of the life insurance in force consisted of group policies. And yet much of the individual life insurance sold today goes to large face value policyholders, for whom tax sheltering and estate planning is emphasized, where the role of selling agents becomes more like investment counseling. Commission expenses can be reduced for larger policies, and this is reflected in negotiating coverage and rates.

Various kinds of annuity policies (with fixed or variable returns, perhaps linked to equity security markets) are offered as vehicles for investment/insurance. This has become an expanding part of the life insurance business; 70 million people were covered by life insurance pension plans in 1998. Banks have offered increasing competition in annuity investments, so that their share in this area has expanded, too.

Health and disability insurance is an outgrowth of the life insurance business, generally without formalized rate bureaus. Group policies and coverage are predominant in this area. Standard cost plus markups have become customary for these group policies, although discounts are sometimes conceded by insurers to obtain the group life insurance coverage commonly associated with an employers' package of fringe benefits for employees. Health Maintenance Organizations (HMO's) are increasingly important, however, as vehicles for cost control and means to wider affordability, although their restrictions on access to procedures are controversial with patients.

Ocean marine insurance is another branch of coverage where rating bureaus do not normally govern. This reflects diverse risks and strong international competition, where insurers want flexibility. Inland marine insurance, however, is commonly regulated through rate bureaus, along with the bulk of property-liability coverage.

4. FINANCIAL REPORTING

While state enforced financial reporting is essential to identify insolvent insurers, some insurers, especially in the life area, would prefer more accounting leeway to show stronger growth and profit performance. Certain consumer advocates, on the other hand, want better profit data (including investment income) in order to limit premiums and rate increases, particularly for property and liability insurance. The American Institute of Certified Public Accounts has developed more liberal accounting guidelines for life insurance companies, which should be welcome to some of them. For the property-liability portion of the industry, however, accounting procedures are more controversial, and involve the issue of rate making policies. And now that the Gramm–Leach Financial Modernization Act of 1999 allows financial conglomerates into insurance, securities, and banking, there are needs for greater coordination of financial reporting across all three industries.

5.   STANDARD CONTRACTS AND CUSTOMER PROTECTION

A major achievement of insurance regulation has been considerable standardization of the more common insurance contracts, such as conventional life insurance and home-fire protection. Through a blend of regulatory pressure, responsible company leadership, and market competition, the harsher features of earlier insurance contracting were eliminated. Non-forfeiture provisions and surrender values for life insurance, the standard fire policy, and limitations upon cancellation treatment are examples of this effort. On the other hand, conflicting pressures for insurance product innovation, new kinds of coverage, economical and low-cost premiums, marketing incentives and commissions encourage policy variation. While insurance departments and consumer groups can monitor basic policies fairly easily, it is difficult to review provisions for every contract and all lines of insurance, including commercial and business property, liability, marine, fidelity, and surety coverage. For business insurance, however, we presume enough competence to negotiate contracts intelligently, so that consumer protection efforts are most important for basic policies widely used by the general public.

State insurance departments also regulate unfair trade practices. The NAIC Model Unfair Trade Practice Bill has been influential in defining unfair methods of competition and deceptive acts or practices. They include misrepresentation, false advertising and financial statements, intimidation, coercion, boycotts, defamation, unfair price discrimination, commission rebates to customers, questionable stock operations, suspicious advisory board contracts, and unsound self-dealing by company officials. State insurance departments have the responsibility of investigating consumer complaints with respect to rates, claims cancellations, dividends, underwriting, misrepresentation and fraudulent activities and other grievances. Limited efforts along these lines are made in most states, although some insurance regulators also believe they are responsible for limiting excessive competition or unsound practices that might undermine insurer solvency.

C. SOCIALIZED RISK COVERAGE

Not all risks should be insured. Many are bearable adversities of living, better and less expensively absorbed in the ordinary course of business or family life. A considerable range of risks has been insured, however, at affordable rates by commercial private insurers. This is the established private insurance system—with life, annuity, health, disability, property, marine, liability, surety and fidelity coverage. But some risks are insured or compensated, in part at least, by government insurance or relief programs. This is the area of socialized risk coverage, which, in a pluralistic society, is often somewhat controversial.

Table VI–2

Socialized Insurance

Funded Government Insurance or Compensation Programs

Old Age Survivors, Disability, and Health Insurance (OASDHI)

Railroad Retirement (Federal)

Unemployment Compensation (Federal and states)

Workmen's Compensation (States)

Temporary Disability Income Benefits (some states)

Government Employee Pensions

Military Pensions, Benefits

[Proposals to Expand National Health Insurance (NHI)]

Crime Insurance (Fed. Insur. Admin.)

FAIR plans (Riot reinsurance)

Flood Insurance (Federal)

Crop Insurance (Federal and states)

Financial Institution Insurance (FDIC, FSLIC, NCU-SIF)

Securities Investor Protection Corporation (SPIC)

Pension Benefit Guaranty Corp. (PBGC)

War Risk Marine Insurance

Assigned Risk Plans for State Auto Insurance

State Auto Insurance (a few states)

State Title Insurance (a few states)

State Property Insurance (some states)

State Solvency Insurance Funds

Government Assistance Programs

Aid for Dependent Children (AFDC)

Assistance to the Blind (AB)

Aid to the Permanently and Totally Disabled (APTD)

Food Stamps

Black Lung Program

Veteran's Benefit Programs

Student Loan Programs

Housing and Urban Development Subsidies

Disaster Relief and Credit Subsidies

Superfund (chemical wastes)

International Aid (Bilateral)

IMF, World Bank, and IDB Contributions

Eximbank

Export Credit Guarantees

The reasons for government insurance or relief may involve heavy cost or extreme risk that most private parties cannot readily absorb, even through private insurer risk pooling. Exceptional natural disasters, earthquakes, massive floods, insurrection and war costs are examples. Social costs from depressions and heavy unemployment, export financing and international credit risks, chemical waste disposal or drastic accidents at nuclear power plants also illustrate these problems. Other reasons for government insurance or relief include limited incomes and lack of affordability, which have prompted old age and survivors insurance, medical care and hospitalization for the elderly and poor, workmen's accident or sickness compensation, aid to the blind and disabled, poverty relief and assistance, food stamps, and so on. In these government programs it may not be easy to draw neat lines between the "insurable" portion, which could be supported by reasonable assessments and contributions related to benefit and risk, and the "relief" or transfer payment portion supported by tax revenues. Log-rolling politics in pluralist societies, especially with affluence, have found difficulties in setting limits on socialized insurance and relief programs. There is disagreement on the extent to which they should be fully funded by intended beneficiaries, whether progressive taxes or internal subsidies should be involved, and the degree to which general budget revenues should be drawn upon for these purposes. Broader affluence clearly encourages generosity. Ultimately, though, excessive liberality for social insurance and relief increases tax loads, may strain incentives for the heavily taxed, and divert investment and tax resources from capital formation and economic growth into income maintenance and welfare programs. Social insurance also competes with other government spending priorities. In other words, there are some limits to social affordability, even for humane and beneficent purposes.

Under-funding is not uncommon in socialized insurance programs, along with a gradual expansion of benefits and beneficiaries. Thus, even with socialized insurance designed to be self-financing, such as Old Age and Survivor's Insurance (the core of "social security"), additional benefits and disability assistance were tacked on, along with generous inflation-indexed cost of living increments, that made this program more expensive. Meanwhile, increased longevity, uncertain economic growth, and a bunching of projected retirements for "baby boomers" in the 21st century, make some of the funding assumptions unrealistic. Since social security and medicare are the biggest single elements of socialized risk protection and transfer payment activity, their handling carries special significance. But social security financing is merely part of a continuing struggle over spending priorities, tied in with budget and tax controversies. Few doubt that government should provide a basic floor of social insurance protection, or what President Reagan called the "social safety net." The problem is to achieve reasonable consensus upon its content and distribution among competing constituencies and their alliances. No one can deny the importance of these issues, because about 10 percent of the gross national product is involved in government insurance and relief programs (federal, state and local), which is roughly compared to the total of all insurance premiums paid through private insurance companies (the latter amounted to roughly 10 percent of GNP in the early 2000's).

D. POSSIBLE REFORMS AND FEDERAL REGULATION

Modern insurance protection in the U.S. is a blend of private insurance company activity regulated by the states, and largely federal social insurance and relief programs. Many proposals for improving this system emphasize the shortcomings of state regulation, and doing something, one way or another, about social insurance, its size, benefit distribution, or financing support. Changes in federal programs, stronger regulation (federal or states), and greater antitrust discipline (with less exemption under the McCarran–Ferguson Act) are common proposals.

1. SHORTCOMINGS AND REFORMS

Proposals for changing insurance regulation and social insurance come from three directions: (i) consumer oriented proposals to reduce excess profits, prices, and waste, and expand benefits for the public; (ii) conservative proposals to reduce socialized risk protection, lower tax support, and increase contributions from beneficiaries; and (iii) technical-minded proposals from moderate experts that blend specific elements from each of the foregoing, and emphasize improved spending discipline and efficiency.

Automobile insurance, its growing cost, wasteful litigation, and limited net compensation has received criticism for many years. Auto insurance premiums accounted for 1.5 percent of the GNP in 2003 or $176 billion, and less than half of this amount goes to pay valid claims for injury and damage. Litigation costs, selling expense and commissions, fraudulent and nuisance claims, and administrative overhead use up some 50–60 percent. Various proposals for no fault liability (or at least reduced liability) are made to cut the litigation and nuisance burden (e.g. "whiplash" injuries) somewhat, but these ideas have been implemented only to a partial degree. Major cuts in premiums probably would entail reductions in claims benefits and trial lawyers strongly resist any drastic changes in tort liability. (With perfect information reasonable claims could be processed more efficiently, but bargaining conflicts and litigation make this difficult.) Part of the cost burden also results from inflated medical and hospitalization expenses, together with expensive automobiles, parts and repairs.*

Rate bureau and cartel pricing practices in the property-liability area have been criticized. While direct writer competition has helped in many states for some lines of insurance, this discipline could be broadened. Mandatory rate bureau pricing might be outlawed, either by state or federal legislation (e.g.

* Many states recently have tried to limit or roll back auto insurance rates, with great resistance from insurer lobbies. In some areas, costs and rates seem clearly excessive, but a serious solution requires a combined effort on expenses, broad-ranging tort "reforms", and improved insurance supervision.

McCarran Act amendments to eliminate their anti-trust exemption).

In the life insurance area other financial institutions wanted to enter which could narrow sales margins and commissions somewhat further. Until 15 years ago only some MSB's and credit unions offered life insurance policies. But now many thrifts and commercial banks sell annuities and/or some life insurance, and more competition results. Yet, it should be emphasized, reasonable life insurance reserves have to be maintained, in any event, by new competitors. Larger banks and financial institutions will probably find it easier, therefore, simply to make acquisitions of life insurance companies, and perhaps expand their sales (and absorb their profits).* This is what Gramm–Leach "reforms" achieved in allowing financial service conglomerates in 1999.

Industrial life insurance policies (small value policies, with high expenses and commissions) have been a target of criticism for several generations. But their importance has declined substantially, with increasing worker incomes and enlarged group life insurance coverage. Credit life insurance has even greater selling and commission expense, with

* Some states recently began in the 1990's to allow banks into insurance underwriting or marketing (some via special affiliates). Major BHC's pushed strongly for such authority as beachheads for expanded activities. But most insurers, and especially independent insurance agents, feared these incursions, and lobbied to limit them. (See Chapter VIII for more discussion.) Bankers contended that economies of integration or scope may be involved, yet insurance interests worried about displacement effects, especially in marketing.

low payout benefits, and has been extensively criticized. Some suggest minimum payout requirements to reduce credit life insurance charges.

Health insurance costs have been increasing rapidly, along with inflation in medical and hospital charges. Private insurers do not have enough incentive to resist this overall inflationary pressure, because of their cost-plus service contracts. But the problem of cost containment for health care is broader, and politically difficult. It involves larger outlays for socialized health care (medicare, medicaid, and government support for hospitals and medical research), speciality certification and high charges for medical services, malpractice litigation, defensive medicine, expensive drugs, and substantial waste and duplication in hospitals. Even so, many complain of inadequate health care for a minority without sufficient health insurance or government supported medical and hospitalization care. Therefore, proposals to expand socialized health insurance have been made, including at least catastrophic insurance coverage and a basic floor of health insurance for all citizens. Such enlarged care would be expensive, and additional tax revenues required, unless the waste in present practices can be eliminated. In the meantime, HMO's have been performing some of the gatekeeper and cost-control responsibilities under "moderate" and "lower income" health insurance plans. And the federal government tried to limit medicare-medicaid expenses with incomplete success and considerable bickering. All of these inter-related problems make health care

and insurance controversial and awkward politically, as the country learned in the Clinton and Bush
presidencies.

Another complaint of consumer advocates is that
insurance company rates on policies or premium
charges are not sufficiently reduced for investment
income on reserves and other assets. They contend,
in other words, that profits and executive compensation (even for mutual companies) are more generous than necessary for adequate reserves. The
growth of insurance companies, with some new
entrants, reflects this fact, they argue. Insurance
industry people deny these contentions, and say
insurance industry returns are not exceptional, or
at least that rates of return are justified by risk
factors in a competitive economy. At issue is a basic
disagreement over the effectiveness of price competition in this regulated industry.

From a conservative standpoint and that of the
insurance industry, the present state regulatory
system functions reasonably well. The main problems of cost increase are external forces, i.e., tort
litigation, excessive awards and risks, together with
inflated medical care, auto repair, and prices generally. They view diversity in premiums, policies, and
service as part of healthy market competition over
the long run.

Conservatives find more problems, and greater
waste, generally speaking, with socialized insurance
and government relief programs. They insist that
log rolling politics has carried these efforts to ex-

cess, and that social security, medicare, food stamps, welfare, and other programs need pruning to offset over-spending. Hence, the major task of insurance reform is to discipline public sector insurance and relief programs, not private insurers who already meet a market test for performance.

There is sharp conflict between the opposing camps on these issues. Some experts take a middle view, finding considerable waste, overpricing, and generous profit in much of the private insurance industry, yet condemning socialized insurance for appreciable waste, under-funding, and an aggregate contribution to government deficits and inflation. The current literature on insurance regulation has ample expressions of all these viewpoints.

2. FEDERAL REGULATION

The state regulated insurance system has strong conservative momentum, with great industry influence. It has resisted federal regulation, and even antitrust enforcement. Most insurance industry people question the need and desirability for any major federal regulation. On the other hand, a considerable range of federal insurance programs has been accumulated (including social security, medicare, unemployment compensation, military and government employee pensions, crime and riot insurance, flood and crop insurance, disaster relief, FDIC, NCUSIF, SIPC, PBGC, export credit guarantees, and war risk marine insurance).

Under the Federal Emergency Management Agency (FEMA), the Federal Insurance Administration already exists to supervise flood and riot insurance, and provides limited planning efforts. The U.S. Fire Administration conducts training and research activities within FEMA, and the Mitigation and Research Office deals with earthquake and civil defense plans. These organizations could be expanded into a more active insurance supervision and coordinating effort, at least for property and casualty insurance. The Department of Transportation also does studies on automobile insurance, and the Federal Trade Commission has published a few reports on insurance.

An interesting precedent for limited federal regulation of insurance is the Risk Retention Act of September 25, 1981. This was prompted by manufacturing industry concern about the expanding burden of product liability litigation and insurance costs. This legislation facilitates the establishment of manufacturer self-insurance groups on a nationwide basis, so that risk management can be developed more efficiently, at lower costs by industries affected with product liability risks.

There have been other proposals for selective federal regulation to deal with particular problems. Federal "no fault" insurance for automobile liability claims was suggested some years ago, but the states handled this issue with a varied range of legislation, or no action at all.

The McCarran–Ferguson Act of 1946 is another example of selective regulation in a way, although its goal was to largely insulate state insurance regulation and rate bureaus from federal antitrust prosecution. The McCarran Act exemption can be reduced to allow more direct writer competition, and provide encouragement for self-insurance groups in other areas. Mandatory participation in rate bureaus could be made unlawful this way.

Selective federal regulation, at this stage, is the most likely method by which major changes could be made in the present pattern of state regulation. But this may require a more consumer oriented Congress and President than existed in most of the 1980's and 1990's. However, we must recall that insurance industry groups have urged "friendly" federal regulation at times as an alternative to legislation that seemed more threatening. Such proposals were made in the later 1860's as a response to state law restrictions, but Paul v. Virginia inhibited that approach for many years. More recently, the Research Institute of the College of Insurance (funded by some leading insurance companies) offered a tentative suggestion for federal insurance regulation in the fall of 1976, when it seemed possible that a more consumer oriented Congress and President could be elected. In 1975 a White House task force also had proposed repeal of the McCarran Act, and its replacement with federal standards for state regulation of insurance. In this context, the Research Institute suggested a Model Bill, with more limited revision of the McCarran Act, allowing substantial joint preparation of cost, risk, and reserve data by insurance company associations, and preserving the opportunity for state regulation at rates that were adequate, not excessive, and not unreasonably discriminatory. This suggests the insurance industry will seek to retain as much as possible of the present state regulatory system that is favorable to insurers, one way or another.

While a more consumer-oriented system of insurance regulation could be installed, over time, at the federal level, the history of other financial industries suggests that some degree of industry-friendly regulation is hard to avoid over the long run. Consumer advocates will press for their reforms, but the insurance industry's track record for influencing its own regulatory environment has been reasonably successful. Nonetheless, sparked by a recent increase in insurance company insolvencies, Rep. John Dingell proposed in 1991 a national insolvency protection system (a Federal Insurer Solvency Corporation—FISC), funded by insurers with stronger supervision and enforcement powers. In 1991 Sen. Howard Metzenbaum also proposed a federal Insurance Regulatory Commission (IRC), to set minimum capital and surplus standards. Several General Accounting Office (GAO) reports carefully probed the problems of insurance company insolvencies.

But the NAIC moved forward as well, with stronger solvency and risk-based capital proposals, the IRIS accounting system, and a new certification program for state insurance departments. Results so far have been considerable, with capital enhanced, and the frequency of insolvencies declining. If any significant enlargement of the solvency problem develops, however, a push for federal regulation and/or tougher NAIC action may be expected.

A bigger challenge to the state oriented insurance regulatory tradition is the new opportunity for banking-securities-insurance industry holding companies. When the Gramm–Leach Financial Modernization Act of 1999 authorized Financial Service Companies to have subsidiaries in all three fields together, it contemplated regulation of each field in their present form. Banking is regulated mainly by the Federal Reserve, OCC, FDIC, and to a modest extent, by state banking regulators; securities markets are regulated mainly by the SEC, NASD, stock and options-trading exchanges; insurance is regulated mainly by the state insurance departments and their commissioners, along with the National Association of Insurance Commissioners (NAIC). The increasing "leadership role" of the NAIC (under prodding by Congressional watchdogs and GAO reports) during the 1990's is remarkable as a regulatory achievement.

But we need to better harmonize financial accounting, oversight, and responses to problems (such as financial holding company failures; mergers involving foreign banks, insurers, and/or securities firms; tax treatment for these conglomerate enterprises; difficulties posed by tax havens and claims for privacy; illegal and drug money laundering; and speculative capital flows in world markets).

A serious complication with the NAIC-state insurance regulation system in its present form is the lack of speedy, national level decision-making for insurance policy. The Fed, OCC, FDIC, and SEC can work together within a few days for emergencies. The insurance industry regulators really need comparable-rapid decision-making. A wide range of crises and messy challenges probably will force more national coordination of insurance regulation in some form or other. A transitional arrangement might be a 3 to 5 member National Insurance Coordinating Board, with a chairman appointed by the president that coordinates NAIC activities. Another variant could be a Federal Insurance Commission (FIC) appointed by the president to coordinate and supervise the NAIC (like the SEC loosely supervises and works with the NASD and the securities exchanges). How this works out will depend on the particular political leaders in the White House, Congress, the financial industries, and the other financial regulators (Sec. Treas., Fed Chair, Comptroller, FDIC Chair, SEC Chair, etc. Finally the insurance industry may want a stronger, more equal voice in federal financial markets and policies (more comparable to the banking and securities industries). Without a strong federal insurance agency, the banking and securities agencies dominate policy at the national level for these industries.

An interesting development over the least 10 years has been international insurance supervisory collaboration. The International Association of Insurance Supervisors (IAIS) was formed in 1994, with a Secretariat now located at the Bank for International Settlements (BIS) in Basel, Switzerland. The IAIS promotes principles and standards on insurance supervision, together with training, textbooks, case studies, and issue papers. IAIS tries to collaborate with the IMF, World Bank, and International Accounting Standards Board. Recent topics for discussions have been natural catastrophes, terrorist disasters, growing litigiousness, capital adequacy, insolvency, bankruptcies, reinsurance, money laundering and e commerce. By 2003 a total of 107 countries were represented in the IAIS. Their impact, along with IOSCO, the BIS, IMF, and World Bank will be to gradually improve accountability, responsible performance, and resiliency in global insurance markets. (The NAIC in the U.S. actively promotes and encourages these IAIS developments.)

3.   BANKING AND INSURANCE CONTROVERSIES

Meanwhile, beginning with Garn bill proposals in 1983–84 to allow interstate financial conglomerates (including insurance), elements of the banking industry sought insurance underwriting and/or marketing powers. Although insurance companies and independent insurance agents resisted this effort, and the U.S. Senate rejected bank insurance powers by a lop-sided majority in 1984, insurance authority remained a goal for some banking interests. Gradually, a few states began to allow banks to sell or underwrite insurance. Comparable legislation was offered in other states, along with recurrent bills in Congress to allow financial service holding companies.* But few experts believed any major integration between banking and insurance could come quickly.

A "turf war" over boundaries and diversification among commercial banks and thrift institutions raged for 15 years since the early 1980's. When failures became widespread among banks and thrifts in the late 1980's, most states relaxed their restrictions on interstate banking. Later big banks won further branching relaxation under the Riegle–Neal Act in 1994 (see Chapters III and IV).

In this context, many believed that bank-insurance interpenetration could only come incrementally. Recent OCC rulings attempted to widen bank powers and allow more insurance activities by banks. U.S. Supreme Court decisions like Nationsbank v. VALIC in 1995, where the court allowed banks to sell annuity insurance policies, and Barnett Bank v. Nelson in 1996, where the court overruled a Florida law attempting to limit bank sales of insurance in small towns (in conflict with an older federal statute), illustrated how gradual opening of insurance markets could occur by regulatory and court decisions. A complication for the insurance industry was that no strong federal regulatory

* For example, in 1991 the Bush administration proposed general authority for "universal-style" financial service holding companies (allowing bank, insurance, and securities affiliates), but Congress did not agree. Later the Clinton Administration endorsed proposals along this line, but it was not until Gramm–Leach in 1999 that Congress accepted this opportunity for financial service holding companies.

agency (like the Federal Reserve, OCC, or SEC) existed to represent their interests; those Federal regulators allowing banks to expand into insurance activities were the *banking* agencies (especially the OCC, and to a lesser extent, the Federal Reserve).

Why did some banks and BHC's want insurance underwriting or marketing authority and powers? Many banks feared consolidation, retrenchment, and computerization pressure, and believed that financial service operations could be leaner with fewer employees. Accordingly, some banks favored expansion into insurance as an offset growth channel, even though this came at the expense of insurance agents (and, to some extent, insurance companies). In addition, some banks saw economies of integration for banking, asset management, and customer services (including insurance). While most smaller banks would get little growth from insurance, a sizable number of large BHC's could make profitable mergers with insurance companies as financial service holding companies. Remember that 72 percent of U.S. bank deposits in 2003 were held by the largest 100 U.S. bank organizations; many of these were potential acquiring firms, on the lookout to buy insurance companies at good prices.

Many insurance industry experts, however, saw less bank expansion potential into the insurance field. Most independent insurance agents, however, fear that many ordinary auto, home, life, and health care policies could be sold in bank lobbies. Over time, they worry, that traditional independent insurance agents could be marginalized and replaced by insurance policies sold in bank lobbies, or tied in with bank loans, title insurance, checking account, annuity sales, and mutual fund services offered by banks. For these reasons independent insurance agents (hundreds of thousands of them) resisted any Glass Steagall reforms that allow banks to enter freely and take over insurance marketing. From their viewpoint, such a banking takeover would be a "death sentence" for independent insurance agents—that only benefits less than a hundred large BHC organizations. Life insurance sales slowed in recent years, and banks were less suited for sophisticated business and estate planning arrangements (that need to be carefully tailored for client needs). For group life policies, margins are thinner, and group policies are often packaged with health insurance for larger employers (and often tied in with HMO's). These areas may be less appropriate for bank marketing, although some BHC's might find profitable mergers with selected life insurance companies. Nonetheless, annuity policies and investments were becoming attractive sales vehicles for large banks in the insurance area. In the diverse network of property and casualty insurance, with many specialized lines of insurance and thinner markets, banks would not find many large scale markets. Only the auto and home insurance markets offer major marketing opportunities for standardized policies, and plenty of insurance competition already exists in these areas. Thus, it would seem that the main potential for BHC's in the insurance industry is not so much large sales increases for policies, but rather in selected merger opportunities with stronger insurance companies (or alternately, under-priced insurance companies with low stock prices that allow profitable mergers). From this perspective, however, financial service holding companies could be formed just as well by strong insurance companies acquiring BHC's as by BHC's acquiring insurance companies.

Finally, with respect to socialized insurance, transfer payments, and "excessive" spending outlays, these are big federal budget and tax policy issues. (Almost 10 percent of the U.S. gross national product is now involved in government or "socialized insurance" programs in one form or another. This compares to about 10 percent of GNP that flows through the private insurance industry. Many insist that as much, if not more waste occurs through these government programs as in the private insurance industry regulated by the states. The proper guideline for any government outlay, regulation, tax subsidy, insurance or guarantee program is that net social benefit should result, and that government intervenes only when it improves the marketplace. The political process is supposed to resolve these questions responsibly, but the disorderly, sometimes incomplete compromises of recent years are disturbing. Unfortunately, there are major, unresolved budget problems for the U.S. with respect to long-term social security and pension funding, government subsidized disability insurance, nursing homes, medicare, medicaid, and overall health care and its insurance. But, these budget and government financing issues are dealt with also in the next two chapters, Pension Fund Regulation, and Controversies and Prospects.

CHAPTER VII

PENSION FUNDS, RETIREMENT ACCOUNTS AND SOCIAL SECURITY

Pension funds, retirement accounts, and social security benefits are an increasingly important part of the economy. From relatively modest beginnings with private pensions before the social security system was established in 1935, the benefits paid under these arrangements have grown, as a share of U.S. GNP, from .6 percent in 1940 to 3.9 percent in 1960, reached 8.2 percent in 1980, and could be 9 or 10 percent now. (See Table VII–1.) Reserve assets held for pensions and retirement accounts are growing substantially, and pension funds (in one form or another) are major financial intermediaries. In 2003 private, state and local government pension funds held about $10,000 billion assets. If social security were funded comprehensively, its current benefits might need another $10,000 billion assets (but social security is financed mainly with current payroll taxes, and only limited trust fund reserves). Thus, the collection of funds for pensions, retirement, and social security are major elements in the network of financial intermediation and saving for prosperous industrial societies like the United States.

Table VII-1

U.S. Pension Facts

Growth of Pension Benefits, 1940-2003 (millions)

Year	Private Plans	Public Plans	OASI	Total	Percent of GNP
1940	$ 140	328	35	503	.6
1960	$ 1,720	2,997	10,667	15,393	3.9
1980	$35,177	37,379	105,074	177,650	8.2
1988	$125,00	75,000	206,000	406,000	8.4
2003	n.a.	n.a.	470,800	n.a.	n.a.

Pension Fund Assets and Reserves, 1950-2003 (millions)

Year	Life Insurer Plans	Other Private Plans	R.R. Retirement	Federal Civilian	State and Local	Social Security (OASDI)
1950	$ 5,600	6,452	2,553	4,343	5,154	13,721
1960	$ 18,850	33,138	3,740	10,790	19,600	22,613
1970	$ 41,175	97,011	4,598	23,922	58,200	38,068
1980	$ 165,845	256,898	2,086	75,802	185,226	26,453
1986	$ 440,555	826,300	6,265	167,381	437,229	46,861
1989	$ 878,460	1,169,000	8,906	225,963	620,000(e)	162,968
1994	$ 878,460	2,356,400	12,629	358,012	1,151,000	436,385
1998	$1,608,000	4,479,000	18,600	479,000	2,370,000	762,000
2003	$1,744,000	4,194,000	24,200	960,000	2,284,000	1,530,700

Growth of Pension Coverage, 1940-2003

(thousands of people)

Year	Life Insurer Plans	Other Private Plans	R.R. Retirement	Federal Civilian	State and Local	Social Security (OASDI)
1940	695	3,565	1,349	745	1,552	22,900
1960	5,475	17,540	1,654	2,703	5,160	91,496
1970	10,580	25,520	1,633	3,624	8,591	120,014
1980	26,080	n.a.	1,532	4,459	13,900	153,632
1986	n.a.	n.a.	1,268	4,938	15,426	164,438
1994	n.a.	n.a.	1,084	5,340	17,000	182,179
2003	[108,000 combined]		n.a.	5,241	17,264	192,400

Types and Number of Private Pension Plans

Defined Benefit Plans (1995) — 27m. participants (1973) 44 m. participants (2003)

Defined Contribution Plans — 11m. participants (1973) 64 m. participants (2003)

45.2m. IRA'S (persons participating — (2003)

1.29m. Keogh's (persons with accounts — (2001)

IRA'S, 401(K's) and Keogh's, Amounts Outstanding, 2003 (billions)

	Life Insurance Companies	Mutual Funds	Commercial Banks and Thrift Institutions	Self-Directed Brokerage Accounts	Totals
IRA'S	$315	$1,306	$268	$1,117	$3,007
Keogh's	n.a.	n.a.	n.a.	n.a.	133
401(k)'s	n.a.	n.a.	n.a.	n.a.	922
Totals	n.a.	n.a.	n.a.	n.a.	$4,062

Sources: 1986 *Pension Facts* and *Life Insurance Factbook, 1991, 1999, and 2005* American Council on Life Insurance, Washington, D.C.; Alicia Munnell, *The Economics of Private Pensions*, Brookings, Washington, D.C., 1982; *Statistical Abstract of the U.S. 1991, 1999, 2004-2005*, Census Bureau, 1991, 1999, and 2005; *PBGC Annual Report, 2003*, Pension Benefit Guarantee Corporation, *2004*.

A. HISTORICAL DEVELOPMENT

The broadening of pensions for the elderly reflects increased affluence among industrial societies, a shift from rural living toward more dispersed urban families, and greater longevity. Before the last 60–100 years, pensions were limited, and considered a reward for special services. Successful military leaders, injured soldiers and sailors, some government officials, courtiers, and ecclesiastics, or others deserving favor were typical pension recipients. Individual family resources were the principal means of support for older people in traditional societies, which prevailed until the last several generations.

In the U.S. pensions were first developed as compensation for war veterans, starting after the Revolutionary War, and major wars thereafter. Some government officials and judges also received pensions, but they were not extended to the majority of government employees until the last several generations. Private pensions were pioneered by a few large corporations in the later 19th century, with American Express and a few large railroads as leaders. Early company pensions were often disability related, or restricted to long-term, senior and "deserving" employees and executives. Because companies frequently used them against unions (and limited access to union members), the American Federation of Labor and Sam Gompers tended to resist company pensions in this period. Unions tried to develop their own pension and death benefit plans in the early 20th century, but union benefits were usually modest.

Meanwhile, social insurance and old age assistance was introduced by Bismarck, the conservative German leader in the 1880's, by Denmark in 1891, New Zealand 1898, Australia 1900, Austria 1907, Great Britain 1908, and France 1910. Bismarck's program included sickness insurance 1883, accident insurance 1884, and old age and disability insurance 1889, financed by contributions from employers and employees. Such social insurance programs became a standard package of legislation sought by social democratic and liberal reformers throughout most of the world in the last several generations.

In the U.S., however, there was greater resistance, which lasted for a longer period. In America the traditions of voluntarism were well established. Higher wages prevailed, farms were larger, and there were more business opportunities. The federal system made it difficult for individual states to experiment with more expensive forms of social insurance, such as old age pensions, because the necessary payroll taxes would handicap their state's employers against those in other states.

Workmen's Compensation laws for industrial accidents were the only type of social insurance to be widely enacted in the U.S. before the Great Depression. They began with Maryland 1902, Montana 1908, New York 1910, and a limited federal law in 1908. And courts declared most early laws unconstitutional. But successful enactments followed rapidly in 26 states between 1911–14. Private liability insurance quickly developed for employers, and they soon preferred the definite and limited costs of scheduled workmen's compensation laws to the indefinite risk of unlimited tort liabilities. Such workmen's compensation laws ultimately spread to all states.

During the 1920's private pension plans proliferated, especially those offered by large corporate employers. By 1929 3.7 million American workers were covered by nearly 400 company plans (roughly 10 percent of the non-agricultural labor force). More trade unions also developed pension plans, though with less resources. Although company pensions became common for larger employers, early vesting was rare, 20–25 years service usually required, and only one tenth of the employees got benefits. Most plans were financed entirely by the employers, with no employee contributions. Financing was from current company revenues in the majority of plans, i.e., "pay as you go", and only a minority of plans collected serious reserves in advance for potential obligations. With respect to industries, railroads had the strongest pensions, with roughly 85 percent of their employees covered, but pension plans were also common among utilities, and the steel, oil, chemical, rubber, machinery, and banking industries. By this time pensions were established for the military services, the federal civil service, some state and local government workers, many schoolteachers and university faculties, and some of the clergy. The idea of pensions was spreading rapidly for "good" employers with public approval. Company stock-option plans were also common, and served some retirement purposes, though mainly for higher salaried executives.

The Great Depression greatly weakened this budding pension movement. Unemployment reached one fourth of the workforce, many businesses and farmers suffered reduced income, and family resources to cushion adversity and old age were reduced. Many companies and governments were forced into retrenchment, and found their pension obligations very expensive. A large number of pension plans failed, and many were discontinued. Severe financial strain confronted the railroad industry pensions. Their pensions covered 90 percent of railroad employees. A large share of railroad employees were older, with nearly a quarter of their workers retiring in a few years. Hence, the leading industry for pension progress, railroads, faced the likelihood of massive default on their pension commitments.

This emergency of widespread economic distress and reduced income for many families and older people brought three Congressional responses, which greatly expanded American social insurance: (i) unemployment compensation; (ii) federal support for the railroad industry retirement system (the Rail Road Retirement Acts); and (iii) social security (old age and survivors insurance). Only sickness or health insurance failed of enactment at this stage, with weaker support and strong opposition from the medical profession.

Unemployment relief had been considered a problem of local poor relief, generally speaking, and Great Britain's unemployment compensation insurance of 1911 was the only national system established before the Great Depression. Such laws did not get much U.S. support until the early 1930's. Then it became clear that a nationally coordinated approach to unemployment and old age pension insurance was needed. For unemployment insurance, Congress established as part of the Social Security Act of 1935 a federal payroll tax, minimum standards, and administration for unemployment compensation insurance. Every state has its own plan under this framework, with some more liberal than others. Experience ratings are used, so that employers with lower layoff rates pay less in payroll taxes.

Some states had already enacted limited old-age assistance laws (10 before 1930, and 20 more before the Social Security Act of 1935). They provided modest relief for elderly people meeting a residency and means test. But only 250,000 people were receiving such benefits in 1934. President Roosevelt's Committee on Economic Security (with staff support and advisory committees) developed a compromise program in early 1935 to strengthen state old age assistance, and create a national system. Originally, the federal government would pay half the amounts granted by the states. Means tests were continued, but the nationwide system was designed to reach most workers (including all states). Payroll taxes were 1 percent initially for employers and employees, with scheduled increases later. Some supporters were disappointed at the low scale of early benefits, but liberalizing amendments gradually enlarged benefits, extended coverage, and increased the payroll tax rates over the years.

Although strong trust funds were contemplated initially, social security policy soon shifted toward cash-flow financing or "pay as you go", with more limited contingency reserve funds. Among the reasons for this evolution were a desire for faster, higher benefit payments than would have been feasible with large advance reserves, and some uneasiness about the deflationary effects of draining off substantial liquidity from current national income to build up big reserves. With enlarged national income, fuller employment, renewed economic growth, and more younger workers as population increased, there was widespread confidence in this current financing method.

With growing affluence Congress felt greater benefits were desirable and affordable, even though payroll taxes had to be raised to some degree. Over the years survivor and dependent benefits were added, along with disability insurance. Earlier retirement was allowed for women, and then for men also. Eventually, in the later 1960's, medicare (health insurance) benefits for older people were tacked on with a separate trust fund. The social security system was extended to cover farmers, domestics and the self-employed, and became nearly universal. The net result has been a substantially increased level of basic old age pensions for almost all citizens.

In addition, state and local government pensions, along with private employer, union, and self-employed plans, grew substantially to supplement the rising "floor" of basic social security benefits. Increased profits and wages during World War II encouraged employer pension plans, especially because war-time excess profit taxes and wage restraints could be avoided this way. Since income taxes remained higher in the post-war era, sustained by bracket creep, these incentives continued to encourage company pension and stock-option plans, especially for upper level executives and technical talent. Corporate contributions to such plans were deductible business expenses, and the income earned by these accumulations normally was sheltered from taxation against the recipients until benefits were withdrawn. Unlike social security, most company pension plans provided benefits closely related to individual contributions, so that high salary employees could gain substantial tax savings this way.

The stronger unions also sought pension plans from employers as fringe benefits and wage hikes in the years right after World War II. The United Mineworkers, Steelworkers, Autoworkers, Teamsters, and Ladies Garment Workers led the parade. Many multi-employer and company plans were established because of such collective bargaining pressures. The National Labor Relations Board and the courts strengthened the pension movement by requiring employers to bargain in good faith over demands for pensions and related fringe benefit packages under Section 8(a)(5) of the National Labor Relations Act.

State and local governments broadened pension plan and other fringe benefits in this postwar era, too. Some plans remained independent of social security, while others merely supplemented social security benefits. But many state and local pension programs built up considerable reserve funds, like the stronger private pension plans.

As this movement for pension plans gathered momentum, Congress provided for the self-employed to receive tax sheltering opportunities through H.R. 10 or Keogh plans in 1962. Insurance companies also developed tax deferred annuity (and variable annuity) policies for the self-employed market, along with high salaried employees. Mutual funds began to encourage special investment accounts for this purpose. The tax laws were revised to facilitate supplemental contributions to company and government pension plans. And in 1974 individual retirement accounts (IRA's) were authorized under ERISA to provide wider opportunities for tax sheltered savings for many tax-payers. Additional liberalization of Keogh plans and IRA tax sheltering opportunities followed recently, in 1976, 1978, and with the Economic Recovery Tax Act of 1981 (ERTA). However, the Tax Reform Act of 1986 cut back on the deductibility of IRA contributions for higher income participants in employer pension plans.

The cumulative result of this pension and retirement account movement was to create supplementary pension income, above and beyond social security benefits, for the majority of workers. Roughly half the private sector employees obtain such pension benefits. While government social security programs provide the bulk of benefits paid to ordinary retired people with limited incomes, these additional private, state and local government pension funds and retirement accounts have expanded greatly. (See Table VII–1.) Between 1950–1988 pension benefits paid by private plans increased from $370 million to more than $125 billion annually, while benefits paid by public plans (federal, state and local apart from social security) increased from $833 million to more than $75 billion annually. Assets held by these private and public plans amounted to $10,000 billion in 2003, or 6 times more than social security trust funds. Hence, the private and public pension funds are important financial intermediaries with large funds to invest (counting all forms of mutual funds there could be more than $12,000 billion of "retirement assets," although some of this will also be passed along to heirs in the next generation).

B. PENSION PLAN AND FUNDING REGULATIONS

Early regulation of pension plans involved compliance with Internal Revenue Act requirements or tax qualification. Since the early 1920's employer contributions to trusts for stock-bonus or profit sharing plans were deductible expenses, and not income for the beneficiaries until actually received by them. Similar deductibility for employer pension fund contributions was later allowed. And insurance annuity policies established by employers received comparable treatment. Some restrictions were placed on these arrangements, however, because of their potential for corporate and executive income tax evasion. Firm commitment or irrevocability was required. The Revenue Act of 1942 added further regulations, because heavier war-time income and excess profits taxes made these "tax loopholes" very attractive for business. The new requirements included at least gradual vesting of pension benefits, participation by 70 percent of the employees in a pension plan (except for temporary and seasonal workers, and those with less than 5 years seniority), and non-discrimination in favor of executives (although contributions and benefits proportionate to compensation were permissible). Subsequently the vesting of benefits was required before plans could be terminated. Apart from these tax qualification requirements, the only other significant law regulating pensions was the law of trusts in each state for funds taking the form of legal trusts, and state insurance law for insurance contract plans developed by insurance companies. Note that commercial banks and trust companies commonly serve as trustees for pension plan trust funds, and banking law indirectly affects their activity, too.

The Welfare and Pension Plans Disclosure Act of 1958, with substantial amendments in 1962, provided for pension plan participants and employees to receive information about their plans. This was intended to discourage malpractices and fraudulent administration. The Secretary of Labor received investigational and anti-fraud enforcement authority. But instances of funds misuse, particularly concerning union pension and welfare funds, aroused continued public controversy. Improved remedies for breach of fiduciary duties were needed for pension funds generally.

Many funds lacked sufficient funding or reserves, and when a company went out of business or its plan terminated, this could leave many workers with greatly impaired pension benefits. Studebaker closed down this way in a well-publicized case, and this led to demands for stronger funding, improved reserves, and better safeguards against plan termination. Only a minority of pension plans were funded comprehensively, and many used a substantial degree of current or "pay as you go" financing.

Other problems concerned delays in vesting benefits. Job changes, layoffs, mergers, or other breaks in pension accrual could substantially reduce pension benefits. A 1972 study reported that, while half the private sector labor force was covered in pension plans, only one third of them had vested benefits (and some of latter were only partly vested). Many hardship cases were documented, some reflecting employer harshness, which generally showed the shortcomings of late vesting practices.

In contrast, the early vesting and full portability of the Teacher's Insurance Annuity Association (TIAA) pensions for college, university, and private school faculties and staff, stimulated criticism for the delayed vesting in many company plans, and the lack of "portability" in most private plans. Other complaints developed about incomplete participation, and workers left out of tax qualified plans.

These problems and complaints led Congress to enact the Employee Retirement Income Security Act of 1974 (ERISA). ERISA increased private pension and benefit plan reporting and disclosure, improved vesting and employee participation standards, strengthening funding and fiduciary discipline, created more retirement opportunities for the self-employed and a new individual retirement account (IRA), and established the Pension Benefit Guaranty Corporation (PBGC) to ensure that vested benefits would survive plan termination. The Internal Revenue Service continued its regulatory role, but with new responsibilities for enforcement of the enhanced participation, vesting, and funding requirements. Meanwhile, the Labor Department received responsibility for enlarged pension plan supervision, reporting and disclosure, and fiduciary oversight. This allocation of jurisdiction grew logically out of previous legislative experience, and reflected a compromise between business and labor interests. The impact of ERISA has been to substantially strengthen private pension plan benefits and their reliability, though at the price of some increase in funding contributions for many pension plans.

1. PARTICIPATION AND VESTING

Eligibility was broadened under ERISA, so that new employees must be allowed to participate and accrue benefits after only one year of employment. Only two major exceptions are now allowed: (i) employees under 21 may be required to wait until that age; and (ii) a two year waiting period can be imposed if benefits are vested 100 percent after that time; (iii) Older workers may not be excluded from pension plans on the basis of age.

Vesting was substantially improved and accelerated for many employees by ERISA. Under many employer pension plans vesting had been delayed until 15–20 years service, and/or reaching the age of 45–50 (or some combination along these lines), and some plans delayed even further. Under ERISA a pension plan must vest 100 percent of the employee's contributions immediately, and the employer's contributions originally had to vest at least as early as one of the following:

(i) A 10 year vesting schedule, after which all accrued benefits are 100 percent vested; [This was most widely accepted for convenience, and referred to as the "10 year cliff", because many employers required the full period before complete vesting occurs.]

(ii) A 5–15 year vesting schedule, with 25 percent vested after 5 years service, 50 percent after 10 years, and 100 percent after 15 years; or

(iii) A rule of 45 vesting schedule, under which benefits were 50 percent vested, when employees with 5 years or more of service reach a combination of age and years service equal to 45, and another 10 percent vests each year for the next 5 years.

Some critics wanted full portability for pension plan benefits, but ERISA did not go that far. ERISA merely encouraged portability by allowing 60 days within which an employee could transfer or "rollover" his lump sum distribution of vested benefits to an IRA, if the new employer would not accept these benefits under its plan (or if the employee became self-employed).

But vesting was liberalized substantially and made more rapid by the Tax Reform Act of 1986, partly to help women and minority employees (which had higher turnover and less frequent vesting). The new vesting regime (in effect since December 31, 1988) provided only two alternatives: (i) 5 year cliff vesting (for multiemployer plans, 10 years service allowed for employees covered by a collective bargaining agreement); or (ii) graded vesting, 20 percent a year after the second full year (so that full vesting is completed after 7 years).

2.   FUNDING REQUIREMENTS

The requirements for funding are most demanding for "defined benefit" plans, i.e., where the pension liability of the employer, union, trust, or insurer is expressed in specific amounts for retirement, survivor's benefits, etc. Before ERISA it was sufficient to pay current pension liability, plus interest on unfunded accrued obligations. This meant the capital base or reserves need not be provided in advance for the larger part of potential liabilities, and that something close to "pay as you go" financing was allowed. Under ERISA pre–1974 plan obligations must be funded with additional contributions to amortize them over a 40 year period; for new plan obligations additional contributions must be amortized over 30 years. Reasonable actuarial procedures and estimates must be used for these amortization programs, taking into account projections of asset values and fund portfolio earnings.

For "defined contribution" plans no additional outlay is required by ERISA, i.e., where a specific amount is vested or set aside for each employee's account. In these pension, stock purchase, or profit-sharing plans, there was little problem of misrepresenting the adequacy of plan reserves to achieve certain benefit goals, and the employee's account merely grows to the extent of such defined contributions. Many of these plans were better funded, though, because sponsors and participants often selected contribution levels in competition with defined benefit plans, so that some comparability in yield would result for plan beneficiaries. ERISA merely requires defined benefit plans to cover their obligations with 30–40 year amortization programs, and appropriate levels of funding and contributions.

Expanded participation and earlier vesting requirements have funding implications for many pension and benefit plans. To the extent additional employees are included, greater contributions have to be made by employers (and perhaps employees). And where vesting occurs earlier for many employees, this increases the pension plan's liability exposure, and enlarges funding requirements for pension and benefit plans.

Where business conditions impose hardship on employers in making their plan contributions, the Treasury (IRS) may waive funding requirements. But no more than five waivers in 15 years are allowed, and underpayments should be made up in not less than 15 years.

To enforce these funding obligations, substantial excise taxes may be imposed (up to 100 percent of the accumulated deficiency), and in extreme situations a pension or benefit plan could be forced into termination by the Pension Benefit Guaranty Corporation (PBGC). If a plan is terminated, the PBGC may enforce a lien to the extent of 30 percent of an employer's net worth, in order to reimburse the PBGC for satisfying deficiencies in vested pension funds. If an employer decides to terminate an under-funded pension plan, this may be allowed, but only subject to PBGC reimbursement (i.e., up to 30 percent of the employers' net worth in meeting vested deficiencies).

Congress relaxed and modified ERISA, to some extent, in the Multiemployer Pension Plan Amendments Act of 1980, affecting some 2,000 plans and 8 million covered workers. This gave some relief to multiemployer plans developed by labor unions, and was designed to ease burdens for declining industries with special difficulties in meeting ERISA funding requirements. This legislation relaxed some funding obligations, allowed for hardship withdrawal by employers (and fair share contributions thereafter), provided for reduction of certain benefits to prevent plan insolvency, attempted relief of plans with overloads of retiring employees, made "unavoidable insolvency" an insurable event for PBGC assistance, and authorized premium increases for PBGC insurance coverage. However, "sick industries" continue to be a problem for private pension plans generally, with awkward financial dilemmas, affecting many individual employer plans, as well as union-developed and other multiemployer pension and benefit plans. Because of recently increased premium charges for the PBGC, a surplus of some $7 billion accumulated by early 2000. Some years before the PBGC was forced to increase annual premium charges from $2.60 to $19 per participant to cover PBGC deficits in the later 1980's-early 1990's. This premium charge may have to be increased again to cover another surge of losses for sick industries in 2001 thru 2003.

3. INVESTMENT REGULATION

Three kinds of managers are used by private pension funds. (1) A large number of plans are "insured" and managed by insurance companies, with up to one-fourth of the private pension assets, including many smaller plans. State insurance regulation applies to this sector, and its restrictions upon assets, bonds, mortgages, equities, and loans. (2) Banks manage a large chunk of the majority of other private pension trust funds, and handle many of the bigger plans. The national and state banking laws, together with the state law of trusts, provide guidelines for investment management. (3) Many remaining private pension funds involve mutual funds, or perhaps union collective bargaining trusteeship arrangements, where there was sometimes a lack of guidelines or investment standards for pension fund managers. Unions often attracted the greatest publicity as to malpractices, misuse of funds, and breach of fiduciary duties. But mutual fund and securities account misuse can become serious, since these are often set up informally.

ERISA mandates fiduciary responsibility for investment managers, trustees, or any other person with control over the pension plan or its assets. The standard for investment is the skill and diligence of a "prudent man", loyal to the plan, and without significant conflicting interests. Reasonable diversification is required, and no more than 10 percent of a plan's assets should be invested in securities of the employer for defined benefit plans. Fiduciaries are liable to the plan for losses resulting from breach of fiduciary duties. Some civil penalties apply with respect to prohibited transactions, mostly involving self-dealing practices. Suits to enforce these fiduciary liabilities may be brought by the Secretary of Labor, plan participants or beneficiaries, or other fiduciaries. Remedies may include damages or injunctive relief, and attorneys fees may be obtained along with relief. Criminal penalties may also be applicable for intentional or willful violations of ERISA requirements.

Thus, ERISA broadens and complements the fiduciary responsibilities already existing for many pension trusts, and extends these fiduciary liabilities to employers, pension plan managers, trustees and others controlling such funds. Remedies and relief for breach of these duties have been strengthened. Significant litigation since 1974 has applied ERISA to a variety of pension and benefit plan arrangements, including insurance contracts, and has enforced fiduciary duties against employers, managers, trustees and others with responsibilities for such funds.

Generally speaking, ERISA provides that pension fund managers, trustees, or officials with control over such funds must be bonded. Because such people are all liable to participants. beneficiaries, and their funds for breach of fiduciary duty, and may involve their company or organization in expensive liabilities, this would be normal prudence in limiting the risk of such loss. Specific exemptions, however, apply to bonding for insurance company, bank, and trust company fiduciaries, but their executives are often bonded anyway, and these financial institutions would be liable themselves for any breach of fiduciary responsibilities.

4. REPORTING AND DISCLOSURE

The reporting and disclosure obligations for pension and benefit plans were substantially enlarged by ERISA. This information provides the basis for IRS, Labor Department, and PBGC supervision, and allows participants, beneficiaries, and other fiduciaries the opportunity to protect their interests. Plan summaries must be given to all participants. Every plan should be audited by independent accountants annually, with annual reports (including actuarial certification if appropriate). Participants must have at least annual access to accrued benefits. Most reports to the IRS or Labor Department are public information, except benefit data on particular individuals. Civil penalties apply to plan administrators failing to make specified reports, and there are criminal liabilities, fines or imprisonment for knowing or willful violation of these disclosure and reporting requirements. The Secretary of Labor is primarily responsible for enforcing these obligations, but participants or beneficiaries also may obtain disclosure or reporting relief where appropriate.

5. PENSION BENEFIT GUARANTY CORPORATION

ERISA created the Pension Benefit Guaranty Corporation (PBGC) as an insurance agency protecting vested pension benefits within the Department of Labor. If a pension plan is terminated, the PBGC guarantees the payment of most basic, vested benefits (*on defined benefit plans*) to appropriate participants or beneficiaries, up to a certain limit of monthly benefits. (The current monthly limit for 2004 is $3,699 based on an indexed formula.) PBGC insurance does not apply to defined contribution plans. The PBGC allocates assets available upon termination of a plan according to priorities, but it pays off deficiencies in satisfying the basic benefits which have vested (within the specified limits). Most pension plan terminations are voluntary, and generally these plans have been financially sound.* Mergers, reorganizations, plant closings, liquidations, or the cost of making contributions are normal reasons for voluntary plan termination. But where plan assets are insufficient, or when termination is sought by the PBGC to protect the interests of plan participants and beneficiaries, a sponsoring company (or companies) will be liable for up to 30 percent of their net worth. Stock-market values, earnings, or, if necessary, the equity for a bankruptcy proceeding, can be used to calculate the sponsor's net worth.

* Voluntary terminations totaled more than 100,000 between 1975–95, and normally the benefits are annuitized or paid off as lump sums to beneficiaries.

Unfortunately, when a sponsoring company becomes insolvent (in a balance sheet sense), and its liabilities exceed assets, net worth is normally negative or non-existent. In these circumstances, the PBGC's lien on 30 percent of net worth may be an "empty bag." In effect, other corporate creditors have priority over vested pension participants and beneficiaries when balance sheet insolvency occurs. Strictly speaking, it would be wise for the PBGC to intervene before actual insolvency, and get some net worth for reimbursement. But thus far, it has not been the PBGC's practice to monitor potential employer (or multi-employer) business failures, and precipitate insolvencies in order to get the maximum reimbursement values. Almost all plan terminations have been voluntary (often involving mergers, closings, or changes in business organizations). Between 1975–1995 only 2,100 distress or involuntary terminations occurred, which required trusteeships for insufficient plan assets. Multiemployer plans (about 2,000 of them) with 8.7 million beneficiaries have been a special concern. But potential PBGC liabilities increased substantially in the 1980's (especially in "sick" industries like steel), and forced a major increase in premium charges.

More recently, another upsurge in PBGC plan termination losses came in 2001–2003. Steel and airlines accounted for most plan losses, aggravated by under-funding that had not been sufficiently remedied. The PBGC's 2003 Annual Report indicated deficits of some $20 billion in these three years.

Now the PBGC wants stronger accountability and disclosures by employers and plans.

Evidently, the PBGC and Labor Department believe it was better to absorb an addition to loss expenses and substantially raise insurance premium charges, than to aggravate the likelihood of business failures, plant closings, and unemployment with an aggressive monitoring program. But more observers now see a danger of renewed corporate business failures with underfunded pension plans, and are concerned that PBGC losses could reach many billions of dollars. The PBGC in 2003 estimated under funding of $450 billion. This could require even larger premium charges for PBGC insurance than most businesses had been expecting, though such premium costs probably could be absorbed by the private pension system. Continued controversy over pension plan funding is likely, with some suggesting stronger PBGC supervision and remedies.* Note that no PBGC supervision is devoted to defined contribution plans, which are becoming the larger portion of U.S. private pension coverage. In 2003 defined contribution plans had 64 million participants, while defined benefit plans had only 44 million participants.

The Pension Benefit Guaranty Corporation (PBGC), while comparable to the FDIC, NCUSIF, and SIPC as a financial institution insurance agency, is weaker than most of these other agencies. It

* One approach would enhance the PBGC's claims in bankruptcy from that of a mere unsecured creditor to become a priority creditor (say up to 50 percent of unfunded liabilities).

does not have as active a monitoring role for financial soundness of pensions, partly because the IRS has some of this financial responsibility. It does not have comparable corrective order authority, and limitations with respect to the 30 percent lien on net worth constrain its use as corrective leverage. Nor does the PBGC guarantee all pension benefits; it merely insures basic benefits up to the monthly limits, and covers only "defined benefit" plans, not "defined contribution" plans.

C. INDIVIDUAL RETIREMENT ACCOUNTS

In 1962 Congress enacted the Self–Employed Individuals Tax Retirement Act of 1962 (more commonly known as H.R. 10 or the Keogh Act). This legislation allowed self-employed people, professionals, and proprietors to establish tax-deferred retirement accounts for themselves and their employees. It was intended to "equalize", somewhat, the opportunities for tax-sheltering through pension and benefit plans already enjoyed by corporate leaders, high-salaried executives, and their employees. H.R. 10 authorized defined contribution "Keogh" plans for the self-employed (and their employees) under which tax-deductible contributions could be made amounting to 10 percent of annual (earned) income up to a maximum of $2,500 each year. Such sheltered accounts could accumulate income free of income tax until drawn upon for retirement many years later.

ERISA increased these contribution limits substantially in 1974, so that Keogh plan "participants" could enlarge annual contributions up to 15 percent of earned income or a maximum of $7,500 annually. In 1981 this limit was raised to $15,000 on annual contributions (still 15 percent of earned income) by the Economic Recovery Tax Act (ERTA). Keogh accounts may have reached $120 billion at the end of 1998.

In 1974 ERISA also authorized the new individual retirement account (IRA). The IRA allowed individual workers not covered by pension plans to set aside income for similar tax-sheltering and retirement purposes. (Participants in terminated pension plans also could convert their lump-sum benefits into IRA's.) The annual limits on IRA contributions were $1,500 or 15 percent of earned income, but these were increased to $2,000 or 100 percent of earned income (whichever is less) by ERTA in 1981. (An amendment in 1977 raised the maximum deduction to $1,750 for individuals with a nonworking spouse, and this "spousal" deduction was increased to $2,250 by ERTA in 1981.) More importantly, ERTA generalized access to IRA's by allowing all employees under $70\frac{1}{2}$ years of age to open such accounts, including people already covered by existing employer, union, government or Keogh plans. Thus, IRA's are available now to most of the working population (instead of merely the 35–40 percent not previously covered by private or government employee pension plans), and to most low and middle income employees in the country. As a result, major new funds have flowed into IRA's. Estimates for IRA fund accumulations by the end of 1998 reached $2,000 billion. (See Table VII–1 for estimated accumulations in Keogh and IRA accounts.) The Tax Reform Act of 1986, however, cut back heavily on IRA incentives for upper-middle and high income families participating in employer pension plans. Although all the profits from IRA and Keogh accounts remain sheltered from income taxes, full deductibility on contributions is retained only for $25,000 individual incomes or those without pensions. [For participants in pension plans deductibility is phased out entirely for individuals earning $35,000 adjusted gross income (or $50,000 for joint returns).] This somewhat reduced the rate of growth in IRA's.

Important limitations apply to Keogh and IRA plan accumulations, though, with respect to early retirement. Substantial tax penalties are imposed on premature distributions or withdrawals before age 59½ (unless one is disabled or transfers benefits due to divorce). This tax penalty is 10 percent of the premature distribution, which eliminates a considerable part (if not most) of the tax benefits received.

In addition, participants in many established pension plans can make substantial additional contributions to their retirement accounts for tax-sheltering purposes (often termed SRA's or "supplemental retirement annuities"). (Internal Revenue Code, Sections 401–415, especially Sections 401–403.) Many of these additional contribution options have existed for years, but the spread of IRA's make this concept more widely known. SRA's offer advantages, including greater convenience, avoidance of IRA fees and charges, earlier withdrawal, and broader options to purchase annuities on retirement. Hence, SRA's and related supplementary benefit plan contributions should be considered as part of the expanded scope for tax-sheltering of retirement income in recent years.

The economic significance of self-employed, individual retirement accounts, and supplementary retirement options is substantial. These accounts broaden the access to retirement savings among financial intermediaries, and allow more competition for these funds. Banks, MSB's, savings and loans, insurance companies, mutual funds, and money market funds compete for these funds, along with many established pension plans (through SRA's and related options), and securities brokerage firms offer "self-directed" Keogh investment accounts for stocks, bonds and other securities. More savings may result from Keogh, IRA, SRA and related accounts, although funds in this category may have less liquidity, and are often subject to financial institution management and service fees. The widening of access to these tax-sheltered savings and investments may be influential politically. This may prove to be a popular, broadly desired tax concession for many families. Conceivably, the taste for "individualized" pension plans could alter group pension and benefit plans for employers, unions, and government (including some elements of social security).

Another legislative development, the Tax Equity and Fiscal Responsibility Act of 1982 (TEFRA), was important for executives, professionals, and small business pension plans. For high-income earners (like many consultants, doctors, and lawyers), the constraints upon tax sheltering through Keogh plans had encouraged incorporation. Although ERISA set some limits on annual contributions to pension plans for high-income "employees", these limits were not very low. Thus, there were tax incentives to use the corporate form, and substantial differences in access to tax-sheltering. TEFRA achieved more equal treatment for contributions to pension plans, and reduces the limits on tax-sheltered plans for high income earners (whether or not they are self-employed or "corporate" employees.) Some corporate plan participants complained that "equity" had been achieved by reducing their access to tax sheltering, but Congress felt this was desirable, and that high income tax sheltering could be cut back somewhat.

D. SOCIAL SECURITY, PENSIONS AND FUNDING CONFLICTS

Although the U.S. evolved a general system of social security pensions and disability insurance (OASDI) for most people, supplemented by expanding private pensions and retirement accounts, many aspects of funding and tax support remain controversial. Four issues have provoked conflict: (i) The extent to which progressive taxation and transfer payments should be built into the system, or the degree to which benefits are linked to an individual's contributions; (ii) The role of government old age and disability insurance and pension benefits versus private pension plans; (iii) The scale of benefits and sources of tax support for the "socialized" or government portion of pensions; and (iv) The proper response to recent strains upon social security financing, including an increasing proportion of the elderly, health care inflation, immigration flows (including "illegals"), and the risk of slowed economic growth, enlarged unemployment, and less prosperity than had been expected.*

Social security and disability insurance (or "social security") in the U.S. represent a compromise achieved by Congress, and worked out over the years. Most politicians accept the established momentum of a socialized insurance system for the elderly, which includes a basic floor of benefits, together with additional private benefits reflecting individual earnings, savings, and retirement plans. Congress has been generous in both directions, with budgetary support for social security, and tax subsidies to private pensions, insurance, and retirement accounts.

Naturally there has been dissent. From conservative viewpoints, we have proposals to reduce the socialized, transfer payment element, and narrow

* In the mid–1930's when social security was established, the average U.S. life expectancy was 64 years; 65 year olds were only expected to live another 12 years. In 2001 the average U.S. life expectancy was 77 years; 65 year olds were now expected to live another 18 years. Thus, longevity has increased dramatically.

the scope for progressive taxation in social security payroll taxes. Some conservatives suggest privatizing a large part of social security, retaining only a residual safety net of assistance for the elderly. One method frequently mentioned is to convert social security for "younger" people, say those below 45, into retirement bonds, allocated according to earnings. Poverty relief or a negative income tax could take care of the less fortunate. A complication with such conversion plans, however, is the lower wage earner, a rather numerous category. Under present social security arrangements their basic pensions are subsidized through progressive taxes. How would this continue? If the lower wage earners should lose net pension benefits, are such reforms politically realistic? An answer, suggest many conservatives, is to substitute "more productive investments" (with little or no income tax, such as private pensions) for the current employer-employee payroll taxes, so that greater yield results. But these extra investment earnings would go predominantly to the higher income workers, still leaving many low wage people with reduced pension benefits (unless supplemented by progressive tax-transfer payments in some fashion).

Table VII-2

Social Security Taxes, Interest, Benefit Payments and Trust Fund Assets, 1937–2003 (millions)

Fiscal Year	Social Security Taxes	Interest Income on Trust Funds	Benefit Payments	Administrative Expenses	Trust Fund Assets
1937	$ 765	2	1	—	766
1940	$ 325	43	35	26	2,031
1945	$ 1,310	124	240	27	6,613
1952	$ 3,881	365	2,194	88	17,442
1960	$ 10,830	517	10,798	234	22,995
1967	$ 23,138	896	21,418	515	26,251
1974	$ 58,906	2,659	58,521	1,082	45,885
1977	$ 77,795	2,659	82,406	1,371	39,615
1981	$131,605	2,289	136,266	1,703	27,226
1986	$208,704	3,447	193,964	2,209	45,857
1990	$291,396	14,909	243,342	2,281	214,900
1994	$344,695	31,103	316,812	2,674	436,385
1998	$430,174	49,333	374,969	3,467	762,460
2003	$533,500	84,000	470,800	4,600	1,530,700

NOTE: OASI alone until 1957; OASDI combined for later years. Hospital Insurance not included.

Sources: Joseph Pechman, Henry Aaron, Michael Taussig, *Social Security Perspectives for Reform,* Brookings, Washington, D.C., 1968; *Social Security Bulletin,* Social Security Administration, March, 1983, March, 1991, and Annual Statistical Supplement 1999, 2004.

A collateral question is the efficiency and productivity of private pensions versus social security taxes and disbursements. Private pensions can attain higher yields with investment portfolios (with some variance in success), but management fees and profit margins for private entrepreneurs must be included. Social security has been operated primarily as a current cash flow system (with less interest income), but its administrative costs have been low. Administrative expense for combined OASDI operations has been less than 1.5 percent in recent years, an impressive achievement for a system of its size and complexity. (See Table VII–2.) Some complain of mistakes and confusion by social security in individual cases, but no system can be perfect and the appeal and hearing procedures improve performance considerably.

There are limits, of course, to the social security tax burden that is bearable. Many believe social security taxes have reached (or exceeded) this limit already, and that any further retirement income gains must come from increased personal saving and investment (mainly from more prosperous citizens). Because of constraints upon social security payroll taxes, some liberals believe general tax revenues should be used to help support social security (and related social insurance and health care). But business interests, the insurance industry, most financial institutions, and, thus far, the majority of Congress have resisted this idea. They argue that social security disbursements cannot be properly disciplined (and limited) unless they are tied to some self-contained payroll-tax contribution mechanism like the present system. At issue is the basic level and distribution of pension and retirement benefits that society believes it can afford.

With this background on the funding controversies for social security and private pensions, we should review recent concerns for the "adequacy" of social security finances. (See Table VII–2). Social security benefits and administrative expenses have exceeded interest income since 1940, and their trust fund reserves were never intended to fully support disbursements. Current cash flow or "pay as you go" became the primary method of social security financing. But trust fund assets for OASI (and later DI) were built up considerably, for awhile, as a partial revenue source, and as a contingency reserve. The OASI trust fund assets reached $17.4 billion in 1952 (for $2.2 billion benefits), but grew more slowly thereafter. Benefits grew faster than reserves in subsequent years, financed out of current social security taxes. In 1974 the combined OASDI trust funds peaked at $45.9 billion (but benefits of $58.5 billion exceeded reserves). By 1981 the OASDI trust funds had fallen to $24.5 billion (with benefits enlarged to $139.4 billion). Between 1974–81 OASDI trust fund contingency reserves had been substantially depleted to low levels (barely sufficient to cover the next monthly benefits). Temporary borrowing from the health insurance and supplementary medical insurance trust funds (with some $26 billion in assets in 1982) helped ease immediate difficulties, but this situation could not go on much longer.

A "short-term crisis" in social security finance grew from the fact that annual benefits slightly exceeded social security tax revenues, a condition persisting between 1974–81. The gap each year was not very large (in most years), but this violated the "pay as you go" principle of social security finance. What produced this gap? Most commentators emphasized three factors: (i) an overly generous indexing formula to offset inflation that added somewhat to benefits; (ii) unexpected rates of inflation for the later 1970's and early 1980's; and (iii) reduced levels of social security tax revenue caused by increased unemployment and slowed economic growth. In other words, if the economy had enjoyed full employment, healthy growth, and low inflation, there would have been no short-term financing crisis for social security in 1974–81.

While this realization helps understand the problem, the financing gap had to be closed. The short-term crisis could only be relieved by reducing benefits, increasing social security taxes, or taking money from general tax revenues. None of these options were popular in Congress or the Administration. But some solution had to be found. Borrowing from health and supplementary medical insurance trust funds could only be a temporary expedient.

Meanwhile, a "long-term crisis" in social security financing was developing for the years 2012–35 and beyond. The projected deficits in "pay as you go" financing become substantially larger when the "baby boomers" of the 1940's–1950's reach retirement age in the next century.* This problem is partly demographic, but also reflects greater longevity and an increasing proportion of the elderly in the population. Thus, "promised" benefit streams (with inflation indexing) exceed social security revenues generated by projected tax rates. Longer run social security financing assumptions are too opti-

* Meanwhile, between 1995–2010 social security "surpluses" are generated. Fewer babies were born 1930–42, because of the depression; many of these are retiring later, too. Thus, benefit payout burdens are eased for 1995–2010.

mistic, and require more economic growth, improved productivity, and employment than the economy actually generates. Four choices exist: (i) Cut benefits somehow and/or increase the retirement age; (ii) Raise social security taxes and/or mandate additional savings; (iii) Draw upon general tax revenues; (iv) Increase investment earnings by full or partial privatization of OASI funding.

President Reagan organized the earlier National Commission on Social Security Reform in 1981. This commission reviewed many options, and its compromise report led to the Social Security Act Amendments of 1983. Benefits were reduced by immediate delays in cost-of-living adjustment (COLA), eliminating some windfall benefits for uncovered employment, and increasing the retirement age somewhat. Taxes were increased by a series of adjustments: (i) raising payroll and self-employed taxes slightly; (ii) taxing some OASDI benefits for higher incomes; (iii) extending social security coverage to non-profit and new federal employees; (iv) preventing state and local employees from opting out; (v) shifting tax rates between OASI and DI trust funds, and (vi) allowing OASDI borrowing from the hospital insurance trust fund through 1987. These amendments were designed to generate $165 billion between 1983–1989 (when a $150–200 billion shortfall was feared). This much "progress" was a substantial achievement, considering the conflicting interests and political stakes for Republicans and Democrats. In the context of controversy about social security finance, the National Commission report and the prompt enactment of its recommendations by Congress can be taken as a renewed commitment toward the principle of "pay as you go" financing, and the need for social security benefits to be kept within the payroll tax revenues provided for them.

These measures relieved the short-term liquidity crisis (1974–81) for social security finance. OASDI reserves grew back substantially from $27 to $762 billion between 1981–99, and up to $1,530 billion by 2003. Increased taxes and funds transfers were important remedies. Much depends upon continued economic growth, and prospects for additional retirement savings. With respect to the 21st century, it is now time for serious study. But an important breakthrough was achieved in 1982 by scheduling increased retirement ages, and this form of benefit reduction. More must be done later with an adjusted schedule of delayed retirement ages to reflect improving health and longevity. And it would be very helpful to improve the yield of social security fund "investments," and to achieve more like equity (or long term bond) yields on a reliable basis.

The problems of elderly people and retirement have received more sophisticated study in recent years. Among the important insights are that increased longevity and improved health can be relied upon to some extent, yet the variance among people is substantial. Thus, some people weaken and need support earlier than 60, while others are going strong well into their 70's. Retirement policy needs to encourage longer productivity and reduce dependence, but respond to real disability in a humane way. More could be done with adjustments to social security (and related health care) that increase incomes, and improve investment yields, without raising social security taxes to meet these objectives.

In any event, social security finance needs continued attention. OASDI disbursements of $533 billion in 2003 amounted to roughly 4 percent of GNP. Federal health insurance programs (medicare and medicaid) added $500 billion or 3 1/2 percent of GNP. And if federal income security outlays of $240 billion (including unemployment compensation, poverty assistance, food stamps, and the earned income tax credit) are taken into account), about $1100 billion or 10 percent of the GNP goes toward federal retirement, social insurance or welfare payments in a broad sense. Meanwhile, private pension contributions absorbed around 3 percent of GNP. Private health and life insurance took $850 billion more or another 6 percent of GNP. Such large outlays are major financial commitments for the nation and a substantial charge upon its resources.

CHAPTER VIII

CONTROVERSIES AND PROSPECTS

Banking and financial institutions law is an evolution of compromises. The development of money and banking law, banking market regulation, thrift institutions, securities markets, insurance companies, pensions and social security funding was set forth in previous chapters. But a number of important issues are controversial now, and being dealt with by Congress and the regulatory agencies. While outcomes cannot be predicted with certainty, the issues and arguments can be summarized. This provides considerable insight into the challenges for banking and financial market regulation in the coming years.

A. CURRENT CONTROVERSIES

Major controversies for financial market regulation include: (i) Government Deficits, Finance, and Monetary Policy; (ii) International Banking and Finance; (iii) Restructuring Financial Markets; and (iv) Changing Regulatory Organization and Guidelines. The interests affected, political alliances, industries, regions and states, large and small institutions, and elements of the public—are struggling over these policies. Key agencies, including Treasury, Federal Reserve, Comptroller (OCC and OTS), FDIC, NCUA, SEC, and their leaders, along with influential legislators, have tried to fashion appropriate compromises. Significant changes in financial institutions law and policy have been implemented already by the year 2005, with far reaching consequences for the economy and politics.

Formulating goals for monetary, banking, and financial institutions policy is helpful, and it reveals the conflicting interests at stake. These arrangements should promote healthy economic growth, ample savings and productive investment, full employment and low inflation. Interest rates and financial service charges should be adequate for these purposes, but not excessive or unreasonably discriminatory. Competition among financial institutions is essential, with relatively easy entry, but we should insist that participants be responsible and properly capitalized. Large multinational institutions are desirable for many purposes, yet we should avoid excessive concentration or dominance by these firms. Decentralized enterprise and healthy local institutions are important in a federal democracy, and their vitality should be encouraged.

A continuing flow of international trade, investment, credit and financial services is necessary for world prosperity. Adequate liquidity, access to borrowing, reliable debt service, and responsible national economic policies should be linked together.

Financial policies, therefore, of the more important countries are interdependent, and should be harmonized. The benefits of productive financial intermediation should be spread more widely among developing countries. Healthy economic growth, with low inflation, and a minimum of disruption or defaults is desirable for the community of nations.

Regulatory authorities should work to achieve these objectives. Continued integrity of financial institutions and public confidence is indispensable. Equitable treatment of customers and institutions has been established as legal policy, and this should be maintained. Institutions must be carefully supervised, with appropriate disciplines for accountability (including their international activities). Regulatory organizations, legislative oversight, and executive coordination should function smoothly and expeditiously to achieve these ends.

Obviously, problems arise in giving detailed emphasis to these general goals. Even this much is controversial to some participants in financial markets, and for other nations (particularly debtor countries wanting generous renewal of credits and foreign assistance). Most banking and financial trade associations have more specific agendas of gains, relief, and "turf protection" against each other. There are real, important and unavoidable conflicts of interest in framing monetary, banking, and financial institutions policy.

B. GOVERNMENT DEFICITS, FINANCE, AND MONETARY POLICY

Many economists and financial people saw large U.S. fiscal deficits ranging between $150–300 billion (or 2–4 percent of GNP) continuing through the 1980's-mid 1990's, and on into the next century, as dangerous.* Government borrowing, if persistent at these levels, competes with private sector investments, keeps interest rates higher, weakens economic growth, and sustains "inflationary" momentum. Large and costly foreign borrowing is required. More than $–5,500 billion in additional federal debts already accumulated between 1982–2004. The U.S. became a net debtor nation in 1985 again (the first time since before World War I). Net U.S. external debts (owed to foreigners) grew rapidly and may have exceeded $–3,500 billion by 2005 (30 percent of GNP). Annual debt service charges, if allowed to increase this way, will become a serious burden on U.S. national prosperity. Fiscal and trade balance discipline must be restored somehow.

Earlier in the 1980's, U.S. economists had less problem with big deficits, with a peak of 10 percent unemployment and only 70 percent of industrial capacity utilized. Politicians hoped, in these circumstances, that stronger fiscal discipline (the "right" combination of spending cuts and tax increases)

* Surging economic growth between 1997–2000 eliminated U.S. fiscal deficits, but deficits resumed in 2002–2005, and perhaps beyond.

might come soon after the 1984 elections, when the public selected its President and another Congress. Unfortunately, political gridlock on spending priorities and tax loads made it difficult to cut back on large deficits between 1985–96. Conservative emphasis on adequate defense spending, resistance to tax increases, and insistence upon further cuts in civilian government expenditures conflicted with many Democrats, who wanted less defense, more civilian spending, and more progressive taxes.

Unfortunately, the 1984, 1988, and 1992 elections failed to break the political impasse. Although the Administration and Congress tried to reduce budget deficits with the Gramm–Rudman Act of 1985 (a five year gradual process), implementation proved difficult. (See Chapter II, infra, pp. 80–97) Budget deficits continued between $150–250 billion in the years between 1989–96, much less progress than originally scheduled. Conflicts between spending cuts for defense, social security and welfare, and other civilian outlays, and/or various tax increases proved hard to resolve without Presidents and Congress willing to compromise more realistically.

Nonetheless, a need for greater budget discipline, and more limited deficits with economic recovery was recognized by the early 1990's among U.S. economists, financial and business leaders. Federal Reserve Board members, Treasury officials, and many Congressional leaders took this view. (European Union countries were coming to similar conclusions, and they enforced tougher budget discipline with their fiscal "convergence criteria" employed to implement European Monetary Union (EMU) in the mid-late 1990's.) Fortunately, defense needs declined during 1991–92 after liberalization and partial break-up of the U.S.S.R. into a looser federation. But large budget deficits of $200–250 billion between 1982–96 could not be relieved by defense cuts alone. Health care, social security, and other "social" programs were increasing. More domestic discipline (spending cuts and/or moderate tax increases), and/or more economic growth would be needed somehow. Without better fiscal discipline, most agreed that economic growth would be somewhat limited, hesitant, and with risks of renewed inflation.

Somewhat by surprise, however, improved U.S. budget discipline, stronger economic growth, and even subsequent budget surpluses developed through the mid-late 1990's. First, in 1993–94 came improved revenues (with a modest Clinton tax increase and economic recovery), along with the failure of an expensive health care reform by the Clintons, which prevented a surge in health care outlays. Ironically, the Republican capture of Congress in November, 1994 also promoted better discipline in spending, and allowed some welfare reform. Although Clinton won some renewed popularity in the 1995–96 budget battles with Congress, Republicans managed to contain spending increases, and ease pressure on interest rates. Increased economic growth followed, and the U.S. and many foreign stock markets moved up a lot. Thus, the Dow Jones industrial average surged from 2600 in 1990 to

11,700 by early 2000; the NASDAQ went up from 410 to 5,000 in the same period. Increased "wealth" in the stock market in the later 1990's added economic growth momentum and helped attract substantially more foreign investment in U.S. securities.

Oddly, somewhat higher interest rates imposed by the Fed in 1998–99 to cool an "excessive" boom managed to enhance investor confidence that stronger economic growth in the U.S. was still sustainable. And, very importantly, higher interest rates in the U.S. than the EU and Japan helped boost short-term confidence in the dollar. This encouraged even more foreign investment into the U.S. Of course, a high dollar encouraged more imports into the U.S., slowed U.S. exports, and widened the U.S. trade and current account deficits, which grew from 2 percent of GNP in 1993 to 4 percent in 1999–2003, and averaged 5 percent between 2004–2005. While many economic experts warned that such large U.S. external account deficits were "unsustainable," the U.S. stock market "bubble" of 1995–2000 only seemed to promote increasing foreign capital inflows to cover these U.S. trading deficits. Meanwhile, a troubling series of disruptive financial booms, bubbles, panics, currency crises, and devaluations abroad brought further "confidence" in the dollar and U.S. capital markets *as a safe haven*. Crises and devaluations in Mexico (1994), Thailand, Malaysia, Indonesia, S. Korea (1997–98), and later Brazil, Russia, Ecuador, Argentina, and other "emerging markets" fostered capital movements into the U.S. And, at least initially, the new "Euro bloc" used easier monetary policy and lower interest rates and monetary policy (from 1999–2002), so that capital flight from emerging markets moved mainly into the dollar and U.S. capital markets, and not that much into the euro. More recently, the U.S. dollar weakened substantially in 2003–2005, especially against the euro.

A temporary aid to U.S. budget discipline was a demographic "accident" for the medium term. Fewer babies, relatively speaking, had been born in the U.S. between 1930–42, and the retirement age for many workers recently has been extended beyond 65. This means a slowdown in U.S. social security benefits paid out from the mid–1990's through perhaps 2010. Meanwhile, payroll taxes for social security have been increasing more rapidly, due to broader prosperity, and growing baby boomer incomes (people now in their 40's and 50's) entering peak income years. This phenomenon is producing a large annual *surplus* in the social security trust funds *for awhile*. Sadly, when the big "baby boomer" cohort (those born between 1943–63) retires in large numbers, say between 2012–35, this U.S. social security *surplus* gets used up rapidly, and big annual *deficits* threaten the social security trust funds. This projected social security "crisis" is very serious, and must be dealt with by cutting benefits, raising retirement ages, increasing taxes, or by "investing" more productively the social security payroll taxes and trust funds.

This is a major U.S. social security reform challenge, a controversy already being argued out among experts, the press, Presidents, and Congress in the later 1990's and the early 2000's. Finding a sufficiently reliable, constrained compromise could be hard politically.*

Meanwhile, in any event, sound U.S. macroeconomic policies, sensible monetary and banking arrangements, and healthy industrial and technological progress should be continued (insofar as possible). Broadly speaking, the 1982 recession (with more than 10 percent unemployment) called for Keynesian and/or Supply–Sider budget deficits and stimulus. By 1999–2000, however, a sustained boom had greatly reduced unemployment, brought some inflation pressures (including higher oil prices), and greatly increased stock prices. This suggested the U.S. had reached the opposite end of the business cycle, perhaps even a "speculative bubble." Experts were divided, though, on how much technological progress had occurred, and how much room for further economic growth might remain.

Four viewpoints emerged: (i) *Onward and Upward*—with faster growth and room for greater prosperity; (ii) *Unstable Stagnation*—with big swings in stock prices and little real gain for some years; (iii) *A Soft Landing*—achieved by Federal Reserve tightening and budget discipline, with slow

* Neither the status quo (no social security changes) nor complete, unregulated privatisation (too risky) is likely to be acceptable. But some partisan ideologues in Congress and the executive branch resist compromises.

growth for a few years; and (iv) *A Crunch and Slow Recovery*—featuring a major drop in U.S. stock prices, and substantial devaluation of the dollar, followed by a slow, difficult recovery, complicated, very likely, by a global recession. Obviously, U.S. policy makers would be debating these alternative scenarios (or projected prospects). Significant disagreements already existed. The next few elections for President and Congress will be crucial, too. Sharply partisan conflicts could undermine sensible teamwork. But the lessons of previous macro-economic experience and contending schools of thought would form the basis for policy-making in the next 10–15 years. (See chapter II, pp. 62–118).

Finally, recent trends to more open global capital markets and international trade add a major complication. It constrains what *national* policy-makers can do. People might hope that better multilateral collaboration would be forthcoming, but experience from the last 25 years shows that consensus among nations is not always achievable, and can be hard to implement.

C. INTERNATIONAL BANKING AND FINANCE

Over the last 45 years the global economy prospered with greatly enlarged international trading activities and capital movements. But there have been stressful difficulties. During the 1970's a surge of price inflation hit most global markets. Oil prices trebled (OPEC I, 1973–74) and trebled again (OPEC

II, 1978–79). Food and many other commodity prices more than doubled. A wage-price spiral of "stagflation" ratcheted upwards in most countries. And inflation hit countries quite unequally. Non-oil nations generally suffered, but oil rich exporters often prospered. Big petro-dollar profits, especially from the Persian Gulf, had to be recycled through leading international banks. These banks, flush with swollen liquidity, loaned generously to multinational corporations (MNC's)and many less developed countries (LDC's). Debt loads for many developing nations built up rapidly. And yet, the global inflation was deeply worrisome to most countries. Most economists felt that inflation had to be disciplined and brought under control somehow.

By the early 1980's all this led to a crackdown on inflation among the leading banking nations (including the U.S., Germany, U.K., Japan, Switzerland, and others). A major global recession and slump followed for many countries, along with high interest rates, serious debt servicing strains, and an extended debt rescheduling crisis. This required a stretch-out of international financial obligations for more than 60 countries during the 1980's, together with tougher fiscal discipline and slowed growth. Slumps followed for many LDC's around the world, but Japan, Taiwan, S. Korea, and most of the ASEAN group prospered. The U.S. mainly prospered, though some of its "rustbelt" and manufacturing areas slumped. Europe prospered unevenly, too, with a mixture of slumps and progress. But Latin America and Africa, for the most part, failed to match East Asian and Indian growth rates. Through it all, however, most multinational banks did well, and the global economy was growing faster than most nations.

In contrast, in the late 1980's the U.S.S.R.'s communist economic-political system broke down in the late Gorbachev years. Liberalization and "market oriented" reforms followed (at least to some extent) for Eastern Europe and the former USSR. China moved more successfully toward market decentralization, although democratic reforms were resisted. Meanwhile, the European Economic Community deepened their market integration. Most of Western Europe joined the Maastricht 1992 treaty arrangements, and formed a wider European Union (EU) that began admitting central European states into closer linkages with the EU.*

By the early-mid 1990's, a movement toward more open, integrated world markets achieved great momentum. Multinational companies (MNC's) now invested more widely in developing countries, with encouragement and legal safeguards from their governments. Privatisation and market-oriented reforms became fashionable. The Uruguay Round and WTO Agreements of 1994 offered more support to open markets, although not to the same degree everywhere (significant asymmetries remained a

* A much stronger, long-term economic performance for democratic Western Europe, and most of Asia, than the U.S.S.R. and its East European satellites, was decisive in the collapse of centralized communism as a political-economic system. Decentralized, market incentives and greater personal freedoms had brought broader growth and prosperity to most Western countries.

serious problem.) "Emerging markets," many of which suffered painful slumps in the 1980's, now welcomed foreign direct investments. Unfortunately, speculative euphoria got out of hand in some countries, e.g. Mexico (1994) and some Asian countries (1997–98), with nasty banking and currency devaluation crises. And although there were widespread complaints about the "excesses" of the globalization, few believed that any broad breakdown or general retreat from world markets was likely or desirable.

On the other hand, frequent adjustment strains, devaluations, and threats to jobs and incomes in many countries brought concerns about appropriate "limits" to globalization. Thus, when an ambitious effort at a new WTO Millennium trade round was launched at Seattle in 1999, these meetings broke down. Also the Doha WTO round "progress" was slow. Most developing nations want to limit further market opening, and many LDC's want relief from commitments to stronger intellectual property rights and investment protection for MNC's and the advanced countries. On the other hand, many agriculture, business, labor, and environmental interests in advanced countries also felt that global market integration had gone too far, and needed stronger limits, reciprocity, and safeguard relief. The U.S., EU, and Japan bickered among each other, too.*

* The WTO dispute settlement process, celebrated by some as a means to global harmony and enforcing free trade more fairly, was becoming a new source of stubborn trade conflicts. Little

Meanwhile, in the world's financial markets the recent crises for many countries taught painful lessons. Stronger regulation, capital adequacy, prudential supervision, and transparency were essential safeguards for both public and national interests. Weak regulation, corruption, and poorly informed markets were major elements of fragility that made the global economy more vulnerable and dangerous. Speculative excess, unsound loans and investments, panics, and disruptive capital flows were aggravated by inadequate regulatory supervision. These lessons applied all through banking, securities, and insurance. Widespread mistakes, fraud, and cronyism were suffered in many nations. If the shortcomings in global financial markets are not dealt with effectively, confidence in global trade and finance could be undermined. Sound financial institutions benefit from healthy competition and market reinforcing supervision that enforces responsibility and common sense prudence.

Governments often play a key initiating role in fostering the growth of finance, banking, corporations and securities markets, and various branches of insurance coverage. In crises governments are crucial to relief, reform, and rebuilding healthy finance. But as major nations progress, become highly industrialized and prosperous, the role of governments shifts more to maintaining healthy regulation, surveillance, and corrective action to prevent or limit serious problems.

agreement seemed in sight on "completing" an equally open world trading system.

Meanwhile, the structure of international financial market coordination provokes controversy. The International Monetary Fund (IMF) plays a central role in assisting countries to ease their balance of payments problems. The IMF encourages governments toward more responsible and sustainable economic, fiscal, and monetary policies. As a result countries can live within their means, and engage the global marketplace more successfully in investment and trade activities. The World Bank and regional development banks supplement the IMF's role with longer-term lending assistance for infrastructure, education, technology, and the environment so as to promote healthy economic development. In many ways these efforts were quite helpful over the last 40–50 years, but many nations suffered difficulties and did not do so well. How to improve the less successful nations is a major challenge.

Capital markets have broadened and deepened in many ways. But better statistics, transparency, and risk assessment are needed. Improved market supervision, accounting, and regulation for financial markets is important. But implementation is a continuing challenge.

Less complete are the multilateral institutions for regulating and supervising international trade in goods and services. Although the World Trade Organization WTO) evolved from eight successive rounds of multilateral trade negotiations under the General Agreement on Tariffs and Trade (the GATT from 1947–94), the new WTO is suffering serious difficulties. There is a conflict over voting and decision-making. Unresolved struggles between "consensus" (often lacking) and UN General Assembly voting (one country-one vote), without weighting according to economic strength or population, weaken the WTO. Major asymmetries and lack of reciprocity, which fosters extensive free-riding and limits on further trade opening measures are a problem. Finally, the scope for national regulation in all forms of trade in goods, services, capital, and financial flows is extremely broad. This greatly complicates decision-making at the multilateral level. For these reasons, many nations are going forward with regional and bilateral trade arrangements.

One of the toughest challenges for financial market regulators is the trend to wider financial conglomerates (banking, securities, and insurance), along with an increased number of multinational enterprises in these financial sectors. We've learned through many institutional failures (e.g. BCCI in 1991) that good accountability, comprehensive reporting, reasonable transparency, and sufficient capital are essential for sound finance. Mergers across national boundaries makes this supervision more difficult, and multinational financial conglomerates even more so. Thus, stronger collaboration regimes (including "Source of Strength" doctrines must be established among financial regulators (banking, securities, and insurance), but also across international boundaries. Thus, the Basle Concordat regime (BIS) for global banking should be extended somehow into a multi-dimensional grid of supervision for international finance (banking, securities, and insurance). This is a key priority for global financial markets.

An important development in global capital markets is also forcing this trend. Already substantial cross-investments are occurring by pension and mutual funds through international boundaries. Thus, the pension and investment intermediaries of the world are already investing into international markets. This is occurring among OECD countries, but also into developing country securities and investment opportunities. International trade in goods and services promotes global commerce, but a lot of this is relatively short-term. But international investments by pension and mutual funds is a longer-term network of financial "marriages" and interdependence. When countries commingle their pension fund investments (not unreasonable from a diversification viewpoint), their need for mutual trust is greatly enhanced. Through joint supervision of international pension assets many nations are more closely bound to each other. Implementing this responsibility is a major institutional challenge; it should lead to an important strengthening of international financial supervision, mutual disclosure and accountability.

D. RESTRUCTURING FINANCIAL MARKETS

Until recently each major field in the spectrum of U.S. financial institutions, commercial banking, thrift associations (MSB's, S & L's, and credit unions), securities marketing firms, and insurance companies, was almost entirely specialized to itself. There was little diversification or cross-ownership between these financial industries, and not much ownership of significant financial enterprise (in any of these channels) by outside industrial companies. Each financial sector was supervised mainly by its own regulatory agency or agencies, responsive and friendly to industry needs, along with more general public and consumer interests. Within their respective channels, banks, thrifts, securities firms, and insurance companies performed their intermediation roles, served depositors and customers, and grew within the latitude allowed for their industry. (See Chart VIII–1 for Traditional Market Participation Among Financial Institutions, and Table VIII–1 for U.S. Financial Intermediary Assets, 1929–2003.) Chartering policies, fiduciary responsibilities, business custom, and historical evolution strengthened this pattern. So did the Glass–Steagall Act of 1933, which separated commercial banking from securities marketing and underwriting, and subsequent court interpretations of that legislation. The Bank Holding Company Act amendments of 1970, which kept commercial banking largely confined to this field, were another important strengthening of this momentum. The traditions of dual regulation, federal and state, for banking and thrift institutions, along with state regulation of insurance, also fostered a conservative view of financial market boundaries.

Growing rivalry, however, began between these industries. Commercial banks and thrift institutions always took some savings deposits from consumers in competition with each other. And, to a limited extent, their lending activities overlapped (more so recently). Meanwhile, securities marketing firms sold bonds, stocks, and notes to customers as saving and investment alternatives in partial competition with deposit taking institutions. Mutual funds were developed as a more convenient means to investment accounts, with flexibility and liquidity more like savings accounts. Insurance companies developed life insurance contracts with investment features, and added variable annuity policies close to mutual funds in character. Banks developed pooled trust investment accounts in response to mutual funds. In another area, commercial banks, insurance companies, and labor organizations (along with other professional groups) took active roles in developing pension funds and their management. All this reflected some competition among financial institutions, even though considerable product and service differentiation partly separated banking, thrifts, securities marketing, and insurance companies.

Table VIII–1

U.S. Financial Intermediary Assets, 1929–2003

(billions of dollars)

	1929	1960	1981	1985	1989	2003
Commercial Banks	$71.5	$257.6	$1,674.3	$2,350	$3,299	$6,668
Savings Banks	9.9	40.6	175.6	326	280	354
Savings and Loan Associations	8.7	71.5	663.8	952	1,252	1,073
Credit Unions	negligible	5.7	77.7	137	203	599
Money Market Funds	—	—	181.9	207	429	2,224*
Investment Companies (including mutual funds)	small	17.0	55.2	289	554	6,635*
Life Insurance Companies	17.5	119.6	526.0	938	1,300	3,880*
Property–Liability Insurance Companies	4.0(e)	32.0	212.0	374	527	1,045*
Pension Funds (state and local government)	modest	19.7	226.2	437	674	2,370*
(private)	—	modest	n.a.	n.a.	n.a.	3,686
	$113.0	$601.8	$4,203.6	$6,936	$9,618	$27,500

Gross National Product, Government Spending, Surplus, and Deficits, 1929–2004

(billions of dollars)

	1929	1960	1981	1985	1990	1999	2004
Gross Nat'l Product	$103	$506	$3,052	$3,993	$5,463	$9,000	11,600
Total Gov't Spending	10.3	137	977	1,262	1,697	2,620	3,546
Gov't Surplus or Deficit	+ 1.0	+ 3.1	- 29.7	- 139	- 139	+ 185	–435
Fed'l Surplus or Deficit	+ 1.2	+ 3.0	- 63.8	- 197	- 197	+ 124	–520
State and Local Surplus or Deficit	- .2	.1	+ 34.1	+ 58.3	+ 35.4	+ 61	+ 85
Gross Fed'l Debt	16.9	290	994	1,817	3,206	5,606	7,486

SOURCES: *Statistical Abstract of the U.S. 1982–2005*, Census Bureau, U.S. Dept. of Commerce; *Economic Report of the President*, February, 1986, 1991, 1996, and 2000, and 2005.

Chart VIII–1

Traditional Market Participation Among Financial Institutions

I. Deposit Taking Institutions

Market Structures

COMMERCIAL BANKS
(Generally restricted to single states under established law)

Competitive national banking market serves large customers

Local oligopolies serve small businesses and families

Thrifts—

MSB's S&L's	Expanding to commercial banking	Competitive alternatives to commercial banking, with special role in housing finance
Credit Unions	More limited services, mostly for employee members	Limited competition for banks, other savings institutions

II. Securities Marketing Institutions

Brokerage Firms	Often integrated, national enterprises	Loose oligopoly of nationwide firms, with competitive fringe of smaller and local firms

Mutual Funds
& Investment Co's

Underwriters

Issuers (Corporations, Partnerships)   Includes all enterprises issuing securities

III. Insurance Companies

Life, Health Insurers

Loose oligopolies of nationwide firms, with smaller and local firms as competitive fringe

Property, Liability Insurers

Loose oligopolies of nationwide firms, with smaller and local firms as competitive fringe

IV. Pension Fund Managers

Commercial Banks
Insurance Companies
Labor or Professional Organizations

Loose oligopolies of nationwide firms, with smaller and local firms as competitive fringe

V. Social Insurance System

Federal Social Security   Unitary nationwide system
Other Federal Insurance
State and Local Government Social Insurance Activities   State (or Municipal) programs

Chart VIII-2

Potential Restructuring of Market Participation Among Financial Institutions

I. Deposit Taking Institutions

		Market Structures
COMMERCIAL BANKS (Nationwide enterprises with unrestricted branching and diversification activities)		Nationwide oligopoly of conglomerates, with some local banks surviving as limited competition
MSB's SB's S&L's	Close to commercial banks, but usually smaller	Limited competition, mainly in local areas
Credit Unions	More limited services, mainly for employee members	Limited local competition

II. Securities Marketing Institutions

Brokerage Firms	Nationwide diversification allowed	Nationwide oligopoly of financial conglomerates, and weak competitive fringe of smaller firms
Mutual Funds & Investment Co's		
Underwriters		
Issuers (Corporations, Partnerships)		Closer links between major financial conglomerates and leading corporations

III. Insurance Companies

Life, Health Insurers
Property, Liability Insurers

Nationwide oligopoly of financial conglomerates, and weak competitive fringe of smaller firms

IV. Pension Fund Managers

Commercial Banks
Insurance Companies
Labor or Professional Organizations

Nationwide oligopoly of financial conglomerates, and weak competitive fringe of smaller firms

V. Social Insurance System

Federal Social Security
Other Federal Insurance

Unitary nationwide system

State and Local Government Social Insurance Activities

State (or Municipal) programs

In the mid 1970's thru 1980's, this rivalry among financial intermediaries increased. MSB's and S & L's began offering NOW accounts, with close to checking account convenience and paying interest to depositors as well. In the late 1970's, when Regulation Q limits kept savings account interest rates substantially below rising money market rates, the securities industry responded with money market mutual fund accounts. The MMMF's offered higher interest rates, almost the same convenience, and added limited check writing privileges. Merrill Lynch introduced cash management accounts (CMA's) for large deposit customers with unlimited check writing, followed by other securities broker-age firms. Gradually, commercial banks and thrifts accepted the need to meet this deposit competition, with lower denomination certificates of deposit. Finally the Garn–St. Germain Act of 1982 mandated money market accounts for banks and saving institutions. These developments substantially increased deposit account rivalry among commercial banks, savings institutions, securities marketing firms and mutual funds.

Meanwhile, savings institutions received broader lending latitude (especially S & L's, whose charters had limited them mainly to real estate loans). The DIDMCA of 1980 and Garn–St. Germain were particularly significant (see Chapter IV, supra). Thus, deposit taking institutions became more competitive with each other, and experienced greater competition with the securities industry.

These developments combined with a more free-market, relaxed, and permissive attitude toward mergers and conglomerate business growth held by leaders in the Reagan–Bush–Clinton–Bush administrations. This encouraged inter-market diversifications and related acquisition moves in the financial sector. And the Glass–Steagall Wall between banking and securities was significantly eroded, and later eliminated entirely by the Gramm–Leach Financial Modernization Act of 1999.

Many observers viewed this trend of diversification as moving toward nationwide financial conglomerates. Early leaders in this structural transformation were the largest U.S. commercial banks, Citicorp, Chase, and Bank of America, Merrill Lynch (strongest in the securities industry), Sears'-Allstate–Dean Witter–Coldwell Banker (an early nationwide-retailing-insurance-securities-real estate brokerage conglomerate), Shearson–American Express (brokerage, credit cards, and travel services), and Prudential–Bache (a major insurance securities combination). A continuation of this merger trend and diversification movement, if unrestricted, could produce, within a number of years, a restructuring of U.S. financial markets. (See Chart VIII–2, Potential Restructuring of Market Participation among Financial Institutions.) What had been separate financial industries, broken down into loose oligopolies, with many small and local financial institutions, could essentially become a much more concentrated, nationwide oligopoly of financial conglomerates, with substantially weaker competition from smaller, independent and local institutions.

While competition might continue for awhile, during the process of this structural transformation, the ultimate results could substantially weaken competitive rivalry for small business, consumer, and individual family accounts. Only larger business and wealthy individual accounts would be likely to bargain with enough clout to get the lowest possible rates or good service from giant financial conglomerates. Corporate headquarters for these financial conglomerates would be concentrated into fewer states, and many communities would lose significant financial leadership talent. Such a radical, structural transformation of the financial organization of American society would constitute a major break with past legal and business traditions. The theme of federalism, which dominated the financial development of this republic, would no longer be influential.

To what extent is such a structural transformation of U.S. financial markets at hand? How rapidly could this merger and diversification movement proceed? Would new legal constraints be required to limit this transformation and increased concentration in financial markets? How should state and federal law regulate these developments? To what extent, if any, should the Bank Holding Company Act be modified? Should new limitations be applied to cross-industry penetration (or large mergers) in the financial sector? Should large companies from other industries be allowed to acquire major banks? and establish big financial conglomerates? Can antitrust enforcement be relied upon to set proper limits on the expansion of financial conglomerates? Or should free market forces, unrestricted merger activity, and expansion of financial conglomerates be allowed to proceed without any legal regulation or constraint whatsoever?

These are controversial questions for financial institutions (large and small), their trade associations, and customers (corporate and individual). States have divergent interests, depending upon the distribution of gains and losses to financial institutions, business interests, and the general public in their areas. Such conflicts raise awkward problems for Congress, and the banking and financial institution regulatory agencies.

But all should recognize that substantial increases in aggregate concentration have occurred already within U.S. financial markets. Between 1980–2003 the share of domestic commercial bank deposits held by the largest 100 U.S. BHC's grew from 46 to 72 percent; the top 25 grew from 29 to 55 percent in these years. The number of commercial banks declined from 14,600 to 7,700. S & L's and savings banks declined from 5,000 to 1,360; thrift institution assets declined substantially relative to commercial banks. Credit unions declined from 21,000 to 9,500 although their assets are still growing somewhat. Consolidation and concentration increased as well in the securities industry, among mutual funds, and in the insurance industry. By

1999 the top 25 securities firms had 94 percent of the industry's capital (and six of these were affiliates of multinational banks.)* The top 25 life insurers had more than two thirds of their industry's revenues, while the top 25 property-casualty insurers had more than 60 percent of their industry's revenues. These other branches of the financial sector were always much more nationally concentrated than commercial banking (or depository institutions), and further consolidation occurred in the 1990's-early 2,000. Between 1999–2003 there were 4,564 acquisition-merger deals involving $738 billion in acquired assets.

During the 1990's the U.S. Congress and bank regulatory agencies had greatly relaxed the limitations on financial concentrations. The key steps were Riegle–Neal in 1994 [allowing interstate bank branching], and Gramm–Leach in 1999 (allowing financial holding companies (FHC's) across banking, securities, and insurance]. By 2003, 630 FHC's had been formed in the U.S.; these FHC's controlled 78 percent of the BHC assets in the U.S.

This illustrates a market transformation of financial institutions toward very large, nationwide, and heavily diversified enterprises. But as Congress largely eliminated the Glass–Steagall "wall", there were still concerns about competition, financial con-

* The six multinational bank affiliates were: Credit Suisse–First Boston; Deutsche Bank; Chase Securities; J.P. Morgan Securities; Bank of Tokyo–Mitsubishi; and First Union Capital Markets Co. In addition, by the year 2003, among 630 FHC's, 26 FHC's did insurance under-writing, 165 did insurance agency activities, and 57 did securities underwriting and dealing.

centration, and limiting conflicts of interest. Various proposals for "firewalls" between banking and securities (or other) affiliates, separate capitalization requirements, anti-tying restrictions, and limits on dealings between affiliates have been under review. But Gramm–Leach seems to have left a lot of this follow-up work to the bank, securities, and insurance regulatory agencies, and especially, to the Federal Reserve as lead FHC regulator.

Many of those believing in broader latitude for financial consolidation expect that a lot of the smaller firms will have to merge into larger institutions or fall by the wayside. This outlook assumes substantially increased economies of scale and integration for financial institutions, based on increased electronic funds transfer and computerization. Others favoring this policy are not so sure that large numbers of smaller banks, thrifts, insurance companies, or securities firms need leave the marketplace. But, in any event, these people trust the "market," rather than "regulation", as the better decision-making process.

Few in this camp are alarmed at the decline of smaller financial institutions. Enough large institutions will remain, in their view, to supply adequate price competition. And those enthusiastic about large financial conglomerates do not see much value or importance in decentralized financial industries, with many smaller banks, thrifts, securities firms and insurance companies throughout the country.

On the other hand, the smaller banks, securities firms, and insurance companies (and independent insurance agents) still muster considerable political strength. And many consumer advocates, academic experts, and public-minded legislators are worried that too drastic a reduction in competition will now occur in the U.S. financial sector. From their perspective the public and consumer interests in a wide array of competitive choices, and the need for preserving a strong opportunity for smaller banks, securities firms, and insurance companies scattered through most of the 50 states, are being greatly neglected. The predominant regulatory agencies (Federal Reserve, OCC, and SEC) are wedded too closely to the outlooks of large institutions. The smaller, more local S & L's and savings banks have been greatly weakened; many of their thrift survivors are regional or state-wide chains. Only credit unions (there are still 9,500 of them) remain substantially decentralized, or confined to the employees of particular companies, government agencies, or local communities. In the securities field smaller, regional brokers have not been that strong since the 1960's, although new entry may not be that difficult. (Capitalization for local brokers is not that burdensome.) And in the insurance sector (especially some branches of property-liability coverage) a significant range of smaller-medium sized companies had been able to survive (especially when "protected" by state insurance rate bureaus that kept premiums at "adequate" levels).

When competition among financial institutions is weakened too much there is a direct impact on the rates, charges, fees, interest rates, and yields available to consumers and small business. Already in many cities and states the deposit interest rates have declined for ordinary consumers, while the margins charged by the largest institutions have widened. Only the biggest depositors and borrowers are able to get better deals, i.e., better competitive pricing for many kinds of financial services. If the Federal Reserve, OCC, and SEC are not aggressively supervising the adequacy of financial competition, this responsibility must be taken up by Congressional committees and their investigations. State agencies might do some work on these lines, too, but it is much harder for state regulatory agencies to investigate and get full information from interstate financial institutions.

E. CHANGING REGULATORY ORGANIZATION AND FRAMEWORK

In a period of controversy over monetary, banking, and financial institutions policy, we often hear proposals for change in regulatory organization, consolidation of agencies, and the framework for decision-making. When monetary management, interest rates, and their relation to fiscal policy are in dispute, proposals to change the decision-making structure of the Federal Reserve are frequently heard, or at least there are concerns over methods of appointment and selecting "Fed" leaders (and other regulatory heads). While the "Fed's" substantial independence seems reasonably well-established, critics sometimes raise this issue, perhaps hoping to influence its course of decisions.

Among the possible restructuring options were consolidation of most federal bank regulation activities (other than Federal Reserve monetary policy) into a new agency. This could be called the Federal Banking Commission (FBC) or a broadened OCC. Crucial questions would be its leadership, responsiveness to different elements of the banking industry (multinational banks, regional banks, and independent banks), thrift institutions, and broader public interests. Some proposed reducing (or "weakening") the Bank Holding Company Act's regulation along with such a change, although this is controversial. Few seemed to favor including the NCUA in such a consolidation, at least initially.

Merger policy would be controversial, especially if independent Justice Department review under the Bank Merger Act were altered in any significant way. Because of so many unresolved controversies, many observers of financial market regulation had not expected any really major legislative developments during 1985–99.

But the FSLIC recapitalization of 1989, and the enactment of FIRREA in August, 1989, did lead to some restructuring of bank and thrift regulation. The Home Loan Bank Board was abolished, and most of its regulatory and supervisory responsibilities were transferred to a new Office of Thrift Supervision (OTS) in the OCC. Meanwhile, FSLIC was absorbed by the FDIC, and the insurance funds were divided into the Bank Insurance Fund (BIF) and the Savings Association Insurance Fund (SAIF). This left the NCUA intact as credit union regulator, along with its NCUSIF. In other respects, the financial institutions regulatory structure remained essentially unchanged in recent years.

More recently after Gramm–Leach, the Financial Modernization Act of 1999 (which allows financial service holding companies to operate in banking, securities, and/or insurance), the problems of conglomerate financial oversight must be faced more realistically. The Federal Reserve has been the primary regulator of bank holding companies; its staffing and expertise have been stronger. This is why the Federal Reserve became the primary regulator for FHC's. The SEC, on the other hand, has built a strong tradition for quality supervision of securities markets. By contrast, insurance regulation in the U.S. has been almost entirely left to state insurance commissions, with a mixed performance—excellent in some states, not so good in others. Recently, after investigative probing by Congressional Committees and the General Accounting Office, the National Association of Insurance Commissioners (NAIC) has become more active, responsible, and important as a serious regulatory institution. A crucial question is whether or not the NAIC can rise to the level of an equal partner to the Federal Reserve and SEC in the supervision and regulation of financial holding companies. If so, fine; if not, many (from both within and outside the insurance industry) will urge the need for a federal insurance regulatory agency.

In this context, it should be emphasized that U.S. banking and financial market regulators and industry experts are becoming more aware, interested, and knowledgeable about banking and financial market regulation in other advanced industrial countries, especially Europe and Japan. In these other countries, banking, securities, and insurance regulation has some similar characteristics. Each nation has a Central Bank and Finance (Treasury) Ministry for monetary and fiscal policy. Banking market supervision and detailed regulation is either the central bank's responsibility, or delegated to a banking commission or similar agency. Insurance might be regulated by the Finance Ministry or an independent agency, while securities are regulated by the Finance Ministry or independently. Merger activity is closely supervised, along with significant international bank branching in their territories. Exchange and credit control authority is commonly established, though not used often by moderate and conservative governments. Foreign exchange markets are supervised more carefully (with significant intervention or support by many countries.) Reporting and auditing disciplines are roughly comparable, and guidelines for capitalization and reserves are receiving greater attention. In the EU countries, in particular, there has been an effort toward harmonization of banking supervision and regulation of financial markets. Greater collaboration efforts through the Bank for International Settlements (BIS), the G–12 countries, and annual IMF meetings are evident. An important step was the agreement on risk-based capital requirements in late 1987 among the G–12 nations (U.S., Japan, U.K., W. Germany, France, Italy, Switzerland, the Low countries, Sweden, and Canada), which moved international banking toward a more level playing field. A further step came from the Basle Committee on Bank Supervision (G–12), which established stronger minimum standards to prevent another BCCI failure. The new minimum standards provide: (i) All international banks should be capably supervised by a home country authority with consolidated accounting; (ii) Host countries should impose restrictive measures on unsound operations in their territories that are not well supervised.

Finally, everyone should realize that bankers and financial leaders around the world have become more international minded over the last generation. There is a large functioning market for liquidity and capital that encompasses most of the globe. National economic policies are more interdependent than ever, and the dimension of international finance must be taken into account for many aspects of financial market regulation. There has been a trend of greatly increased mutual contacts and shared insight that includes regulatory leaders and key staff experts. The global economy is becoming a broadly shared field of market experience. This development will enhance mutual understanding and sophistication, and may help ease the economic strains and conflicts that arise inevitably among nations.

*

INDEX

References are to Pages

†

DATE DUE

OCT 0 7 2010	

DEMCO, INC. 38-2931